Swords and Cinema

For Olivia

Swords and Cinema

Ancient Battles in Modern Movies

Jeremiah McCall

Pen & Sword
MILITARY

First published in Great Britain in 2014 by
Pen & Sword Military
an imprint of
Pen & Sword Books Ltd
47 Church Street
Barnsley
South Yorkshire
S70 2AS

ISBN 978 1 84884 476 6

Typeset in Ehrhardt by
Mac Style Ltd, Bridlington, East Yorkshire
Printed and bound in the UK by CPI Group (UK) Ltd,
Croydon, CRO 4YY

Pen & Sword Books Ltd incorporates the imprints of Pen &
Sword Archaeology, Atlas, Aviation, Battleground, Discovery,
Family History, History, Maritime, Military, Naval, Politics,
Railways, Select, Transport, True Crime, and Fiction, Frontline
Books, Leo Cooper, Praetorian Press, Seaforth Publishing and
Wharncliffe.

For a complete list of Pen & Sword titles please contact
PEN & SWORD BOOKS LIMITED
47 Church Street, Barnsley, South Yorkshire, S70 2AS, England
E-mail: enquiries@pen-and-sword.co.uk
Website: www.pen-and-sword.co.uk

Contents

Introduction   vi
List of Plates   xi

Chapter 1   *Troy* and Warfare in Archaic Greece   1

Chapter 2   Spartan Hoplites, the Phalanx, and the Film *300* 23

Chapter 3   *Alexander* and the Battle of Gaugamela   62

Chapter 4   The End of the Roman Republic   89

Chapter 5   Imperial Rome   121

Chapter 6   Roman Sieges and *Masada*   152

Conclusion   177
Appendix: List of Online Texts of Ancient Sources   186
Notes and References   189
Bibliography   201
Index   206

Introduction

Did that really happen? The trend of creating cinematic epics set in the ancient world went dormant in the 1960s and came back with a vengeance in the twenty-first century: *Gladiator* and *Troy*, *300* and *Alexander*. We watch these and other films from the sword and sandals genre over and over again and cannot help but ask, did that really happen? Is the version of the ancient world portrayed onscreen authentic in any way or the mere imagination of filmmakers unsupported by anything approaching historical evidence? If you have ever watched a film set in the ancient world, wondering about historical accuracy while enjoying the spectacle, this book is for you. Its purpose is to help fans of the genre investigate a particular facet of the epic film set in the Greco-Roman world: the battle scene.

Why battle scenes? In part, because the study of ancient battle has evolved considerably over the past twenty years and needs to be re-introduced. Once the study of war was limited to lists of battles and results, a discussion of generals and battle plans that ran the risk of boring students to tears. Units of actual soldiers were treated as automata that manoeuvred and executed plans according to the generals' wishes. If you find yourself less than enthusiastic about reading a book devoted to ancient warfare, it may well be that you were taught military history in this way. Things have changed. The historical community shifted radically in its approach to warfare after historian John Keegan wrote *The Face of Battle* in 1976. In this innovative landmark work, Keegan sought to break with the tradition of discussing battle as a series of top down decisions ordered by generals. Instead, he proposed that a truer study of battle would explore the experiences of the soldiers in the action, the humans who did the actual fighting and dying. Keegan noted:

> I do not intend to write about generals and generalship ... I do not intend to say anything of logistics or strategy and very little of tactics in the formal sense ... On the other hand, I do intend to discuss wounds and their treatment ... the nature of leadership at the most junior level, the role of compulsion in getting men to stand their ground ... and above all, the dimensions of the danger which different varieties of weapons offer to the soldiers on the battlefield.[1]

In short Keegan focused on soldiers' experiences of battle, psychologically and physically. In the field of ancient military history, a number of historians eagerly applied Keegan's approach to their own field and attempted to investigate the battlefield experiences of the ancient soldier.[2] Ancient military history today is an exploration of fear and danger, psychological and physical, which deserves a far wider audience.

Unlike many historical treatises on battle, cinema in particular offers, theoretically at least, a superior medium for displaying the experience of battle, for it captures action in both sound and image. In any scene on film intended to capture the mechanics of a battle, humans cannot easily be abstracted into impersonal units. They must be shown going about the business of battle and that means they must be shown in equipment within formations inflicting and receiving harm and experiencing a variety of emotions.

Judging how a film displays the actual sights and sounds of ancient combat however is, to say the least, an imprecise business. Filmmakers have to create a complete visual world for their audiences, designing all the necessary props even for the smallest details and framing each shot. Books written on ancient combat, on the other hand, are more often freed from such responsibilities. Look at it this way. A book that describes a Roman army in battle can simply leave out a myriad of details without the reader ever missing them: the footgear worn, the size and shape of weapons etc. Consider, for the sake of argument, the following excerpt from a battle scene, written by the author for an earlier book. At this point in the narrative, a Roman army is about to clash with the forces of Hannibal, who invaded Italy at the end of the third century.

> The Roman front line, according to the sources, engaged Hannibal's Spanish infantry, tough veteran soldiers. The centres of the two battle lines fought in close combat for some time without reaching any decisions. Hoping to tilt the scales, Hannibal ordered war elephants to be brought up to the front. The elephants and their drivers assaulted a spot in the line and caused considerable panic among the Romans at the centre. A junior officer, Gaius Decimus Flavus, assessed the situation and acted swiftly to restore his soldiers' morale. He grabbed the standard from a unit of hastati not yet panicked by the elephants and ordered the soldiers to follow him.[3]

If one tries to visualize the scene as described, it becomes readily apparent that the text leaves out any number of details about formations, equipment, clothing, and so on in order to provide a comprehensible and structured narrative that focuses on what the author considers most important at that point of the book. These details may be described elsewhere, readers may be directed to other works that describe these aspects of Roman and Carthaginian armies, or, more likely, missing details might be ignored altogether.

A filmmaker capturing this same battle scene, however, does not have the luxury to omit even small details. In a visual medium all that the camera can see becomes part of the representation, authentic or not. A director will remain responsible for all that is in the scene, intentional and not. To represent this scene from text authentically, filmmakers have to account for armour, weapons, clothing the elephants themselves, not to mention the geography of the battlefield. The formation of units would need to be represented as would the design of the standard the officer seized. The list could continue indefinitely, In short, the filmmaker hoping to recreate a historical episode authentically is accountable for levels of detail that the writer can safely ignore, even when writing a relatively detailed work.

Still, film, especially dramatic epic film, is not history. Its directors, however authentic they may want their works to be, do not intend for their films to mimic prose accounts of the past. To do so would be a waste of the cinematic medium. A conversation between *Alexander* director Oliver Stone and his historical consultant, Robin Lane Fox, illustrates this point. According to Fox, Stone warned:

> Be sure you understand we are not making a history book. This is not a documentary. It is a dramatization, though it should take history as its starting point. There will have to be compromises, because of time, money, drama, and space. If you can accept that, I'll try to keep explaining when we have to depart from that framework. I'll have to run events together, and condense them, but I want to capture the spirit of it.[4]

Dramatic filmmakers can respect history, but they are making dramas, telling gripping stories that will engage viewers. Drama, of course, is not antithetical to history, but there are frequent occasions during the making of a historical film when a choice must be made between accurate historical detail and effective storytelling.

So we must take it for granted that historical epics will have flaws in their authenticity whether because everything visible in a scene is apparent to the watcher – a key feature of the medium – or because the filmmakers sacrifice historical details in the name of building a more compelling drama. One who chooses can pick nits and, inevitably, find flaws and inconsistencies in any given film. This can lead to a boring – and unfair – treatment. Therefore, while this book will point out some flaws in the authenticity of various movies, its purpose is not to condemn historical films for their flaws. Nor does this book focus on why certain filmmakers shot battle scenes the way they did. That is to say, this book does not focus on the modern context of the film, the ways in which the film was written and produced. Instead it uses film as an entry point into thinking about how the armies of Greece and Rome fought and what the experiences of soldiers in these armies were like. Through these films we can consider what is authentic and what is not in a way that broadens our understanding both of the ancient film epic and of ancient battle.

Accordingly a more flexible, not to mention sympathetic, standard is needed for assessing the overall accuracy of a film's scenes of ancient battle. A sort of 'take away' test is needed. Simply put, the fundamental question is this: if a viewer watched a particular battle scene in a film, and this battle scene was their only exposure to how those particular combatants fought, what understanding would they take away with them? In this light the focus remains on the core depiction of the battle, not the inauthentic minutiae that one could dedicate an entire book to listing.

Since this is a book on ancient war and warriors, it will survey Greco-Roman military history in the course of investigating a number of films. The work is organized chronologically according to the period of warfare represented by a film or films. The first three chapters investigate Wolfgang Petersen's *Troy* and the battles of Homeric Greece, Zack Snyder's *300* and the Spartan army in the Persian Wars, and Oliver Stone's *Alexander* and the Macedonian army. Then focus shifts to the Roman world with a chapter on the Late Republic considering movies such as Stanley Kubrick's *Spartacus*, and the HBO series *Rome*. A chapter on the empire considers *Gladiator*, *Centurion*, and *The Eagle*. A final chapter uses the film *Masada* as a foil to investigate siege warfare in the Roman world.

List of Plates

1. A depiction of the infantry soldier on the Mycenaean Warrior Vase.
2. Athenian amphora depicting a chariot, c. 700 BC.
3. Mycenaean blades and spear heads from graves at Ialysos, c. 1450–1100 BC.
4. Bronze Etruscan shield, second half of the 7th century BC. The shape is similar to a hoplite's shield though, unlike the hoplite shield, this has a central boss and handle.
5. Chalcidian-style helmet. Apulia, c. 510 BC.
6. Bronze Corinthian-style helmet, c. 650–570 century BC.
7. Bronze Corinthian-style helmet.
8. A Roman copy of a bust of Pericles showing the wearing of the Corinthian helmet outside of battle.
9. Tomb of Kybernis showing a hoplite spear, shield, and Corinthian-style helmet, c. 480 BC.
10. Corinthian-style helmet from Attica, 5th century BC.
11. Front of Laconian (Spartan) warrior figurine, 6th century BC. The warrior is depicted with helmet, shield, breastplate, and greaves.
12. Side of Laconian (Spartan) warrior figurine, 6th century BC.
13. The Macmillan Aryballos depicting warriors in hoplite gear, c. 7th century BC.
14. Bronze greaves of the type worn by hoplites. Southern Italy, 5th century BC.
15. Bronze Montefortino type helmet of the style used by Roman legionaries in the Republic and early Empire. Apulia, c. 3rd century BC.

16. A bronze votive figurine from Umbria, 5th century BC. Note the reinforced shoulder flaps that were characteristic of later Roman armour styles.
17. A bronze Roman figurine depicted in a *lorica segmentata*, 2nd century AD.
18. A *gladius* from Germany, c. 15 BC.

Chapter 1

Troy and Warfare in Archaic Greece

On the rocky, sun-drenched shores of Phtia, Odysseus makes a final bid for Achilles to accompany the Greek invasion of Troy: 'This war will never be forgotten, nor will the heroes who fight in it.' Of course the movie *Troy* cleverly fulfils its own prediction, retelling Homer's epic thousands of years later. In doing so, the film also raises some interesting questions about its relation to Homer and Homer's relation to historical Greek warfare. The movie claims in the opening to be inspired by Homer, the master Greek poet of the Archaic Age. He composed the epic *Iliad* about the ninth year of a great war between Greeks and Trojans. He was a poet, however, not a historian in any sense of the term. Nor was he the creator of these stories. Rather he was a bard in a long tradition of bards passing down oral stories of heroes in song and poem, generation after generation. Homer achieved lasting fame, however, by committing these stories to writing in his epics the *Iliad* and the *Odyssey*. Ostensibly, his poems are set in the Late Bronze Age, the period when the Mycenaean Greek culture flourished in mainland Greece and the Aegean (c. 2200–1150 BC). The *Iliad* and *Odyssey*, however, have sparked a long debate of their own, ever since ancient times: do they give more than a superficial treatment to the Mycenaean Greeks, a civilization that collapsed centuries before his birth? And if not, what historical period might Homer's works actually describe? Unlike the other movies considered in this book, therefore, *Troy* poses a doubly complicated set of questions: How effectively does the film represent Homer's *Iliad*, and what period of warfare did Homer's *Iliad* represent?

Investigating this problem requires a brief survey of Greek history. The earliest Greeks – by which are meant speakers of Greek – migrated from West Asia to the Balkan Peninsula late in the third millennium. These Greeks, more than 1,000 years before the Athenians built their famous Parthenon, developed a culture historians call Mycenaean, a label based on the name of one of the leading palace complexes of the age, Mycenae. The Mycenaean Greeks were politically organized into small kingdoms centred on places like Mycenae, Tiryns, and Pylos. Each small kingdom had a central palace and citadel complex that served, among other purposes, as a great redistribution centre for the produce and crafted goods of the countryside. The Mycenaeans developed the first form of written Greek, and developed a thriving trade with other powers in the Eastern Mediterranean like the Egyptians and Hittites. They also practised a great deal of what amounts to piracy, raiding the shipping and settlements of neighbours somewhat regularly. For reasons that are not fully understood but were likely quite unpleasant, the Mycenaean kingdoms collapsed between 1250 and 1150 BC. By Homer's day, which was probably around 700 BC, the Mycenaean palaces were ancient ruins, palatial no more.[1]

In the aftermath of the Mycenaean collapse, both mainland and island Greece entered a Dark Age, so called because all written evidence for mainland Greece has disappeared, along with a substantial amount of archaeological evidence. Eventually, over the course of a few centuries whatever had caused the Mycenaeans to fall seems to no longer have been a factor, for in many of the little pockets of fertile land in between the mountains of rocky Greece, new communities formed with a new sense of political organization. An increase in archaeological remains from the early eighth century demonstrates that the Greeks entered a period of growth and revitalization historians call the Archaic Period. These small communities developed into the uniquely Greek form of city state called the polis. Homer was born in this period, somewhere round about 700 BC. He took advantage of – or personally initiated

– the use of a written alphabet to record Greek compositions and composed his two epics. The *Iliad*, which is most important for studying ancient warfare, described the events from a few weeks during the ninth year of a war that was supposed to have, according to tradition, lasted for a decade.

Hence the knotty problem. For centuries, many assumed that the world Homer described, with poetic embellishment, was that of Mycenaean Greece, the Bronze Age (c. 2200–1150 BC). In some respects Homer seems to describe a Bronze Age culture – a culture of heroes from long before his day, armed and armoured with bronze. Accordingly when he talks of Agamemnon, leader of the Greek host, as the king of Mycenae, and describes weapons and armour of bronze, in addition to war-chariots, it appears as if he is describing Mycenaean warfare and civilization from centuries before his day.

If Homer did mean to set the *Iliad* in the days of the warrior kings of Mycenaean Greece, however, he had very little way to access that world directly. Brushing up on Mycenaean history by reading historical accounts was out of the question. Though Homer may not have been blind as later Greek traditions asserted, he lived at a time when the very knowledge of writing had disappeared from Greece. Today we are so tied to written texts as major sources of information that it might seem, at first glance, that the Mycenaean world was closed to Homer. That bard, however, lived in an oral culture. Without the crutch that writing provides for failing memories, oral cultures were capable of preserving cultural memories intact in their rough forms for centuries, perhaps even the five or so between Homer and the last gasps of the Mycenaean civilization. Homer may well have seen remnants of Mycenaean civilization in the form of armour and weapons left over from the Bronze Age as dedications to the gods in their temples. He may have received from his predecessors elements of an oral tradition from the late Bronze Age.[2]

There are significant problems, however, with assuming the *Iliad* in any way directly reflects Mycenaean warfare in the late Bronze Age. Though oral traditions can pass on through centuries, it simply appears impossible to suppose that Homer could have accurately described in detail a world that had disappeared half a millennium before. A much stronger case can be made that the *Iliad* reflects the Greece of Homer's day, or perhaps that of his grandparents. The logic runs like this: Homer's poems came from a long developed tradition about the Greek heroes of old. So the subject matter of the *Iliad* was believed by all to be ancient. Homer knew nothing substantial about truly ancient warfare, i.e. that of the Mycenaeans. What he did, then, is describe the oldest warfare he knew, which, so it is argued, would be somewhere within a century before his birth, the tales his grandparents passed down. To make the poem authentically ancient sounding (since again, these heroes were supposed to be ancient), he added some Mycenaean touches to apply a patina of venerable age to his descriptions of war and society from his own day. So, he put the epic tales together in ways that made sense to him based on what he had heard or seen. Whenever fitting, he added a reference to something antique to remind listeners of the purported antiquity of his story. So, for example, he refers to a helmet made out of scales of sliced boar's tusks of which a Mycenaean example has been recovered by archaeologists.

If one looks at his language carefully, some clear trends appear. First, Homer describes the armour, from helmets and shields to cuirasses and greaves, as made of bronze. He describes shields generally as round, crafted of hide and bronze, and made with a central boss and handgrip. A few times he refers to round shields that seem more like the hoplite shields of the later seventh century. Taken together, this sort of equipment seems to have existed for only a short period in Greek history, about 25 years to either side of 700 BC.[3] It stands to reason, then, that the historical system of warfare modelled in the *Iliad* was actually somewhere close to Homer's own day, about 700 BC.

Like Homer, *Troy, the film*, makes its own blend of various times and places. Indeed the set designer for Troy conceded readily that he mashed up several different civilizations to get the ultimate desired look for Troy.[4] In some cases the influence is not so much from a particular historical period as it is from a Hollywood archetype. To give one major example, the city of Troy itself, historian Peter Green notes, is not representative of the Bronze Age city as we know it from archaeology. Instead it is mired in stereotypical and fairly unhistorical cinematic representations of ancient cities that are themselves products of some unhistorical nineteenth century world views. This did not escape Green's notice when he concluded,

> Despite all the computerized facilities for the creation of virtual reality at his disposal – including a faithful, and highly realistic, reconstruction of Troy made for the archaeologist Manfred Korffmann's Troia Projekt – Petersen's Troy follows the same old formula, if on a lavish scale. He gets the external batter walls right (though he makes them over twice their real height), but inside we have the familiar mish-mash of vaguely Egyptian-looking temples, anachronistic artwork (Hittite, Egyptian New Kingdom, Greek Archaic, fifth century Athenian, etc.), under-furnished public courts and a superfluity of empty platforms.[5]

So not only is the *Iliad* largely unhelpful for understanding Mycenaean warfare, *Troy* does not fare well in this regard either. Instead, to the extent that it draws from Homer, the best candidate for the period of warfare *Troy* represents is the Archaic period of Greece.

Considering the film as a model of Archaic Greek battle, however, enables us to ignore some important but historically suspect features of the film. The first, the depiction of a pseudo-historical Bronze Age city itself, is not too difficult to ignore when exploring Archaic Greek combat. The conflict represented in *Troy*, just as in the *Iliad*, is not fundamentally a siege; there are no siege works, no siege engines, no mining and countermining. Instead it is a series of pitched battles for the fate of a city. The second element to ignore is the massive size of the forces. *Troy* is based on an epic after all, and in this epic

1,000 ships and some 50,000 men came to take the precious city. These are figures that were beyond the capacity of Archaic Greek cities to muster. Nor can one be too concerned about whether the names of the heroes represent specific historical figures. So, to put a fine point on it, leaving out questions of architecture, army size, and the precise historical identity of any particular person named in the film, does *Troy*'s model of combat, the arms and armour, troops and tactics, duels and deaths, represent anything like the warfare of the *Iliad* and of Archaic Greece?

The *Iliad*'s Model of Archaic Combat

To answer this it is important to establish what is known about battle in Homer's age, the late eighth century. The Mycenaeans, following the trends of older civilizations in the Eastern Mediterranean such as Egyptians, Hittites, and Mesopotamians, used chariots as an important combat arm. While the terrain in Greece was decidedly unfriendly to horses, Mycenaean palace records indicate that some of the kingdoms had as many as several hundred war chariots at their disposal. How exactly these chariots were employed on the battlefield and their importance relative to infantry are still matters of significant debate for historians. What seems clear, however, is that chariots were used not for charges into masses of infantry or for head-on collisions with other chariots, but as mobile platforms from which archers and javelin throwers could launch their missiles against enemy infantry with relative impunity. So we might imagine an ancient battle in the Late Bronze Age consisting of masses of infantry with chariots serving as a mobile arm to attack the flanks and rear of the infantry.[6]

As Mycenaean civilization collapsed, this seems to have changed. Based on the archaeological finds of weapons and armour, and images of warriors on pottery and reliefs, the Greeks and their eastern Mediterranean neighbours shifted away from chariots and instead focused on infantry as the most significant combat arm. These infantry, in Greece, became better armoured than before, wearing short corselets of leather or linen reinforced with strips of metal or metal scales. A new type of shield also appeared. The shields of the earlier Mycenaean period were of the tower kind – long, rectangular or figure-8 shields that protected most of the body. Now smaller, round shields developed that had a single central boss and handgrip and a shallow conical shape from boss to rim.[7] Warriors equipped something like this are depicted on a single instance of a Mycenaean pot, the so-called Warrior Krater from the beginning of the twelfth century (see plate 1).[8] A single row of soldiers marches along on the vase, each armed uniformly with a corselet and open-faced helmet topped with a pair of horns. Their shields are not quite round but instead somewhat crescent shaped. This pot is Mycenaean, however, and while it gives the flavour of the kind of armour that may have been employed in the Archaic period, it is very difficult to say whether Mycenaean styles of arms and armour persisted after their civilization collapsed.

Another source of evidence for arms and armour in the Archaic period is the *Iliad* itself. If anything, the poem indicates that the equipment in any particular Greek army would vary widely. Some warriors would use thrusting spears, others javelins, still others swords. Even axes are referred to upon occasion. Slings and bows and arrows have their place, too, though Homer clearly believed them to be morally suspect weapons compared to the up-close and personal swords and spears. As for protection, some warriors wore armour, others none. Shields, when they are described tend to have these characteristics: they were round, made of hide and/or bronze, sometimes reinforced by one or more wooden staves across the back, and had a central boss. These references to central bosses suggest that warriors held these shields out in front of them using a central grip.[9] Some references seem to suggest different kinds of shields existed, longer rectangular or oval shields. Certainly, the variety in armour and weapons would suggest that similar variety existed for shields.

So, how did these soldiers fight? Any answer to this must ground itself in Homer, our only writing that touches on this shadowy period in Greek history. Hans Van Wees, who has written at length about battle in the Homeric Age, considers warfare in the historical period described by the *Iliad* as fundamentally similar to that practised by New Guinea's Dani warriors:

> Depending on his personal preference, a man is armed with spears or bows and arrows. The spearmen carry long, finely crafted stabbing spears and often a couple of cruder short spears which they can throw at an enemy ... Men also carry tobacco nets for times of rest behind the front lines ... At first a few men run towards the enemy, who are still far beyond arrow range. For a few minutes they shout taunts ... wave their weapons and then retire. Some of the enemy reciprocate. Gradually the lines get closer together and soon they are within firing range of each other. ... Men move up from the rear, stay to fight for a while, and then drop back for a rest. Those in the front, in the most vulnerable positions, must keep in constant movement to avoid presenting too easy a target. As men dance up to the front, they can take care of themselves. As they drop back, though, they have a blind side and many wounds are received then. ... Spearmen and archers work together, with the idea that the bowmen will bring someone down with an arrow so that he can be killed with a spear ... The front continually fluctuates moving backwards and forwards as one side or the other mounts a charge.

As the early afternoon wears on, the pace of battle develops into a steady series of brief clashes and relatively long interruptions. An average day's fighting will consist of ten to twenty clashes between the opposing forces.[10]

According to Van Wees, most of the warriors in the film are spaced 5m or more away from their comrades, a loose open formation. He also notes clashes were short-lived, no more than 15 minutes long, and no more than a third of the warriors engaged in these clashes at any one time.[11]

Van Wees essentially adopts this display of Dani combat as a model of Archaic Greek combat. And so, following the model, a historical Ajax would taunt a Hector into a confrontation, throwing spears. If the challenge was accepted the two would close to duel. Their conflict soon brought a gathering of each hero's nearby allies to the forming knot of men. A more sustained combat broke out between these pods of warriors, but not for long. Then the warriors would dissipate again into their loose, open formation. The phenomena of warriors clustering and dispersing would happen up and down the lines simultaneously. Any significant massing of troops, correspondingly, would happen sporadically and through spontaneous generation rather than any orchestration by a commander.

This model of fluid combat seems to characterize appropriately a number of scenes described in the *Iliad*. There are many occasions, however, when Homer refers to both armies clashing and fighting as a whole, something that would, it seems, rarely if ever happen in the heroic model above. Take this example from the *Iliad*:

The armies massing ... crowding thick-and-fast as the swarms of flies seething over the shepherds' stalls in the first spring

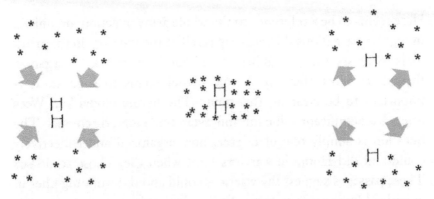

Diagram of van Wees' Model: Heroes (H) initiate a duel, their nearby comrades (*) clump around them and fight, then all disperse.

days when the buckets flood with milk – so many long-haired Achaeans swarmed across the plain to confront the Trojans, fired to smash their lines. The armies grouping now – as seasoned goatherds split their wide-ranging flocks into packs with ease when herds have mixed together down the pasture: so the captains formed their tight platoons, detaching right and left, moving up for action.[12]

Clearly Homer does refer to the common soldiers here in ways that suggest they were organized, fought in lines, and were integral to the battle.[13] A second example of units fighting collectively comes from a passage where Nestor gives advice to Agamemnon at a certain point in the fighting:

But you, my King, be on your guard yourself. Come, listen well to another man. Here's some advice, not to be tossed aside, and I will tell it clearly. Range your men by tribes, even by clans, Agamemnon, so clan fights by the side of clan, tribe by tribe. Fight this way, if the Argives still obey you, then you can see which captain is a coward, which contingent too, and which is loyal, brave, since they will fight in separate formations of their own.[14]

Here seems to be a reference to the whole army in action, organized in regular formations that encompass all of the warriors in the army. This suggests the possibility for Homeric warriors to organize themselves more than the heroic model seems to suggest. It is important to be clear on this point. The heroic model Van Wees offers has significant value for understanding Homeric combat. The question is simply one of degree: how organized and collectively could and did Homeric warriors fight when they chose to do so? These passages suggest the warriors could and did work together in organized formations at times. Still, it is not the case that everyone in these armies was engaged in direct combat at all times. Of course, as is the case in any massive crowd, there would have been those at the front and in the fighting and those farther back and currently out of the fighting. Second, none of these passages, despite their hints at grouping and teamwork, suggests that the infantry fought in well-defined formations, organized into even clean ranks and files. It is simply to suggest that the armies were organized so that commoners fought too, not just heroes, and they did at times engage their opponents as armies, en masse, not only as sporadic clusters of duelists.

Certainly, Homeric warfare was a loosely organized affair. The armies arrived and occupied the battlefield. Each noble brought along with him a retinue of fighters, his subordinates. To this extent there was a vague sense of unit organization. Unlike later Greek warfare, however, there were seemingly no ordered formations, no ranks or files. The collective mass of troops on both sides moved closer, perhaps just out of range of a spear cast. Then came the series of mini-battles. All along the battlefield the bravest fighters, the *promachoi* as they were called, stood in the very front. Any warrior desiring to keep his reputation, or noble wishing to be distinguished by more than birth alone, stood among the *promachoi*. These fighters on both sides would clash along the battle front. One would hit another with a spear cast or even run forward to attack a foe in hand-to-hand combat.

In the transitional period between Homeric warfare and the development of the Archaic phalanx these armies of clumps and individuals begin to coalesce. Tight and orderly formations of rank-and-file were not yet enforced. Still, there grew a collective sense that hand-to-hand combat was superior to other forms and that fighting together side-by-side in a unified formation was the most effective way to do that. Since the development of this attitude was evolutionary, not revolutionary, slingers, archers, and javelin throwers continued to fight alongside the heavy infantry, taking advantage of their comrades' shields to dart in and out for a quick strike against the foe. The heavy infantry, for their part, slowly adopted a concave shield with a characteristic elbow strap and hand grip on the rim. Alongside this shield, they began to insist upon teamwork. This meant attacking the enemy in formation and defending against the enemy in formation.[15]

So what did this look like? At the very least the front rows of fighters would be engaged more often than not. Depending on how loosely units were formed, fighters in the first few rows behind that might engage collectively with the enemy. Without strictly ordered formations and clearly defined lines, however, it must have been relatively easy, and common for that matter, for spaces and pockets to appear between the opposing front lines and dissolve organically as soldiers successively attacked and defended, pressed forward and fell back. These spaces and pockets allowed for heroes to duel as the *Iliad* suggests they did, while still being backed by their comrades-in-arms.

Troy's Cinematic Model of Combat

Now back to the film. How closely does *Troy* represent this sort of Archaic Greek battle? Let's begin with each force's arms and armour. The Trojan forces, certainly, are too uniform in their armour and weapons to reflect a historical Archaic army. Curved rectangular shields that protect their bearers from neck to ankle are found in three standardized varieties. Some sport four bosses near the corners. Others are smooth with a cutout on the soldier's right, the better to allow him to thrust a spear at his foe. An oval shield completes the options for director Petersen's Trojans. They all look fundamentally of the same make – which would, perhaps, make sense for a Bronze Age kingdom's standing army, but not for the citizen militia of Archaic Greece. The armour of each soldier in the ranks is completely uniform. For head protection, the soldiers have open-faced helmets that flare out at the bottom into neck protectors and have nasal guards. Armour corselets protect their torsos. These are crafted of sturdy linen, perhaps, or leather. The material is reinforced with metal plates and decorated with etchings. This armour certainly could have existed in some place and time, but its uniformity, if anything, is out of place for an Archaic army. Indeed with the exception of the shield types, the Trojan army approximates fairly well the soldiers painted on the Warrior Krater (see plate 1). But neither *Troy* nor the Warrior Krater capture the variety of warriors with different weapons and equipment that should be gathered under the army's banners. The main weapon of the infantry is a thrusting spear with a broad, bronze, leaf-shaped head. There are no inter-mixed troop types, no slingers, no javelineers; the archers are actually separated from the infantry. The film version of the Trojan army, in short, has little to recommend it as a representation of Archaic Greek soldiers.

The Greek infantry are armoured similarly to the Trojans as far as functionality. Their armour is much less ornate, however. The Greek cuirass in *Troy* consists of bands of metal or leather connected to one another with smaller shoulder bands. Oddly enough, their armour is similar to that crafted on a bronze (see plate 16) of an Italian soldier from the much later Roman Empire. In addition to this, each warrior also wears a tunic covered by a skirt of leather *pteruges* to guard their lower abdomen and upper thighs. Like the Trojans, each Greek warrior appears to be wearing essentially the same armour – a standardization that, again, fits the Warrior Krater, but not Archaic Greece. The Greek shields, however, show more variety. Many are round with a central grip, appropriately Homeric. The shields are of bronze and some are decorated with simple concentric circles and bosses. Others have a rounded, pie-shaped cutout, while others are in the shape of the rounded crescents found on the Warrior Krater. Still others are of the figure eight variety, which resembles the body of a violin, oval with cutouts in the centre. None are highly decorated. Here the film presents a reasonable approximation of the Archaic Greek shields. That is about the whole of it, however. Like their Trojan adversaries, each Greek soldier has a sturdy thrusting spear and there is none of the variety in weapons that there should be, no javelins, slings, or bows.

What about the depiction of combat itself? *Troy* offers its most elaborate sequencing in its spectacular staging of the first major battle. The Trojan forces are arrayed outside their city, clad in their essentially uniform style. Every so often one can see a standard bearer carrying a pole with a shield mounted on it. In later periods of Greco-Roman warfare such standard bearers would serve to rally soldiers and to guide them in a formation as they manoeuvred. These Greeks, however, do not have any clear organization of rank and file that would suggest the need for such standards. At the head of the host rides Agamemnon (Brian Cox) in his chariot, wearing a more ornate corselet of leather with riveted metal plates highlighted in gold and silver, not wholly unlike that of the Trojan lords. He is accompanied by the other Greek lords also in chariots: Menelaus, Odysseus, Ajax, and so on. The Trojan army stands amassed in front of its city, waiting.

But there is hope that perhaps only one man might die that day. Paris (Orlando Bloom) and his brother Hector (Eric Bana), mounted on horses at the front of the Trojan host, wait for the Greek army. Paris hopes to duel Menelaus (Brendan Gleeson) and, in doing so, bring the war to an end. Menelaus is game enough and accepts the challenge. Up to this point the scene has roughly followed the third book of the *Iliad*. Here, however, the screenwriters must veer widely off the path Homer trod because the film has pointedly eliminated the gods from the narrative. Paris, dominated by the bear Menelaus, is no longer rescued by Aphrodite, but crawls back in defeat, wounded, to his brother Hector. Hector, rather than watching his brother die at his knees, slays Menelaus. Enraged by the seeming treachery of Hector, Agamemnon orders the Greek host forward into battle. Led by their chariot-borne warlords, the Greek infantry trot into battle on the double-quick. They move as a mass but without any particular order – something we should expect of an Archaic army.

This part of the scene is significant for those imagining ancient battle. The run is uncontrolled, each man running at his own pace. The faster and more confident warriors quickly outstrip the slower-paced, and the mass of soldiers develops gaps in its front. This is a dynamic of any mass of people, even horses for that matter; if a conscious effort is not made to stay in a formation, the group will quickly lose cohesion. It is difficult enough in any period and place

---

That's Not How He Died in Homer!

A number of heroes meet different deaths in the ancient sources than they do in the film:

- Menelaus and Paris duel in the third book of the *Iliad* and Paris certainly is bested. His patron goddess, Aphrodite, rescues him and Menelaus goes unscathed, living through the war and returning home with Helen. Since Petersen intended to craft a Trojan war without gods, however, this will not do. His plot: Hector intervenes to save his brother and slays Menelaus.
- Achilles dies during the war, writers many centuries after Homer wrote. During one assault, he fights his way into the city gates and is shot in the heel with a poisoned arrow by Paris. The assault is ended and the Greeks do not yet take Troy. In the cinematic version, Achilles is one of those who sneak into the walls of Troy using the wooden horse. He finds Briseis as Troy is falling, kills Agamemnon to stop him from harming her, pledges his love, then dies.
- Homer's Agamemmnon survives Troy, while the cinematic version dies during the sacking of the city. His return to Myceneae, however, is far from triumphant. In Aeschylus' *Oresteia* trilogy, we learn that his wife, Clytemnestra, has taken a lover. The two murder Agamemnon in his bathtub.

to get infantry to stand and march in an orderly fashion of uniform ranks and files, let alone attack while maintaining such an orderly formation. The warriors in *Troy* as we might expect, do not have such orderly formations, and the dangers of their running attack are illustrated. Simply put, the front runners will reach the enemy unsupported by their comrades, a dangerous position in which to be. Meanwhile the Trojans stand in orderly rows, tower shields planted firmly on the ground and spears thrust forward to receive the charge. The discipline of the Trojan infantry stands in stark contrast to the Greek warriors who run at their foe in a mob.

And then, the impact. Peterson shifts the camera to a high angle following shot along the front lines to capture the collisions of the soldiers. The foremost Greek warriors smash into the Trojan shields, sometimes breaking into the lines, other times dropping dead from a spear thrust. Spears and shields fly up into the air as the Greeks try to break the Trojan formation through the force of their impact. The camera moves down the front, surveying the devastating collisions. Chaotic knots of men fighting one another form along the front lines of the Trojan ranks. The Trojans attempt to maintain their formations while the Greeks simply pour into their ranks as they are able. This too represents what must have been a natural outcome of a less organized infantry formation charging a body of infantry standing still and in formation. The latter work their way into the ranks of the former; how deeply depended on the space of the gaps between men.

This epic collision in *Troy* draws directly from a simile Homer employed:

> As a heavy surf assaults some roaring coast, piling breaker on breaker whipped by the West Wind, about on the open sea a crest first rears its head then pounds down on the shore with hoarse rumbling thunder and in come more shouldering crests, arching up and breaking against some rocky spit, exploding salt

foam to the skies so wave on wave they came, Achaean battalions
ceaseless, surging on to war.

At last the armies clashed at one strategic point, they slammed
their shields together, pike scraped pike with the grappling
strength of fighters armed in bronze and their round shields
pounded, boss on welded boss, and the sound of struggle roared
and rocked the earth.

Screams of men and cries of triumph breaking in one breath,
Fighters killing, fighters killed, and the ground streamed blood.
Wildly as two winter torrents raging down from the mountains,
Swirling into a valley, hurl their great waters together,
Flash floods from the wellsprings plunging down in a gorge,
And miles away in the hills a shepherd hears the hunger,
So from the grinding armies broke the cries and crash of war.[16]

Though it appears that the majority of the Trojan army remains in
its formation, the entire front line has become of a mass of men
struggling in what amounts to a brawl.

This sort of entropy that drove warriors to abandon formations
and focus on themselves, and made lines of warriors devolve
into scattered pairs of duelists, may have been common in more
organized armies. In loosely ordered armies like those of Archaic
Greece, scenes like this fighting in *Troy* may well have occurred

---

Homeric Wounds

Though Petersen's film is by no means free of violence, the depictions
of violence tend to be far tamer than the scenes described by Homer.
The poet took great pains to describe in detail those strokes that took
a man's life. Achilles inflicts on Demoleon one of the more gruesome
deaths of the *Iliad*. 'He stabbed his temple and cleft his helmet's
cheekpiece. None of the bronze plate could hold it – boring through
the metal and skull. The bronze spearpoint pounded, Demoleon's
brains splattered all inside his casque.' (20.449–54, Fagles trans)

frequently. Odysseus calls for the men to reform their lines – ironic since they really have had none. Hector, on the other hand, bellows for the more organized Trojans to push collectively against the Greek forces. Just so; there is ample evidence that a more organized force pushing against a disorganized force could rout it.[17]

The cameras return to the front line brawls. Close-up shots of swords stabbing and spears thrusting are punctuated by shots of archers drawing bowstrings to ears, then wider shots of the front line. Shields are used to bludgeon opponents, soldiers stumble in the mess. The scene is chaotic. It is difficult to get a sense of who is who and what progress, if any, is being made along the frontlines. The representation of ancient Archaic battles as chaotic, brutal, messy affairs in the zone of hand-to-hand combat is well promoted. Really the call of the commanders for action is the problematic part of the scene, being inconsistent as it is with the disorganization of the melee. It is not clear at all how their voices would be heard above the din or how, for that matter, the troops would even be able to disengage and reform. As for the standard bearers, they seem to have disappeared. Whether this is reasonably authentic or not depends on how well organized the initial forces were and the emphasis the armies put on staying in formation. Given what has been posited for Greek armies of the period, this scene seems credible as a model of how a battle evolved – or rather devolved – from a charge to a mixing mass of men in the front lines.

Thus the cinematic battle moves on as the cameras shift from the clash in the front line to a pocket of space occupied by the mighty Greek, Ajax (Tyler Mane). Armed with a tower shield and a massive war hammer, he lays flat Trojans all about him. Hector sees the damage Ajax is dealing, charges to meet him, and is knocked from his horse by a mighty blow from Ajax's shield. As the two duel in a small open space, the battle continues all around. Though knocked about by Ajax, Hector manages to dispatch him with a spear thrust to the abdomen. The duel won, the Trojans all about cheer for his triumph. Anything like this kind of duel required spaces in the battle to appear here and there, and thus the scene captures this aspect of Archaic warfare well.

Next Hector shouts for the Trojans to push. They lean into their shields and push collectively. Slowly the disorganized Greek combatants are pushed back. Then the lead ranks of the Trojans cast their spears at the Greeks, draw their swords and rush them. As the melee continues we see Hector in the fray killing his opponents. The archers continue their attack and ultimately Agamemnon must order the retreat or risk losing his entire army. The Greeks turn and run, stepping over their dead comrades, driven on by the Trojans at their back. The victorious Trojans drive them to their beachhead where the tables are turned as they come within range of the Greek archers. The victory, however, is with the Trojans. Hector recalls the troops and sends an emissary to the Greeks to allow them to bury their dead.

Really in both epic and film these are matters of emphasis: heroic stories require heroes and heroes are expected to stand out by their behaviour from the backdrop of ordinary people and behaviours. This is what our model of Archaic Greek battle supposes and this style of combat is precisely what Petersen's *Troy* illustrates well. For the most part the Greek forces fight in masses as a collective army but not in any particularly orderly formation. The Trojans, for their part, are more organized and able to close shields and give the massed shove that in the later days of phalanx warfare was called the *othismos*. In the absence of orderly rows and columns of soldiers (the Trojan push not withstanding) there was often considerable space on the battlefield for the *promachoi*, the heroes, to engage in duels. The duel between Ajax and Hector is not an unreasonable representation of this as far as its staging in the battle. Sadly though for fans of Ajax's war hammer, we have little if any evidence of such a weapon in use on Greek battlefields. Swords and spears, javelins, slings, and arrows, yes; two-handed war mauls, no.

Heroic Duels to the Death

Troy also follows in Homer's footsteps in presenting a series of special duels both in and outside normal battles. Some of these duels take place formally before battle or during a pause in the battle. The duel between Paris and Menelaus is one example. *Troy* itself opens with another special duel. The army of Agamemnon has been busily unifying Greece through war and they have reached the borders of a reluctant Thessaly. An arrangement is reached by the two kings that the outcome of a single duel to the death will determine the victor, thereby sparing unnecessary bloodshed. The agreement made, Agamemnon's soldiers shout the name of their hero, 'Achilles.' Arriving late after a night of women and wine, Achilles is reprimanded by Agamemnon. Ever proud, he turns to quit the battle, suggesting that Agamemnon can damn well fight his own battles, but the words of the wise Nestor hold him back: 'Achilles, look at the men's faces. You can save hundreds of them. You can end this war with a swing of your sword. Let them go home to their wives.' Achilles turns back to the battle field and strides toward Boagrius.

It is over almost before it has begun. The lines of two armies mark off a field and Achilles strides coldly toward Boagrius, sword and shield in hand. The latter bolsters his courage by leading the Thessalian troops in a battle cry. Turning to the approaching Achilles, Boagrius casts one of his two javelins at the Greek hero. Achilles calmly catches the shaft in his shield, casts the shield aside, and quickens into a run. Achilles easily dodges the second spear, and the two warriors are almost within arms' length. Boagrius draws his sword, ready for the clash of steel that never comes. Leaping into the air in a seemingly superhuman burst of power and grace, Achilles strikes down into the left shoulder of his enemy, piercing home in a mortal blow too fast for the crowds of warriors to see. As Achilles strides toward the Thessalian army to find another challenger, Boagrius drops to his knees, a corpse before he hits the ground. The King of Thessaly surrenders his royal sceptre to Achilles and the war is over.

In both this duel and that between Paris and Menelaus, the outcome of the duel is to determine the outcome of the war. It is difficult to say historically whether such arrangements happened and how common they may have been. On the one hand the ability to conclude a war with limited bloodshed might be appealing to some. Putting everything into a single duel of champions, however, was pretty risky. There are parallels in other ancient cultures, accounts of duels that were supposedly arranged to determine the outcome of a battle. The account given in the Book of Samuel about David and Goliath falls under these parameters.[18] The Romans too cherished a story about the Horatii, three brothers that fought the three brothers from Alba Longa, the Curiatii to determine which of the two cities should rule the other.[19] These too are of unclear authenticity.

What is reasonably certain, however, is that warriors in the Archaic period, those concerned with having an extraordinary reputation, sought public displays of their valour. Winning a duel with a distinguished enemy was the paramount way to achieve this. And so Hector slew giant Ajax on the battlefield. Later in the film, Patroclus, pretending to be Achilles, leads the Myrmidons to rally the hard-pressed Greeks. Patroclus and his men cut a swathe through the Trojan ranks until Hector checks him. The two duel in a circle as the armies stop and watch. Soon Patroclus is slain, his throat cut by Hector's blade. Of course this will lead to Hector's death in the edge-of-one's seat martial dance that is the duel between Hector and Achilles. Indeed if the *Iliad* emphasizes anything, it is the frequency of clashes between outstanding warriors. As historian J.E. Lendon notes of the *Iliad*:

> It happens again and again: a major hero encounters a minor hero of the enemy. The minor hero is introduced, and then the minor hero is slain, often with a gory anatomical description of the killing ... The encounter between two warriors can be much elaborated. Upon meeting, opposing warriors may exchange threats – 'here you will meet your doom!' – defiances

– 'bragging ox!' – and boastful genealogies. The introduction of the victim and his death are often adorned with epic similes, sometimes heartbreakingly beautiful ... Yet the one-on-one fighting can also be stripped of all adornment and reduced to a mere list of the slain.[20]

Rather than being a sideshow to the plot in the *Iliad*, the duels, with their naming of the heroes are a critical point in the poem, pointing to an ethic in the Archaic age that one should publicly demonstrate one's martial bravery to be worthy of honour. These heroic duels are part and parcel of the loosely organized nature of Homeric armies. In a system where individuals are expected to stand out from their peers and win or die through their own skill, where combat is conceived and described as being fundamentally reducible to a series of duels, it is not surprising at all that armies consisted of heroic leaders and their retinues, and a significant amount of the fighting took place between the leaders, the *promachoi*. This is a feature of Archaic warfare that *Troy* captures very well.

So, how does *Troy*, the film, fare on the take-away test? Though not without a significant share of errors in setting and in some aspects of equipment, *Troy* offers some reasonable models of Archaic combat. A movie-goer who never investigated any other evidence or accounts of Archaic battle would get a not unreasonable portrayal of some of the main combat mechanics. Heroes are at the centre of it all. Whether duelling one-on-one or leading their retinue into battle, they are the catalysts that drive the armies to clash in battle. As they seek out the most dangerous foes their comrades clash beside and around them in loose formations that can disintegrate into swirling masses of men. This sort of battle, which *Troy* captures fairly well, is a far cry from the form of warfare the Greeks developed later in the age: the hoplite phalanx. It is to this type of battle that we shall now turn.

Chapter 2

Spartan Hoplites, the Phalanx, and the Film *300*

Word of the end has reached the Spartan King, Leonidas. He and his small force of elite Spartan hoplites, assisted by Arcadian allies, have thwarted the might of the Persian army for days. By taking advantage of the narrows at Thermopylae, the path constrained by cliffs on one side and the sea on the other, the Greeks have halted the Persian invasion of their lands no longer. The betrayer, Ephialtes, revealed to Persian king Xerxes the goat track that circles behind the Greek defences. Daxos, leader of the Arcadians, now reports to Leonidas that the Phocians guarding the path have been routed; the Persian Immortals will be at the Greek rear lines in the morning. Hearing the news, Leonidas simply shouts his command: 'Spartans, prepare for glory!' An incredulous Daxos replies, 'Glory? Have you gone mad? There is no glory to be had now! Only retreat; or surrender; or death.' Leonidas growls, 'Well that's an easy choice for us Arcadian. Spartans never retreat. Spartans never surrender. Go spread the word. Let every Greek assembled know the truth of this. Let each among them search his own soul. And while you're at it ... search your own.' Ultimately the Arcadians leave, perhaps to fight another day, but the Spartans remain at their post ... and die.

This is one of many dramatic vignettes director Zack Snyder employs in *300* to retell the legend of the Spartan defence at Thermopylae. The story was told and retold among the Greeks, and Herodotus preserved it in his *Histories*, some 2,500 years ago. Three hundred Spartans, as Herodotus told it, along with several thousand other Greeks – a point too often overlooked – held the pass at Thermopylae against tens of thousands of Persian warriors. The story of their defence became legend, the legend of the fearsome and ever-obedient Spartan warrior. In 1998, Frank Miller took up the legend in a graphic novel called *300*. In 2006, Snyder brought the graphic novel to life onscreen. He is clear that this work was not meant to provide a historical representation of the battle, but rather an epic story. In one interview, Snyder notes,

> I'd say *300* is a movie that is made from the Spartan perspective. Not just from the Spartan perspective, the cameras are the Spartans, but it's the Spartans' sensibility of the Battle of Thermopylae. If you had Spartans sitting around a fire and they were telling you before anything was written down what happened at Thermopylae, this is the way they would tell it. It's not necessarily down to the fact that they don't have armour on. Everything about it is just to make the Spartans more heroic.[1]

Heroic they are. Still, the core event depicted is historical and naturally raises questions for viewers. Were the Spartans really that formidable? Why would they fight and die at Thermopylae? Once one strips out the fantasy beasts and the computerized exaggerations, does *300* capture the face of battle in fifth century Greece, what the Greek soldiers wore, how they fought and how they died?

Development of Greek Warfare: Hoplite and Phalanx

The Greek armies of the Archaic age, which we considered in the last chapter, underwent a critical evolution in the seventh century. Once armies consisted of noble warriors accompanied by less well armed followers. Soldiers fought collaboratively but in loose, unordered formations. The new form of fighting, however, was based on a highly organized and orderly formation, the phalanx, manned by uniformly armed soldiers, the hoplites.

Since each hoplite had to supply his own equipment, there assuredly was variety in how each was armed. Still a standard panoply developed in the seventh century and persisted without significant modification into the beginning of the fifth. Most critical of all the new equipment was a round shield, perhaps 3ft in diameter with a wooden core and, by the fifth century, a thin bronze covering. These shields were concave like bowls and perhaps 6in. deep from rim to centre. A hoplite carried this shield using a forearm band and a hand grip near the edge of the shield. The concavity of the shield allowed a hoplite to rest the rim of the shield on his shoulder, an important feature which will be addressed later. A good estimate for the weight of one of these shields is a hefty 15lbs, which may not sound like much until one remembers this was dead weight that would need to be held up in position for lengthy amounts of time.[2]

While the shield was the defining piece of equipment, early hoplites also wore a great deal of body armour. The typical breastplate for a hoplite in the seventh and sixth centuries was crafted from bronze. Front and back halves were attached to the wearer's body by straps. Typically, the armour was bell-shaped, curving out from the waist. This allowed for mobility – the flared bottom of the corselet left the hips unrestricted – and served to catch any downward sword or spear stroke lest it slipped down to the unprotected lower abdomen. By the time of the Persian Wars, new designs of leather or stiffened linen started to be put into use as well as lighter corselets of bronze.[3] Greaves of bronze were worn to protect the lower legs. Shaped to fit the shin with an opening in the rear, they stayed in place due to the elasticity of the bronze. To protect the head, a hoplite wore a bronze helmet, often with some kind of horsehair crest. The most common type of helmet was the Corinthian, which was bell-shaped, with the flaring bottom serving to protect the neck as well as the head. Cheek-pieces came forward to protect face and mouth (see plate 5).[4] Altogether, this panoply was hot and very heavy at 50 to 60lbs, but it unquestionably provided superior protection for close combat.

The primary offensive weapon of the hoplite was a heavy thrusting spear. Ranging from 6–9ft in length, the spear had a wooden shaft 1in. thick and was topped with a bladed point of iron. A bronze spike tipped the butt end. It allowed the spear to be used after the head snapped off – a not uncommon occurrence. More brutally, it allowed the hoplite easily to stab down at an enemy on the ground. A sword would often be carried as a backup weapon.

The phalanx consisted of closely packed rows of hoplites, perhaps with no more than 3ft of space per soldier, in ranks typically eight hoplites or more deep. The key to a phalanx's success was teamwork. It may be instructive for the reader to raise their left arm and imagine a shield attached to it 3ft in diameter with the hand grip a few inches from the rim. Such a shield would offer superior protection for the hoplite's left side but far less protection for his right – it is worth noting, so far as we know, left-handed hoplites were required to fight as right-handers. Therefore, each hoplite received protection on his right from the shield of his comrade. Indeed this arrangement resulted in a phenomenon noted by ancient experts: a large phalanx would tend to drift to the right as it marched, each soldier shifting just a little to the right to gain more protection from his comrade. Leaving that aside, so long as each hoplite maintained his position in the phalanx, he protected and was protected by his neighbours as he used his large thrusting spear to attack the enemy. The key to the success of the phalanx, however, was not so much the front as the rear. Those hoplites in rows beyond the first two or three could not engage directly in battle; their weapons were too short. Consequently these hoplites in the rear ranks experienced a considerable amount of stress with no way to release it. They had a superior position to see those ahead stabbing fiercely, hear the scrape and clang of bronze and the grunts and cries of men, but all they could do was wait and watch. If the men in those rear ranks felt the battle was going poorly, and decided to think of themselves rather than their comrades, they might start to drift away and leave the leaders. Unsupported by the rear, the leaders too might turn to flee. The great irony of this kind of flight was that while it was surely motivated by a sense of self-preservation, it actually increased the likelihood of death since a fleeing hoplite would turn his less-protected back to the enemy and generally cast away his shield to gain speed.[5] For this reason, incidentally, Spartan mothers famously admonished their husbands to come back with their shields or on them.[6]

It is striking that the Greeks, who loved to compete for personal glory in so many other areas, chose a form of combat that emphasized the team player, the one who did not stand out. Recently, though, historian J.E. Lendon has demonstrated that the teamwork of the phalanx was not contradictory to competition. Rather, individual hoplites still competed with their comrades when in battle. Instead of a competition to win the most duels or otherwise excel as an individual fighter, however, the hoplites competed to be thought the most stalwart, most steadfast member of the phalanx, showing bravery and discipline even in the horror of battle.[7] Tyrtaios, a seventh century Spartan general and poet, illustrated how teamwork could be thought of as heroic in a series of elegies he wrote to inspire warriors in their duty.

> For it is fine to die in the front line a brave man fighting for his fatherland ...

> So let us fight with spirit for our land. Die for our sons, and spare our lives no more.

> You young men, keep together, hold the line,

> Do not start panic or disgraceful rout. Keep grand and valiant spirits in your hearts,

> Be not in love with life – the fight's with men!

> Do not desert your elders, men with legs no longer nimble, by recourse to flight:

> It is disgraceful when an older man falls in the front line while the young hold back,

With head already white, and grizzled beard, gasping his valiant breath out in the dust. Let every man then, feet set firm apart, bite on his lip and stand against the foe.[8]

Above all, a hoplite had the duty to be loyal, steadfast in holding one's place on the team. These high standards were the marks of honour that Spartan hoplites, indeed all hoplites, strove to achieve.

Perhaps it is not surprising that just as Greek warfare veered away from the noble-led masses shown in *Troy* to the egalitarian phalanx, so too Greek societies – plural because ancient Greece was always politically fragmented – developed a new form of political organization, the *polis*. Essentially this uniquely Greek form of city state was based on the principles of citizenship. A citizen of a *polis*, which generally, though not always, meant a landowning male whose parents were from the *polis*, enjoyed a certain degree of political participation and legal equality to his fellow citizens. Perhaps the defining feature of any *polis* was its citizen assembly where all citizens had the right to register their opinion on the direction of the state. Though we cannot determine which came first and spurred the development of the other, the two developments, phalanx and *polis*, were surely interconnected. The ideals of egalitarian teamwork in the phalanx crossed over into the ideals of equal voting in an assembly, and vice versa.

Sparta and its Powerful Phalanx

No *polis* had a stronger and more feared phalanx than Sparta, and this was largely due to Sparta's peculiar historical development. The *polis* itself – the actual region was called Lacedaemonia, hence the Λ on the shields – consisted of five small villages along the Eurotas River. A rising power in the seventh century, by the sixth century Sparta occupied the dominant position in mainland Greece and was at the centre of a series of unilateral alliances with most of the *polises* in the Peloponnesus, the so-called Peloponnesian League. Though its power and status were challenged at times, most often by Argos to its north, Sparta consistently remained the most politically powerful and militarily feared *polis*. This was certainly the case when the Persians invaded Greece at the beginning of the fifth century.[9]

The key to Sparta's military dominance, and commensurably weighty political influence in Greek affairs, was its phalanx. Sparta alone of all the *polises* enabled its citizens to engage fully in military life, training regularly in the arts of war and drilling in their phalanx formations. Sparta had this capacity because early in their history, the Spartans came to dominate the Greeks of neighbouring Messenia, located to Sparta's west. In a set of wars that are poorly documented and poorly understood, the Spartans conquered Messenia and subjected the Messenians to the status of *helots*. *Helots* were serf-like subordinates required to deliver half of the agricultural produce they farmed to their Spartan masters. This freedom from the need to produce their own food was what allowed Spartan males to devote their time to participating in the political life of the *polis* and training for military service. Since the Spartans viewed these two practices – civic and military participation – as most critical to the good life of a citizen, keeping the *helots* labouring at agriculture, and the Spartans not, was of paramount importance.[10]

For understanding the battle of Thermopylae there are two main sources, neither of them Spartan. The first is Herodotus of Halicarnassus. Halicarnassus was a city on the southwestern coast of Asia Minor – the ancient Greek name for what is now Turkey. Little is known for certain about Herodotus other than what can be concluded from his writings. At one point it was accepted that he had travelled extensively throughout the eastern Mediterranean in search of evidence for his narrative, but even that no longer seems certain. What is reasonably certain is that Herodotus eventually travelled from Halicarnassus to Athens and seems to have written his history there in the second half of the fifth century. His central topic was the great war between Persians and Greeks, in which the Thermopylae campaign played a significant role.[11]

The second substantial account comes from Diodorus Siculus, a Greek writer from the first century BC. When it comes to his account of fifth-century Greece he is valued mostly because of his use of Ephorus as his main source. Ephorus, like Herodotus, came from Asia Minor and eventually travelled to Athens. He wrote his history in the later fourth century with an emphasis on writing a universal history, one that would describe not only the Greeks but other Mediterranean cultures. Though his level of source criticism was not always as sophisticated as other Greek historians, the importance of his work, preserved through Diodorus, to those reconstructing fifth-century Greek history cannot be denied.[12]

One of the difficult truths of studying ancient Sparta, however, is that the Spartans themselves left very little historical evidence. Though the general and poet Tyrtaios, quoted above, left war speeches from the seventh century, there are no fifth-century Spartan voices in history, theatre, poetry, or any other literary form. What cannot be gleaned from archaeology must be gathered from references to Sparta by other Greeks.

So it is that when it comes to understanding Spartan institutions our most extensive and valuable sources are Xenophon and Plutarch. Xenophon was an Athenian with interests ranging from historical writing to commanding troops as a mercenary. It was in this role that he encountered the Spartan king, Agesilaus, and struck up a fast friendship, even serving with him against Athens at the battle of Koroneia (394 BC). Activities like this earned Xenophon exile from Athens for a time, during which he was able to observe, first hand, Sparta and its customs. These observations were crafted into a treatise on Spartan society and customs that is invaluable to anyone hoping to understand Sparta.[13] Plutarch was a Greek biographer who lived and wrote under Roman rule in the first and second century AD. Among his other work is the biography of the legendary law-giver, Lycurgus, which is full of explanations of Spartan customs. He also wrote works collecting memorable Spartan sayings.

The accounts of the various sources differ on a number of issues, but a good case has been made for the following as the essentially historical narrative of the Thermopylae campaign.[14]

The battle at Thermopylae was part of the second Persian invasion of Greece. These invasions were sparked two decades before, in 499 BC. That year the Greeks of Ionia, in what is now western Turkey, revolted against their Persian king, Darius. The city of Miletus led the way. Milesians sought and received support from Athens in mainland Greece. Together, the Ionians and Athenians managed to sack the Persian capital of Ionia, Sardis. King Darius recaptured the rebel *polises*, then set his sights on the *polis* of Athens. Whether revenge was a sufficient motivation or he simply thought it a good enough excuse for extending Persian control into Europe, Darius launched an amphibious campaign against Athens. A fleet of Persian warships and troop transports crossed the Aegean and landed at the plains of Marathon, a day's march northeast of Athens. A force of Athenian hoplites drove the Persians back to their transports. After a failed attempt to bypass the Athenian walls through treachery, the fleet returned to the east whence it came.

Darius never managed to punish the Athenians. He died sometime in the next decade and was succeeded by his son, Xerxes. Xerxes was fiercely motivated by revenge, according to some ancient accounts, though one suspects he also saw a good opportunity to justify an invasion. He summoned contingents of soldiers from all the subject peoples of the Persian Empire. This large army marched for mainland Greece by way of the Hellespont, the narrow channel of ocean from the Black Sea to the Aegean. Royal engineers, not without difficulty, bridged the Hellespont and the Persian army marched west and south, through Thrace to Thessaly and the doorstep of Greece. The Persian navy, meanwhile, followed along the coast, guarding the flank of the land forces, transporting supplies, and facilitating communications.

Word reached Sparta of Xerxes' plan to invade Greece in the summer of 481 BC. The Spartans reacted by sending envoys to

Apollo's oracle at Delphi and to other Greek *polises*. The message from the oracle was grim indeed. The Persian invasion would only be stopped when Sparta was sacked or one of its kings slain in battle. Ultimately, the Spartans opted for the latter possibility and a fight with Xerxes. The Athenians, meanwhile, got the news from Sparta and consulted the oracle for themselves. The oracle's message this time was more complicated but included an indication that the wall of wood would not be defeated. The Athenian politician Themistocles persuaded the assembly that this wall of wood could only mean the Athenian fleet of triremes, the state of the art warships of the day. Consequently, the assembly voted to fight against Xerxes. With the powerful *polis* Sparta and the up-and-coming *polis* of Athens ready to fight, a conference was called in Corinth with other like-minded Greek states, and the Hellenic League was formed to face the Persian threat.

The League initially planned to send 10,000 hoplites to Thessaly to defend the Vale of Tempe. The flat, open plain made this plan untenable, however, particularly when further word reached the Greeks of the magnitude of Xerxes' army. A new plan was formed: a land force would hold the narrow pass at Thermopylae supported by the fleet nearby in the strait at Artemisium. The Spartan king, Leonidas, exercised his authority to form a small detail of 300 Spartans – men who had at least one son living and thus their line of inheritance intact. He and his 300 set out, leaving the rest of the Spartan hoplites at home. Leonidas also levied 1,000 of the Lacedaemonians, those who lived under Spartan authority but were not themselves Spartan citizens. Though it may seem odd, this small Spartan force also included *helots* acting as camp servants and light infantry. Other Peloponnesian hoplites brought the total expeditionary force to, perhaps, 4,100. Once Leonidas left the Peloponnesus and reached Boeotia, west of Athens, 700 Thespians joined his band – citizens of Thespis that is, not actors. Thebes, meanwhile was forced to contribute 400 hoplites to the enterprise. The *polis'* loyalty was suspect and these hoplites were hostages to guarantee the Thebans' good behaviour. At Thermopylae an additional 3,000 soldiers from Locria, Phocis and Malia joined Leonidas' force. All told, the Greek defenders may have numbered about 7,000 hoplites and several thousand light infantry.

Though the modern shoreline has changed significantly, in the fifth century the pass at Thermopylae was exceedingly narrow. According to Herodotus:

> the narrowest part of this whole region lies ... in front of Thermopylai and also behind it, consisting of a single wheel-track only both by Alpenoi, which lies behind Thermopylai and again by the river Phoinix near the town of Anthela there is no space but a single wheel-track only: and on the west of Thermopylai there is a mountain which is impassable and precipitous, rising up to a great height and extending towards the range of Oite, while on the east of the road the sea with swampy pools succeeds at once.[15]

The narrowest part of the pass, then, was perhaps 7ft wide and reinforced by the remnants of a wall built long before. Seemingly, Thermopylae was the perfect defensive position. Perfect that is until Leonidas learned of a mountain path that circumvented the position. He dispatched 1,000 Phocians to guard the path and, no doubt, hoped its existence would remain unnoticed by the Persians.

The Greek forces, heavily armed and armoured, organized in a phalanx, and aided by an outstanding defensive position held the pass for two days with few casualties received and many inflicted. By the third day, however, the Persians had received news of the mountain pass that undermined the Greek position. They dispatched a force to occupy it. The Phocians were defeated, the summit of the mountain captured, and the Persian force was ready to descend the mountain and strike at the rear of the Greek position. The leaders of the Greek coalition forces met, and Leonidas ordered that all forces should return to the south while the Spartans and their Lacedaemonian subordinates remained to defend the pass as long as they could. The 400 Theban hostages were also required to stay; the valiant Thespians volunteered to stay. This rear guard approximated something close to 2,000 heavy infantry, only 300 of whom were actually Spartans. The *helots* also remained, though probably not by choice. The Persian forces entrapped these Greeks and slew them from a distance with arrows and javelins. What the Spartans and their loyal comrades had brought the Hellenic League was a little more time to prepare a defence and evacuate Athens, which was next on Xerxes' list. But these Greeks also won a resounding moral victory that motivated the Hellenic League in its resistance to Persian domination. The Greeks who died at Thermopylae were buried together in graves marked by five stone markers. Leonidas, 'the Lion' was memorialized by a stone lion. Almost four decades later, Leonidas' bones were transferred to a Spartan grave that was topped by a memorial and a list of the Spartans who had fought at Thermopylae. Annual games in honour of these dead were held at Sparta.

The Origins of the Conflict in the Film *300*

As the film *300* would have it, Persian envoys arrive at Sparta to demand earth and water for their 'god-king' Xerxes. These are the traditional tokens of submission, and so far as the viewer can tell, for the Persians, the Spartans are just another little power in the path of the Persian conquests. King Leonidas of Sparta (Gerard Butler), just finished giving lessons in fighting with honour to his son, is given the news. He opens the doors of his house to reveal a small city centre with Spartans going about their daily business. Councilman Theron (Dominic West) arrives with the envoy who demands earth and water. The historical context, the Ionian Revolt and the battle at Marathon a decade before are omitted entirely. The envoy recounts the vastness of Xerxes' empire and the size of his army, so monstrous that 'it drinks the rivers dry'. Then he relays the god-king's demand for submission.

'Submission.' Leonidas turns the word over in his head, considering. He decides quickly. 'See, rumour has it, the Athenians have already turned you down. And if those ... philosophers and, uh, boy lovers have found that kind of nerve then ...' Theron interrupts, urging diplomacy, but Leonidas continues: 'and of course Spartans have their reputation to consider.' Now the envoy threatens Leonidas to choose his next words carefully. As the music rises, the camera shifts to pan across nearby Spartans. Leonidas considers them, their freedom, and their lives. He reaches a decision. 'Earth and water – well, you'll find plenty of both down there!' indicating a gigantic – and strangely unfenced – well to the back of the Persian messengers. 'Blasphemy! Madness!' shouts the Persian envoy as he and his comrades are driven back into the well, a filmic moment rendered in slow motion. The screams of the falling Persians fade away and we never do hear them reach the bottom.

Leonidas knows well that the Persians must be stopped, and they must be stopped at the narrow pass of Thermopylae where, he says, 'their numbers will count for nothing'. Even the king in Sparta, however, must gain the permission of the *ephors* for such a venture. Historically Xenophon suggests that the position of *ephor* was established,

[The Spartans] had come to the conclusion themselves, that of all the blessings which a state, or an army, or a household, can enjoy, obedience is the greatest. Since, as they could not but reason, the greater the power with which men fence about authority, the greater the fascination it will exercise upon the mind of the citizen to the enforcement of obedience. Accordingly the *ephors* are competent to punish whomsoever they choose; they have power to exact fines on the spur of the moment; they have power to depose magistrates in mid-career – nay, actually to imprison them and bring them to trial on a capital charge. Entrusted with these vast powers, they do not,

---

Cinematic Misleadings

- Leonidas is king of Sparta, but no mention is made in *300* of that unique Spartan institution: a second king.
- Leonidas scoffingly calls the Athenians 'philosophers and boy lovers'. Historically, romantic relationships between adult males and young teen boys were considered a common feature in Spartan male society.
- Great pains are taken by the narrator to tell the story of Leonidas' upbringing in the *agoge*, the Spartan system of education. In fact the kings were exempted from the *agoge*.
- The Immortals were the elite Persian warriors. They are represented on the walls of Persepolis as infantry armed with spears and bows, and protected by wicker shields, loose clothes and turbans. The origin of their name is unclear – but they were not black-robed and gold-masked inhuman warriors.

---

as do the rest of states, allow the magistrates elected to exercise authority as they like, right through the year of office; but in the style rather of despotic monarchs, or presidents of the games at the first symptom of an offence against the law they inflict chastisement without warning and without hesitation...[16]

... Monthly they exchange oaths, the *ephors* on behalf of the state, the king himself on his own behalf. And this is the oath on the king's part: 'I will exercise my kingship in accordance with the established laws of the state.' And on the part of the state the oath runs: 'So long as he (who exercises kingship) shall abide by his oaths we will not suffer his kingdom to be shaken.'[17]

Where the *ephors* are described by Xenophon as stern guardians of the law, however, in *300* they are cast as twisted fiends, 'inbred swine more creature than man'. They keep a mystic, despotic control over Sparta and its actions. Their chief tool is prophecy gained by preying sexually on the beautiful young oracles who tell them the future. Their supposed superstition, and irrationality, evil really, are set foils to the noble rationalism of King Leonidas. Accordingly, after Leonidas shares his plan, the ephors protest:

> *Ephor: We must consult the oracle ... trust the gods, Leonidas.*
> *Leonidas: I'd prefer you trusted your reason.*
> *Ephor: Your blasphemies have cost us quite enough already!*

The oracle, intoxicated by the smoke of the cavern, delivers an ill prophecy, and Leonidas' request is denied.

This scene is part of the writer and director's methodical emphasis. Throughout the film Leonidas and his supporters are portrayed as fighters for reason and freedom. Indeed at the very end of the film, the narrator Dilios tells the Spartan warriors around him, on the eve of the battle of Plataea,

> From free Greek to free Greek the word was spread. That bold Leonidas and his 300 so far from home laid down their lives. Not just for Sparta but for all Greece and the promise this country holds ...This day, we rescue a world from mysticism and tyranny and usher in a future brighter than anything we can imagine.

These claims must be taken with a healthy dose of salt. Though the ancient Greeks are rightly recognized even today for their contributions to reason and logic, they were not modern rationalists and certainly not atheists. Their faith in the gods, fear of forces beyond their comprehension, and surrender to irrationality were much the same as most ancient peoples.

The Spartans, far from being rational atheists, were noted for religious scruples that exceeded those of other Greeks. Herodotus asserted that they 'esteemed the things of the gods as more authoritative than the things of men'. They were known for their respect for divine signs and were willing to offer sacrifice after sacrifice, even in battle, to obtain properly the messages of the gods.[18]

Indeed, Xenophon actively linked their piety with their excellence as soldiers, noting:

> But I will go back to the beginning, and explain how the King sets out with an army. First he offers up sacrifice at home to Zeus the Leader and to the gods associated with him. If the sacrifice appears propitious, the Fire-bearer takes fire from the altar and leads the way to the borders of the land. There the King offers sacrifice again to Zeus and Athena. Only when the sacrifice proves acceptable to both these deities does he cross the borders of the land. And the fire from these sacrifices leads the way and is never quenched, and animals for sacrifice of every sort follow. At all times when he offers sacrifice, the King begins the work before dawn of day, wishing to forestall the goodwill of the god. And at the sacrifice are assembled colonels, captains, lieutenants, commandants of foreign contingents, commanders of the baggage train, and, in addition, any general from the states who chooses to be present. There are also present two of the Ephors, who interfere in nothing except by the King's request, but keep an eye on the proceedings, and see that all behave with a decorum suitable to the occasion. When the sacrifices are ended, the King summons all and delivers the orders of the day. And so, could you watch the scene, you would think all other men mere improvisers in soldiering and the Lacedaemonians the only artists in warfare.[19]

So the suggestion that religious scruples played little role in the more rational world of the Spartans holds no water. Leonidas' categorical rejection of anything not founded in logic is a modern varnish to the story.

The claim that the Spartans fought for the freedom of all Greeks is only slightly more substantial. It is all too easy to forget that Greek society, for all its seemingly progressive features in government and law, was a slave society. Slaves worked the silver mines and tutored

---

Spartan Cold Warriors

1962's *The 300 Spartans* begins with a shot of the Athenian acropolis – an ironic choice really since Athens and Sparta were enemies more often than not and had fundamentally different approaches to political and social life. The narrator's opening words, however, make clear that this will be a film about ideals: 'Greece. That hard and timeless land where even the stones speak of man's courage, of his endurance, of his glory.' Now the camera shifts to a shot of the modern plaque in the pass of Thermopylae, and the narrator continues, 'and none more eloquently than this lonely pillar in a desolate pass some 200 miles north of modern Athens. Across the hush of 24 centuries, this is the story of a turning point in history.' Now the camera captures a single line of Spartans sloping down a gentle hill. They are clad in red cloaks, helmets with red horsehair crests, round bronze shields and spears. Behind them stand a few archers. '... Of a blazing day when 300 Greek warriors fought here ...' The camera shifts to the front of the line and reveals a second line of Spartans perhaps fifty feet behind with some archers. '...to hold with their lives their freedom and ours.' It should come as no surprise that the film is viewed by many as a thinly veiled moral allegory for the Cold War. Here the Spartans are transformed from their controversial ancient selves into the freedom fighters of the West.

---

children even in Athens, that paradigm of early democracy. While the Spartans may not have had chattel slaves as such, they practised their own particular brand of oppression against the *helots*. These were the semi-enslaved inhabitants of Lacedaemonia and neighbouring Messene. They worked the land allotted to each Spartan so that, free from the burden of agricultural labour, he could participate fully in political and military life. Indeed Spartan obsession with military preparedness is explicable in part because of their desire to keep the *helot* population in check. Every year when five new *ephors* took office, they formally declared war on the *helots*. This was not to suggest that the Spartans actively conducted military operations against the *helot*, but rather the declaration effectively put the *helot* population under martial law and made slaying a *helot* equivalent to slaying an enemy combatant, not murdering a potentially innocent soul.[20]

The Ideal of the Spartan Hoplite and the Spartan Myth

300 resoundingly promotes the raw courage and toughness of the Spartan warrior. When Leonidas must bid his beloved queen Gorgo (Lena Headey) farewell, their looks and tones are tender, but not their words. Looking Leonidas in the eye, Gorgo bids, 'come back with your shield or on it', a saying attributed to a nameless Spartan mother by Plutarch in his *Sayings of Spartan Women*.[21] When Leonidas and his 300 join with a few thousand Arcadians, the Arcadian leader Daxos expresses dismay that the Spartans have brought so few warriors, Leonidas points out that he brought more than Daxos – more true warriors that is. When the young Spartan Stelios accompanies Arcadian leader Daxos on a scouting mission, his face breaks out in a mad smile upon seeing the size of the Persian army. When Daxos asks whence the grin, Stelios replies that at last, after so many battles, he may finally find an enemy worthy of him.

The film clearly links this hardiness to the Spartan system of education, the *agoge*. Indeed the film opens to Dilios (David Wenham) weaving a tale of Leonidas' education. Ignoring that the Spartan kings were actually the only male Spartan youths freed from participating in the *agoge*, the cinematic account suggests that only those children who were physically fit were allowed to survive; others were cast aside to die.[22] From selection until adulthood then, Spartan males were 'baptized in the fire of combat'. Shouted at, abused, beaten when they were weak, beaten if they proved themselves defiantly strong, Spartan males were taught systematically 'that death on the battlefield in service to Sparta was the greatest glory he could achieve in his life'. Then when his upbringing was largely complete, the Spartan child underwent his initiation by surviving alone in the wild. In Leonidas' case, Delios tells, this involved a night in the snow with only a loincloth and a desperate fight for survival with a large, ferocious, and quite hungry timber wolf. Historically, it also involved the Krypteia. Those Spartans who, during their time in the *agoge*, showed themselves fit for leadership in Spartan society were gathered into the Krypteia, a secret police made up of promising youths. The special charge of the Krypteia was to keep the *helots* suppressed. Quite often this meant that the men of the Krypteia identified and murdered select helots both to weed out potential troublemakers and to terrorize those left alive into submission. Roaming the countryside with only a dagger, they preyed on the helots in order to demonstrate their Spartan manhood.[23]

Through this description of the Spartan *agoge* and elsewhere throughout the film, *300* raises the perennial historical problem of the 'Spartan mirage', as one historian dubbed it many decades ago.[24] As noted earlier, the Spartans left essentially no written evidence about themselves. Rather, all our written information, save a few inscriptions, comes from outsiders, these mostly Athenian. But the Spartans had a vested interest in appearing as formidably trained killers to the rest of the Greek world. Hence the mirage. Was Spartan life as tough as this or did the Spartans simply find it suitable to let the rest of Greece think so?

Our best account of the *agoge* comes from the Athenian Xenophon's observations. Here he describes the system set in motion, as the Spartans believed, by the semi-legendary lawgiver Lycurgus:

Lycurgus ... gave the duty of controlling the boys to a member of the class from which the highest offices are filled, in fact to the 'Warden' as he is called. He gave this person authority to gather the boys together, to take charge of them and to punish them severely in case of misconduct. He also assigned to him a staff of youths provided with whips to chastise them when necessary; and the result is that modesty and obedience are inseparable companions at Sparta. Instead of softening the boys' feet with sandals he required them to harden their feet by going without shoes. He believed that if this habit were cultivated it would enable them to climb hills more easily and descend steep inclines with less danger, and that a youth who had accustomed himself to go barefoot would leap and jump and run more nimbly than a boy in sandals. And instead of letting them be pampered in the matter of clothing, he introduced the custom of wearing one garment throughout the year, believing that they would thus be better prepared to face changes of heat and cold. As to the food, he required the prefect to bring with him such a moderate amount of it that the boys would never suffer from repletion, and would know what it was to go with their hunger unsatisfied; for he believed that those who underwent this training would be better able to continue working on an empty stomach, if necessary, and would be capable of carrying on longer without extra food, if the word of command were given to do so: they would want fewer delicacies and would accommodate themselves more readily to anything put before them, and at the same time would enjoy better health.[25]

Enduring physical hardship and having the resourcefulness to survive in the midst of scarcity were critical parts of the *agoge* and Spartan boys learned these skills through practice, not theory.

The *agoge* however, was not simply a curriculum designed to produce tough Spartan warriors, though that was certainly a goal. Learning obedience, propriety, and respect were equally important:

In order that the boys might never lack a ruler even when the warden was away, [Lycurgos] gave authority to any citizen who chanced to be present to require them to do anything that he thought right, and to punish them for any misconduct. This had the effect of making the boys more respectful; in fact boys and men alike respect their rulers above everything. And that a ruler might not be lacking to the boys even when no grown man happened to be present, he selected the keenest of the prefects, and gave to each the command of a division. And so at Sparta the boys are never without a ruler.[26]

Upon reaching young adulthood, Xenophon says, a final round of restrictions was imposed on a youth lest he get ideas about independence and individualism:

... When a boy ceases to be a child, and begins to be a lad, others release him from his moral tutor and his schoolmaster: he is then no longer under a ruler and is allowed to go his own way. Here again Lycurgus introduced a wholly different system. For he observed that at this time of life self-will makes strong root in a boy's mind, a tendency to insolence manifests itself, and a keen appetite for pleasure in different forms takes possession of him. At this stage, therefore, he imposed on him a ceaseless round of work, and contrived a constant round of occupation. The penalty for shirking the duties was exclusion from all future honours. He thus caused not only the public authorities, but their relations also to take pains that the lads did not incur the contempt of their fellow citizens by flinching from their tasks.[27]

Xenophon's account, whether embellished or not, is that of an eyewitness, albeit one observing the Spartan system a hundred years after the period that concerns us. And while certainty remains out of reach, the broad outlines of the educational system have been reasonably well established.[28]

So, Sparta's *agoge* was, in fact, a systematic and brutal effort to eliminate a boy's ties to family and his desire to act independently. In place of these drives the *agoge* substituted loyalty to the *polis* and strict obedience to the elders in the state. Everyone was subordinate to someone or something in Sparta. The citizens were subject to their elders, as revealed in the Spartan policy that the citizen assembly's vote could be overturned by the council of elders, the *gerousia*.[29] The kings could be thwarted by the *ephors*. The *ephors* are the best candidates for leaders in Sparta but even they swore oaths to follow Spartan law. Obedience was a cardinal virtue in Sparta. Young lads, Xenophon noted, were required to walk in silence, eyes down, not venturing a word or a glance lest it appear disobedient.[30] Again it's worth noting that the kings were exempt from the *agoge* – perhaps since the position of king was inherited it would not do for a royal child to wash out of the system. Besides this point, however, Delios' discourse on education in *300* is essentially consistent with the historical system.

In a society where obedience, duty, and conformity to *polis* laws and authorities were so paramount, it is not surprising that military operations were an area in which a Spartan's worthiness could be judged. When Spartans returned from campaigns one of the critical roles of Spartan women was to praise or shame each publicly according to his performance in battle. Indeed honourable death in battle, above all, was the mark of a true Spartan. Unlike other *polises*, which clearly designated areas away from the living for the dead to be buried, Spartan dead were buried in places where the living still gathered. The only graves that were actually honoured with a mark, a simple grave stone, were those whose occupants had died in battle.[31] And to be the relative of such a Spartan was a great honour. In short, while the film is undeniably over-the-top in presenting Spartan attitudes, the core presentation of Spartans as dutiful warriors seeking worthy battles in which to show their skill and service to their *polis*, fits the ancient evidence well.

Hoplite, Phalanx, and the Battle at Thermopylae

Even the historical account of Ephialtes, the Greek traitor, shifts considerably under the treatment of author Frank Miller, preserved in the film *300*. Herodotus offered only the following report on Ephialtes:

Now, as [king Xerxes] was in a great strait, and knew not how he should deal with the emergency, Ephialtes, the son of Eurydemus, a man of Malis, came to him and was admitted to a conference. Stirred by the hope of receiving a rich reward at the king's hands, he had come to tell him of the pathway which led across the mountain to Thermopylae; by which disclosure he brought destruction on the band of Greeks who had there withstood the barbarians. This Ephialtes afterwards, from fear of the Lacedaemonians, fled into Thessaly.[32]

In *300*, however, Ephialtes is a caricature, a horribly, seemingly impossibly, deformed man. Parting ways again with the evidence, he is even a Spartan. Or rather, he was born to Spartan parents in Sparta, which is not the same thing. His tale is a sad one to modern ears. He would have been abandoned to die at the command of the Spartans for his horrible disfigurement but his mother loved him too much. And so, she and her husband secreted Ephialtes out of Sparta, he tells Leonidas. He has his father's shield, helmet and cloak, however, and he proudly declares that his father taught him to fight, 'to make spear and shield and sword as much a part of me as my own beating heart'. It is the case, Plutarch records, that Spartan elders ultimately decided the fate of each male child: life for those deemed physically fit to survive and thrive as warriors, and death for the rest. This feature of Ephialtes' story is consistent with Spartan practice.[33] Leaving aside that any child with the physical challenges displayed by Ephialtes would assuredly not survive in an ancient world with ancient medicine, Ephialtes was clearly not a true Spartan. And not to be a true Spartan was not to be a Spartan at all.

Despite its almost complete lack of historical grounding, this transformation of Ephialtes from a nobody to a Spartan outcast allows for a deeper illustration of the overruling conventions of Spartan society, most important of all, that a true Spartan must serve honourably in the phalanx.

Leonidas is moved, clearly, by Ephialtes' tale; his look betrays a hint of sympathy for this tortured body with a determined soul. When Ephialtes finishes his story with a few exemplary thrusts of his spear, however, Leonidas simply says, quietly, 'Raise your shield.' 'Sire?' Ephialtes questions. 'Raise your shield as high as you can'. Ephialtes strains at the effort, but he physically cannot bring the shield to cover his shoulder. Leonidas then notes: 'Your father should have told you how a phalanx works. We fight as a single impenetrable unit. That is the source of our strength. Each Spartan protects the man to his left thigh to neck with his shield. A single weak spot and the phalanx shatters.' Then he looks down at Ephialtes and raises his hand above him; 'Thigh to neck, Ephialtes.'

Carrying the wounded, removing the dead, and bringing water, these things Ephialtes can do. He cannot be part of the phalanx, however; he is not the equal of the Spartan citizens. The rejection wounds Ephialtes deeply, and in his rage he turns to the Persian king and reveals the secret path around the Greek lines.

This short episode introduces audiences to the principles of the phalanx, that characteristically Greek fighting formation. The principle as Leonidas states it is historically sound and recalls words from Tyrtaios' war poems:

Abide then, O young men, shoulder to shoulder and fight; begin not foul flight nor yet be afraid, but make the heart in your breasts both great and stout, and never shrink when you fight the foe. And the elder sort, whose knees are no longer nimble, fly not ye to leave them fallen to earth.[34]

The phalanx depends on each soldier standing his ground fighting with his colleagues and living or dying together.

How well, though, does theory play out in *300*'s battle scenes? First, consider the equipment of the Spartans and Persians in the film. The Spartans certainly cut imposing enough figures as hoplites. Equipped with shield, helmet, and greaves, wearing the archetypical

---

Ephialtes the Spurned Lover?

The 300 Spartans of 1962 directed by Rudolph Maté gave a different spin to Ephialtes that, while less fantastical, still deviates from the ancient accounts. In this cinematic version, the young Spartan Phylon has been denied the right to fight alongside the 300. He and his love Ellas follow the army as it moves north and eventually come across a couple living in the hills near Thermopylae. The elderly couple have taken in a man name Ephialtes without asking too many questions. Ephialtes is spurned in his advances toward Ellas. In revenge and for gold, he tells King Xerxes about the mountain track that circumvents Thermopylae. It seems that for both filmmakers the historical Ephialtes needed a stronger motive of personal revenge to justify informing the Persians about the back route at Thermopylae.

Spartan red cloak, and armed with spear and sword, they have most of the historic panoply. The helmets may be a bit fantastical, but are basically sound. A look at various models from the British Museum shows that the Spartan model, with its faux-visor, cannot be confirmed but still stays reasonably close to what we know of such helmets (see plates 5–7 and 10). The lack of breastplates is more problematic. It is not that warriors could not fight without them, but so far as can be determined, the breastplate was typical for the early fifth century hoplites *300* portrays. Even the Arcadians fight without the cuirass and it seems more likely that the director wanted to enhance the heroic material of the graphic novel by portraying the heavily muscled Greek torsos. If anything, the limited archaeological evidence suggests a reversed situation. Sixth century metal figurines of warriors, crafted in Sparta, all show the hoplite armed with breastplate and helmet but completely naked from the waist down. This does not seem like an appealing mode of dress for modern sensibilities but at least would have offered significantly greater protection than *300* allows its warriors. The Spartans are countered by all manner of Persian warriors. Historically different nations provided different troops whose capabilities and costumes span the spectrum, as a survey of Herodotus' descriptions reveals.[35] The film follows suit, though most of the infantry are variants on a theme. Some wear what appears to be leather armour of a sort. Most tend to wear no armour at all, relying only on tunic, cloak, and trousers for protection. Most carry wicker shields, serviceable enough to deflect the errant arrow or sword but of little use against a determined spear thrust. In these attributes they resemble Herodotus' description of the Persian infantry: 'about their heads they had soft felt caps called tiaras, and about their body tunics of various colours with sleeves' and 'about the legs trousers' although he notes that the tunic sleeves have 'the appearance of iron scales like those of a fish'. Next he goes on to note that 'instead of the ordinary shields they had shields of wicker-work, under which hung quivers; and they had short spears and large bows and arrows of reed, and moreover daggers hanging by the right thigh from the girdle'.[36]

When the main Persian force arrives, the ground shakes from the weight of their numbers. Since Herodotus' day the Persian army has been estimated at sizes up to and including 2,100,000 soldiers, which was essentially Herodotus' estimate. A great deal of energy has been invested by historians trying to constructively revise these hyperbolic numbers. Some aim for about 50,000, others for 200,000 or 300,000.[37] In any case, the first Persian warriors appear. The lead soldiers carry oblong wicker shields with cutouts in the middle that give them the appearance of a violin body. They wear turbans, shirts and trousers, and corselets of what appear to be leather embossed with metal plates. Spears are their primary weapons. Leonidas looks back at his soldiers, arrayed in the phalanx and roars: 'This is where we hold them! This is where we fight! This is where they die! Remember this day, men. For it will be yours for all time.' Only Spartans hold the pass; there are no other Greeks to be found. The Persian commander demands the Spartans lay down their weapons. He receives a spear through the chest for his effort. The Spartans raise their shields into a wall, thrust forth their spears and Leonidas taunts: 'Persians, come and get them,' a saying historically attributed to that Spartan King.[38]

The battle begins. The Persian warriors charge as a mass not unlike the Greek host in Petersen's *Troy*. They have no defined ranks or columns; as a result the fastest runners start to outstrip the rest. The Spartans meanwhile, wait to receive the charge. The first two lines hunker behind their shields in a combat stance, chests perpendicular to the shield and the rim resting on their left shoulders. They are covered in their crouch, as Leonidas noted, from thigh to neck and then some. Spears are at the ready in underhand grips, the iron heads extending over the fronts of their shields. The camera shifts to the Persians charging, then changes to a top view close-up that emphasizes the contrast between the disorderly Persian charge and the Spartans, holding their positions as their captain bids them.

Then comes the impact. Wicker shields raised, the Persian infantry collide with the Spartans. The Spartans dig their heels in the sand, pushed back ever so slightly by the force of the massive charge. The front ranks of hoplites lean into the concavity of their shields. They are too close to their enemies to use their weapons. Instead a shoving contest develops. The camera closes in on a handful of combatants shoving back and forth, the Spartans leaning into their shields. There is very little killing. One Spartan in the third row receives a cut to the arm from a spearhead which he returns by stabbing his enemy in the chest. This is the exception, however, not the rule. The focus is on pushing with shields. The weight of the enemy numbers pushes the Spartans back, but then they dig in and halt. Dramatically, and quite unrealistically, the Spartans use their shields to throw back the leading Persians then follow up with stabbing spears to dispatch their foes. This begins a cycle: shove back, move shield aside, stab and move forward a few inches. There are instances of individuals lifting their shields and slashing with sword, but the shield wall of the phalanx quickly reforms and most of the killing work is done with spears.

Certainly, the close-ups of Spartan warriors shoving their enemies back with their shield arm, raising their shields over them and unleashing murderous spear thrusts makes for outstandingly heroic cinematography. Still the practical limitations on such a tactic make it unlikely this was how Spartans, or anyone else for that matter, fought. First, though the push, pull, and shove of the infantry lines did occur in these battles, this also presumably involved soldiers leaning into their shields and using their bodies to push. Throwing back something the size of a man with the back of a shield arm is a feat of strength most cannot accomplish and certainly not repeatedly. Second, even if each and every Spartan were appropriately Herculean for this task – as the movie really does suggest – the tactic of lifting one's shield high and exposing oneself to stab essentially negates the very purpose of the shield, to defend. Instead we should reject this aspect of the scene in favour of other shots that capture fierce scrabbling and pushing with Spartans thrusting spears over or to the side of their shields. These kinds of attack were devastating enough. When Greek fought Greek and all wore comparable bronze body armour, the casualties would have been minimal. The effect of the Spartans' iron spearheads against the wicker shields and cloth armour of the Persian warriors, however, must have been devastating.

The Spartans' rhythmically methodical killing creates breathing room between the opposing lines. Now there is more space, perhaps 3–6ft. The Spartans continue their grim work following a tempo. Shields move aside and spears thrust forward. The camera shifts to a high angle shot showing a wave of Persian troops checked by the slow and orderly Spartan advance. It is worth noting that the Persians are not massed but still flowing irregularly up against the Spartan wall individually or in small groups. One cannot help but wonder if the Persians would really have sacrificed their great advantage in numbers by sending soldiers so haphazardly against the phalanx. Essentially, though, that is what the ancient sources said they did and in the absence of any means to circumvent the Spartan line, there probably was little else to try other than steadily increasing the numbers assaulting the Spartans. Whether orderly or haphazardly,

Spartan Sayings

Plutarch, a second century Greek living in the Roman Empire, collected and wrote the *Sayings of the Spartans*. A number of rough-and-ready aphorisms he attributed to those involved in the Thermopylae campaign. These two make their way into *300*:

- 'When someone said, "Because of the arrows of the barbarians it is impossible to see the sun," [Leonidas] said, "Won't it be nice, then, if we shall have shade in which to fight them?"'
- 'When Xerxes wrote, "Hand over your arms," Leonidas wrote in reply, "Come and take them."'

Plutarch also ascribes to Spartan mothers in general, a saying other Greeks attributed to Queen Gorgo: 'Come back with your shield or on it.'

Finally, Plutarch records a number of other sayings attributed to the Spartan king Leonidas at Thermopylae:

- 'When someone else said, "[The Persians] are near to us," he said, "Then we also are near to them."'
- 'When someone said, "Leonidas, are you here to take such a hazardous risk with so few men against so many?" he said, "If you men think that I rely on numbers, then all Greece is not sufficient, for it is but a small fraction of their numbers; but if on men's valour, then this number will do."'
- 'He bade his soldiers eat their breakfast as if they were to eat their dinner in the other world.'

(Plutarch *Moralia 225B-D*)

however, the Persian shields and armour were simply not up to the task. They could not stop the thrust of Spartan spears.

The same probably should be noted about the Spartans and their equipment in *300*. If the historical Spartans had been as naked as the filmic ones, they would have suffered a far greater number of wounds. This is not to suggest that hoplite shields and a phalanx formation alone were flimsy defences. Clearly they were quite the opposite. Diodorus points directly to the critical role of Greek shields and phalanx in his description of the fighting:

> The fight which followed was a fierce one, and since the barbarians had the king as a witness of their valour and the Greeks kept in mind their liberty and were exhorted to the fray by Leonidas, it followed that the struggle was amazing. For since the men stood shoulder to shoulder in the fighting and the blows were struck in close combat, and the lines were densely packed, for a considerable time the battle was equally balanced. But since the Greeks were superior in valour and in the great size of their shields, the Medes gradually gave way; for many of them were slain and not a few wounded. The place of the Medes in the battle was taken by Cissians and Sacae, selected for their valour, who had been stationed to support them; and joining the struggle fresh as they were against men who were worn out they withstood the hazard of combat for a short while, but as they were slain and pressed upon by the soldiers of Leonidas, they gave way. For the barbarians used small round or irregularly shaped shields, by which they enjoyed an advantage in open fields, since they were thus enabled to move more easily, but in narrow places they could not easily inflict wounds upon an enemy who were formed in close ranks and had their entire bodies protected by large shields, whereas they, being at a disadvantage by reason of the lightness of their protective armour, received repeated wounds.[39]

Still, even an unintended sword or spear blow against naked flesh stood a good chance to cripple or kill. So it's important to remember that while this part of the film illustrates the effectiveness of shields and formation, historically the Spartans did have their panoply at Thermopylae. This meant historically their protection from wounds was significantly greater, and their cinematic defensive formation was even more effective in reality. After all, the Spartans and their allies did hold firm against a vastly numerically superior force for days.

So far, though some of the shield work is puzzling, and the lack of armour sticks out like a sore thumb, the phalanx has worked exactly as Leonidas described to Ephialtes and very much how many historians think it did. Each hoplite protects his comrades; all work together. 'A single weak spot and the phalanx shatters,' Leonidas had said. So far, the phalanx works like a phalanx. The less organized and less well protected Persians are devastated. Then something changes. The shot shifts from the organized phalanx to Leonidas and his captain moving ahead of their comrades. Gaps in the shield wall remain where they once stood, and the two sally as much as 10ft in front of the line, like Homer's *promachoi*. No longer part of a team, the two engage in a brutal display of individual spear-work, presented in slow motion. Leonidas launches into a murderous dance, spinning about, using his spear to strike with swings as well as stabs, and flipping Persians over his shield. The camera focuses on him now. He has outstripped his captain and moves forward perhaps another 10ft. Still the Persians are loosely grouped, flowing toward Leonidas in small groups of two and three. Shifting from an underhand stab to an overhand throw, Leonidas knocks a Persian to the ground, impaled on the spear. Spear gone, he draws his sword, a reasonable facsimile of a Greek sword. He flips a Persian over his head and cuts into several more. Finally the foremost phalanx fighters are but a few steps behind. There is nothing even approximating, however, the unified phalanx wall from only a minute before. Yet Leonidas catapults forward again with no indication of any concern for his comrades.

This is not a phalanx battle. Indeed it looks very much like an *aristeia*, a display of battlefield excellence that Homer often employs in the *Iliad*. One of the more memorable *aristeias* is that of Diomedes, who is energized by Athena to go on a killing spree:

So raging Diomedes mauled the Trojans. There – he killed Astynous, then Hypiron, a frontline captain. One he stabbed with a bronze lance above the nipple, the other his heavy sword hacked at the collarbone, right on the shoulder, cleaving the whole shoulder clear of neck and back. And he left them there, dead, and he made a rush at Abas and Polyidus, sons of Eurydamas, an aged reader of dreams, but the old prophet read no dreams for them when they set out for Troy – Diomedes laid them low then swung to attack the two sons of Phaenops, hardy Xanthus and Thoon, both men grown tall as their father shrank away with wasting age ... he'd never breed more sons to leave his riches to. The son of Tydeus killed the two of them on the spot, he ripped the dear life out of both and left their father tears and wrenching grief. ... Next Diomedes killed two sons of Dardan Priam careening on in a single car, Echemmon and Chromius. As a lion charges cattle, calves and heifers browsing the deep glades and snaps their necks, so Tydides pitched them both from the chariot, gave them a mauling – gave them little choice – quickly stripped their gear and passed their team to his men to lash back to the ships.[40]

The passage is similar enough in flavour to Leonidas' onscreen performance. Leonidas has personally slain or wounded at least thirteen enemy soldiers in the span of one minute to Diomedes' eight, and if the names of every Persian he had slain were included, the script would read still more like this passage from Homer. Leonidas plunges his sword into the final fallen body, then looks up to see a mass of Persian soldiers keeping their distance, perhaps 12ft away. Apparently at no point do these Persians see fit to occupy the open space and use their far greater numbers to slay the lone Leonidas. This episode is a purely cinematic construct.

Now that Leonidas' *aristeia* is done, the Spartans reform with the goal of pushing the remnants of the Persian attackers off the cliffs and into the sea. This focus on duelling, however, seems to make a mockery of Leonidas' emphasis on teamwork. And while it may have been the case that some hoplites at Thermopylae or in other battles did break ranks and engage in individual duelling, this was clearly not the expected behaviour. Each person who left the line weakened the line. If anything, our sources indicate that the Spartans did not lose discipline; they simply closed ranks. Certainly that is the gist of Diodorus' account above. And while Herodotus suggests that the Spartans in particular were not static fighters but would lure the enemy in by faking retreat then turning to attack, both he and Diodorus, when they say anything at all about the Greeks' formations, say that they were orderly and close ranked.[41]

Returning to the film, after Leonidas' *aristeia* the skies indeed darken with the arrows that blot out the sun, so numerous are they. The camera reveals another advantage of the Spartan shield – it stops arrows. The Spartans crouch under their shields, the arrows lodging in the shields and piercing their cloaks but doing no damage to the men. Next the Persians try a cavalry charge. Leonidas, standing in the front rank looks back at his soldiers and growls, 'Today, no Spartan dies.' The phalanx reforms to await the charge – this time in a wedge. Cavalry were used in very limited capacities by Archaic Greeks engaging one another in phalanx battles. The phalanx itself is essentially the best defence against mounted units since, so long as the infantry keep their nerve and hold their place, a horse will not be coaxed or driven to a collision with a wall of men.[42] The wedge as a formation was normally used by certain ancient cavalry formations, not infantry, to penetrate an enemy formation; there may not have been any disadvantage for the Spartan infantry to adopt this defensive position, but there is no easily graspable advantage either. It may be that the wedge provided a better scene setup for taking shots of the cavalry troopers' attacks. In any event, attack is what they do. The Persian cavalry armed with sturdy spears or swords, metal helmets, oblong wicker shields and metal breastplates on top of tunics and trousers. They wear a reasonable enough panoply for heavy cavalry. Herodotus, however, says the Persian cavalry were equipped the same as the infantry except for metal helmets; he makes no mention of breastplates.[43] There is an authentic moment where the Spartan captain's son looks nervous and his father bids him to be calm – a nod to the morale impact of a cavalry charge. While horses will not normally collide with clusters of men, the men may not be aware of that fact and it surely must have taken steel nerves to hold one's place as animal and rider bore down.

The cavalry close and flow to each side of the Spartan wedge, slashing and stabbing as they pass – authentically enough avoiding collisions. The Spartans stab and slash back as they pass. The shots of this cavalry pass illustrate an important element of cinematic versions of ancient battle. Individual cavalry troopers and soldiers are shown fighting, not the group. Though the establishing shot indicates that a whole formation is attacking, what the audience sees is a series of one-on-one battle shots. The cinematic perspective often highlights such individual attacks, personalizing the battle, bringing it close to the viewer in a way that would be lost if the camera pulled back far enough that all the engaged soldiers were in the shot. What is lost is a sense of the direction of the whole battle at that point. What is gained, however, is a visceral sense of the many individual encounters that made up a unit battle.

At this point in the film the Spartan captain says their Greek allies want to be part of the battle. Leonidas agrees that the Arcadian commander Daxos and twenty of his hand-picked soldiers should ready themselves. It's a reminder that the battle at Thermopylae was not, by any means fought by Spartans alone. Herodotus and Diodorus are clear throughout their narrative of the first battles that the Persians were fighting 'the Hellenes' not simply 'the Spartans'. They do not suggest any difference in the type of service: all the Greeks are referred to as the troops of Leonidas. With such a narrow space to fight, it seems likely that different contingents of Greek hoplites rotated into the battle as time passed, but our sources are silent on the matter.[44]

More than twenty minutes of film time have been devoted to the first day of battle. The Spartans have handled everything the Persians have launched at them and slaughtered an enormous number of their foes. Now it is time for Xerxes' best troops: The Immortals. This follows roughly the account in Diodorus:

> Xerxes, seeing that the entire area about the passes was strewn with dead bodies and that the barbarians were not holding out against the valour of the Greeks, sent forward the picked Persians known as the 'Immortals', who were reputed to be preeminent among the entire host for their deeds of courage.

The Immortals, however, fared little better than their comrades-in-arms:

> But when these also fled after only a brief resistance, then at last, as night fell, they ceased from battle, the barbarians having lost many dead and the Greeks a small number.[45]

These immortals as Diodorus notes, were an elite unit of soldiers chosen for their courage. Herodotus also refers to these soldiers, even providing an explanation for their name:

> These picked ten thousand Persians ... were called Immortals for this reason: when any one of them was forced to fall out of the number by death or sickness, another was chosen so that they were never more or fewer than ten thousand. The Persians showed the richest adornment of all, and they were the best men in the army.[46]

He agrees essentially with Diodorus:

> When the Medes had been roughly handled, they retired, and the Persians whom the king called Immortals, led by Hydarnes,

attacked in turn. It was thought that they would easily accomplish the task. When they joined battle with the Hellenes, they fared neither better nor worse than the Median army, since they used shorter spears than the Hellenes and could not use their numbers fighting in a narrow space.[47]

He does provide the additional piece of information that the Immortals were spear fighters. This is corroborated earlier in his account when he describes the standard equipment of the ethnic Persian units, to which the Immortals belonged: sleeved tunics and trousers, wicker shields, spear and dagger, bow and arrows. This equipment suggests that the Persians served as heavy infantry, but with flexible weaponry for ranged attacks.

300 transforms the historical attack of the Immortals into something almost unrecognizable. Indeed, if the narrator did not refer to the attacking group as Immortals there would be no reason to identify them as such. In the film, night falls before the Immortals attack. They are shrouded in black from head to toe, each with a golden mask cast in a fearsome grimace and a metal breastplate. These warriors wield two katana-like blades as their only weapons. Further embellishment appears when one raises his hand. It is shrivelled and blackened like that of a mummy with long, almost talon-like fingernails. The narrator notes:

> They have served the dark will of Persian kings for 500 years. Eyes as dark as night. Teeth filed to fangs. Soulless. The personal guard to king Xerxes himself. The Persian warrior elite. The deadliest fighting force in all of Asia. The Immortals.

There is little else to consider in this almost completely fanciful encounter. The Spartans fight the immortals individually and take some casualties. From the perspective of building a good story, the individual duels highlight that of all Xerxes' troops, only the Immortals can come close to beating the Spartans. From the perspective of illustrating systems of combat, the Spartans have abandoned the very formation Leonidas himself said gave them strength and the formation that, historically, allowed the Greeks to hold the pass for as long as they did. After a bit of fantastic duelling, the Spartans return to their phalanx and the film shows a close-up of hoplites and Immortals struggling.

In its account of the second day, the film embraces the fantastic side for a time. To the crunch of distorted guitars belting out hard rock rhythms, the audience sees a monstrous war-rhinoceros, explosive magical grenades from the magi, a giant man who has crab claw hands, and of course, a gigantic King Xerxes. Eventually the film returns to simpler encounters of Spartans and Persians, but the phalanx again has been abandoned for the more dramatic and less historical duelling. Two Spartans, Stelios (Michael Fassbender) and the captain's son Astinos (Tom Wisdom), slaughter Persians as a pair, standing perhaps 6–10ft apart from one another. The corpses spread out in the open space around them and a line in the dusty distance is the Persian army. The logic of this scene would suggest that Persians only dispatched skirmishers to fight in this round. By now it should be clear that this fundamentally misrepresents the issue. Historically the Persians en masse were not able to penetrate the phalanx; it was not a matter of individuals duelling. Diodorus highlights this feature again in his account of the second day fighting:

Xerxes, now that the battle had turned out contrary to his expectation, choosing from all the peoples of his army such men as were reputed to be of outstanding bravery and daring, after an earnest exhortation announced before the battle that if they should storm the approach he would give them notable gifts, but if they fled the punishment would be death. These men hurled themselves upon the Greeks as one mighty mass and with great violence, but the soldiers of Leonidas closed their ranks at this time, and making their formation like a wall took up the struggle with ardour. And so far did they go in their eagerness that the lines which were wont to join in the battle by turns would not withdraw but by their ceaseless endurance of the hardship they got the better and slew many of the picked barbarians. The day long they spent in conflict, vying with one another; for the older soldiers challenged the fresh rigor of the youth, and the younger matched themselves against the experience and fame of their elders.[48]

Fundamentally though, this scene serves the narrative of the film. Astinos will soon die duelling, overwhelming his father the captain with shattering grief and rage. In retaliation, the captain himself goes on a killing spree and the imagery of the phalanx is again left far behind.

Of course, the tragedy of this story, in the historical narrative and the fantastically embellished film, is that the Greeks that stay will die. In the end, Ephialtes, pride wounded by Leonidas, is lured by Xerxes and his appeal to sensual pleasures to betray the location of the goat track that goes over the mountain and circumvents the Spartan position. The other Greeks leave to seek safety – though in reality a number of other Greeks remained at their posts alongside the Spartans.[49] A final dialogue between Leonidas and King Xerxes heightens the tragedy and the men, still all Spartans, are pierced by hundreds of arrows raining down on them from all directions. The film ends on a triumphant note, however, for Delios, the narrator of these events has survived. After the loss of one of his eyes Leonidas judged Delios could best serve not by dying with the 300 but by delivering the news. 'Remember us,' he tells Delios, 'Remember why we died.' And so Delios speaks the words that Herodotus says were carved on a memorial stone, 'Go tell the Spartans, passerby, that here by Spartan law we lie.'[50] The brief final scene of the film shows Delios speaking to his Spartan comrades at Plataea, the site of the decisive Greek victory against the Persians. Dilios wraps up his story: 'From free Greek to free Greek the word was spread. That bold Leonidas and his 300 so far from home laid down their lives.

Not just for Sparta but for all Greece and the promise this country holds.' The Greek army now numbers 30,000 with 10,000 Spartans and Delios encourages, 'The enemy outnumber us a paltry three-to-one. Good odds for any Greek. This day, we rescue a world from mysticism and tyranny and usher in a future brighter than anything we can imagine.'

There are so many intentionally fantastical elements in *300* that one might well wonder why even include it in a search for models of ancient battle. Indeed even if all magic, all grenades, all fiends, and the 8ft tall god-king Xerxes himself were struck from the film, the frequent return to the deeds of the individual as a warrior fighting alone, undermines the concept of the phalanx. But it is in those moments, when the camera homes in on the phalanx, its members working together and staying in formation, that the film offers a helpful image of the mechanics of hoplite warfare. It is not based on complicated manoeuvres or stratagems, nor is it based on the technical skill of the combatants. In the moments of pushing and pulling, grunting and screaming, and metal clanging on metal, *300* illustrates, first and foremost, that fighting in a phalanx is a test of will, and a test of camaraderie. Secondly, this formation on the right terrain was unstoppable by the looser organizations and weaker equipment of the Persians. Indeed it remained the characteristic formation of Greek armies, though it would undergo something of a transformation under Alexander the Great, to whom we now turn.

Chapter 3

Alexander and the Battle of Gaugamela

Oliver Stone's *Alexander* (2004) begins at the end. Alexander (Colin Ferrell) is at death's door, lying in his sick bed, surrounded by his ambitious generals. He makes one dramatic effort to pass on his signet ring and bestow legitimacy upon one of his successors, but dies before he can do so. The scene jumps ahead forty years from Babylon to Alexandria, Egypt. Here we witness a much older Ptolemy (Anthony Hopkins), one of those generals, dictating his account of Alexander to a scribe, Kadmos. Ptolemy laments that, after Alexander's death, his generals tore the short-lived Macedonian empire apart. Now, Ptolemy laments, 'there is no one left to remember' the great deeds of Alexander. 'He was a god,' says Ptolemy of Alexander, 'or as close as anything I've ever seen. He changed the world. Before him there were tribes and after him all was possible. There was suddenly a sense that the world could be ruled by one king and be better for all.'

Ptolemy continues his dictation and the scene shifts to Macedonia in the days of Alexander's youth. He is loved fiercely by his mother, Olympias (Angelina Jolie), and admires but comes to resent deeply his father, King Philip II of Macedon (Val Kilmer). In his schooling he learns to wrestle, learns about geography, learns how to win and lose well in competitions. His father takes him down into the royal Macedonian catacombs and inculcates in him the legends of gods and heroes. In short he is trained to be a hero and a king. And so he shall be. When Philip is murdered, a death many then and now attributed to Olympias, Alexander becomes king of Macedonia.

At the close of these segments covering Alexander's early years, the camera returns to Ptolemy, continuing his account. Philip is murdered and Alexander king. The Greeks who had been subject to Philip broke their treaties under Alexander. Alexander subdued them and destroyed the *polis* of Thebes for its treachery. This object lesson in the dangers of rebellion quelled Greek resistance. Once Greece had been re-secured, Ptolemy narrates,

> At 21 Alexander invaded Asia with an army of 40,000 trained men. Liberating one city state after another, he conquered all of western Asia south to Egypt, where he was declared pharaoh of Egypt, worshipped as a god. It was in Egypt that the respected oracle of Siwah declared him the true son of Zeus. He finally provoked Darius himself to battle in the heart of the Persian Empire near Babylon.

The camera follows Ptolemy's line of sight, panning across and up the large mosaic wall map from Babylon to the plains by the village Gaugamela.

The Battle of Gaugamela, Alexander's greatest single victory, is the critical battle scene for Stone's epic. The director invested a great deal of effort to recreate the battle as authentically as possible. To that end he worked with historian Robin Lane Fox, whose biography of Alexander, now more than three decades old, is still very much the standard treatment of the Macedonian conqueror.[1] Fox, in his commentary on the DVD version, refers to *Alexander* as 'a film which is an epic drama with an unusual reference to history as a springboard,' but also a film that 'was never conceived or presented as a historical documentary'.[2] He makes an important point. One cannot listen to the director's notes without recognizing that Oliver Stone took great pains to learn as much as possible about the historical Alexander and capture the drama of that historical Alexander on film. His consultant is a leading expert on Alexander. We should expect then that when the film diverges from the historical evidence, it does so not through any lack of care on the part of the director and consultants, but because, in the end, Stone made an epic film, not a documentary. *Alexander*, in short, is a perfect case study for the strengths and limitations of film capturing the face of battle and for how historical elements can be transmuted in the making of an epic film.

Macedonian Warfare

Macedonia, the kingdom of Philip and Alexander, was located in the northern part of the Balkan Peninsula. It was a minor power in the days of the Persian invasion of Greece. Culturally Greek though looked on as barbaric by many of the Greeks who found the Macedonian dialect incomprehensible, the Macedonians played a minor role in the political and military struggles of the fifth century. Politically fragmented into the spheres of powerful landed nobles and exposed to constant raiding from the tribes of Illyria to the northwest and Thrace to the northeast, the Macedonian kings were relatively weak. A gradual evolution took place in Greek warfare of the fifth century and the fourth, however, and King Philip II of Macedon (359–336 BC) took advantage of cutting edge ideas in warfare to create the Macedonian army and make Macedon supreme in the Balkans.

Philip, in short, instituted the military reforms that allowed his son to exceed him so in fame. The Macedonian victories against the Persians, not least of all at Gaugamela, were triumphs for a new form of army, one very different from the hoplite phalanx that fought an earlier generation of Persians. He turned the Macedonian army into a standing army with regularly scheduled pay for the soldiers, an important change from the militia armies that characterized most of Greece. Having a professional force allowed him to conduct regular training in all manner of complex manoeuvres that were normally beyond the militia citizen-soldier.[3] He also overhauled the logistical systems of the army, making it more efficient and effective as a campaign army. Previously, and as was common in Greece, each soldier was attended by a servant who helped him with his armour, cooked, and performed a variety of other services. Philip ended this practice and set the standard that every ten soldiers would be supported by one servant, reducing the number of non-essential personnel – and mouths to feed – significantly. Supply trains were streamlined further. Now soldiers were trained to carry their own emergency rations, as much as thirty days' worth, and cover up to thirty miles in a days' march if needed. Any food beyond the bare rations of olives and bread had to come from foraging in the local countryside. These measures made the army swifter on the march and less vulnerable to attacks on its supply lines.[4]

But it is the functioning of Philip's highly trained army in battle that is most important for analyzing the film *Alexander*. The core of the Macedonian army under Philip consisted of three forces: Foot Companions, who provided a phalanx, Companion Cavalry, and Hypaspists. The phalangites of the Foot Companions numbered about 9,000 and normally occupied the centre of the Macedonian battle line.[5] The smallest core unit was the *syntagma* of 256 soldiers.[6] These troops were trained over years of service to shift efficiently their depth and formation as circumstances demanded, from a wide formation, eight soldiers deep, to a column 120 deep. They were also trained to make about-faces and to shift from an open marching order to closed ranks where each soldier occupied less than three feet of space and soldiers' shields fit closely together.[7]

These phalangites were trained to fight equipped with the new panoply Philip had assigned them. Gone were the 7–8ft spears and the 3ft diameter heavy hoplite shields. The former stretched

---

How many eyes did Philip have?

Diodorus Siculus, likely drawing from the fourth century historian Ephorus, reported that Philip lost one eye during the siege of Methone, an Athenian stronghold (16.34.5). While Oliver Stone's Philip has clearly lost the use of an eye, Robert Rossen's Philip from the 1956 *Alexander the Great* has the use of both his eyes.

and the latter shrank. Instead of the spear, phalangites now carried the *sarissa*. A monstrous pike up to 18ft long, it had a foot-long iron head, metal butt spike with a counterbalance, and was made from two shafts of cornel wood joined by a bronze tube at the centre. Armed with this, the first four or five ranks of soldiers could extend their spears past the front line and attack, offering a formidable challenge to an enemy.[8] Managing this pike was a strictly two-handed affair. Gripping a traditional hoplite shield, or any shield with a handgrip for that matter, was impossible. Instead, the phalangites carried the *aspis*. A round shield of bronze about 18in. in diameter, the *aspis* was held by an elbow strap for the left arm and a shoulder strap so that both hands remained free to manage the *sarissa*.[9] In addition to this a phalangite might wear a helmet and greaves.[10] The men in the front of formation were the most heavily armoured with a light corselet of linen or leather that could be reinforced with some metal but was far lighter than the body armour of a fifth century hoplite.

The phalanx had two primary functions. The first was to engage the enemy's infantry, thereby preventing them from manoeuvring and enabling the Companion Cavalry to strike a blow on the flank or rear. The second was to pressure the infantry once it had been disrupted or disordered by cavalry, to give a final shove and break it apart. Though the Macedonian phalanx was generally effective at these tasks, it had its own particular weaknesses. The need for the phalanx to remain tightly knit and orderly meant that it was challenged by anything other than completely flat terrain, which caused it to grow disordered. This was the case even for these professional Macedonian soldiers who had trained for years, testimony to the difficulty of manoeuvring in a phalanx. Furthermore, the *sarissas* were a terrifying enough experience for enemy armies, but less useful should that enemy be able to close within the spear lengths and attack with sword or short spear. Though the phalangites were highly trained, the formations still moved at a very lumbering and limited pace compared to light infantry. Finally, with shields hung from the left shoulder and elbow, the phalangites were extremely vulnerable on their unprotected right flank.[11]

It was to protect the right flank of the slow moving phalanx that Philip formed the Shield Bearers, or Hypaspists. These troops were equipped in a full hoplite panoply of helmet, greaves, cuirass and shield. They bore swords and possibly short stabbing spears. Crack troops, they were normally positioned on the phalanxe's right flank. Thereby they joined phalanx to cavalry and prevented enemy outflanking on the right.[12] Swifter and more flexible than the phalangites, the Hypaspists were employed in a variety of different military roles.

The metaphor of a hammer and anvil is often used to describe Philip and Alexander's tactics. The phalanx was the anvil, the steady base that pinned enemy infantry formations in place. The Companion Cavalry was the smashing hammer.[13] They were an elite group of lords provided by Philip with abundant Macedonian farmland to enable them to train and stable warhorses. When Philip took the throne they numbered perhaps 600. When Alexander succeeded him, that number had increased to 4,000.[14] The Companion Cavalry were shock cavalry, meaning that they were intended for close combat with enemy cavalry and infantry. They were well armoured for fighting up close, wearing a metal or leather cuirass and pteruges to protect the lower abdomen. For head protection many wore what is known as a Boeotian style helmet. An unusual looking helmet, it consisted of a skull-cap with a brim flaring from the cap and rippling to resemble cloth. They carried a spear slender enough that it commonly snapped on impact and a sword for when it did. Like all ancient riders, the Companions had no stirrups and had to have an impressive amount of horse skill to charge and fight without losing their seats.[15]

The Companion Cavalry used the wedge as their core formation and this offered several advantages. First, the pointed formation allowed easier penetration of the flanks or rear of infantry formations. Equally as important, the wedge had only one leader for the riders to follow, allowing the formation to wheel and manoeuvre sharply, much more sharply than could a rectangular formation. So, while the infantry served as anvil in the centre, the Companion Cavalry on the right of the battle line engaged any enemy cavalry on that side, defeated it, then wheeled to hammer the enemy battle line in the flank or rear.[16]

These three forces were the core of the Macedonian army that Alexander inherited from Philip. It was balanced in its types of units – phalanx, cavalry, and a flexible infantry battalion. As needed, Philip and Alexander supplemented these units with foreign specialists. Slingers and archers, light cavalry and infantry, even Greek hoplites, they made the already balanced force even more flexible in its capabilities.[17]

Philip had achieved striking political and military successes during his reign, forcing the tribes around Macedonia and the Greek *polises* to accept Macedonian hegemony. After the defeat of the latter, Philip formed the League of Corinth, which the defeated Greek *polises* had no choice but to join. Ostensibly it was as a general commissioned by the League that Philip prepared for his next great undertaking. He would invade Persia and seek to redress the wrong of Xerxes' invasion 150 years before. When Philip was assassinated in 336 BC, he had already dispatched a small expeditionary force under his loyal commander, Parmenio, across the Hellespont and into Asia Minor.[18] In the aftermath of Philip's murder, Alexander outmanoeuvred rival claimants to the throne and won the blessing of the army to succeed Philip as King Alexander. Then he had to deal with rebellious Greeks, Illyrians and Thracians who took Philip's death as a signal to revolt. Only when he had firmly seized the reigns of the fledgling empire, by the end of 335 BC, could he undertake the expedition against Persia that Philip had planned.[19]

Several major sources for Alexander's campaigns, none of them eyewitnesses, have survived. The most notable are Diodorus Siculus, Quintus Curtius, Plutarch, and Arrian. Diodorus included Alexander in his 'universal' – essentially Mediterranean in his day – history. Curtius and Arrian both wrote histories specifically focused on Alexander's campaigns while Plutarch wrote a biography of Alexander. Generally speaking, Arrian's and Diodorus' accounts are considered the most sound. Arrian is of particular value because he seems to have relied mostly on the best possible original sources for Alexander's campaigns. One was the official history of Callisthenes, that Alexander sanctioned until the end of 331 BC when he had Callisthenes jailed for treason. The hype of this official account was compensated for, historians suspect, by his reliance on the accounts of two of Alexander's generals, Ptolemy and Aristobulus.[20]

Back to Alexander. Though the Macedonian army had perhaps 50,000 soldiers all told[22] and the total forces upon which Persia could draw numbered in the hundreds of thousands, Alexander confidently marched his way into the Persian Empire from western Asia Minor. At the Granicus River in 334 BC, he won his first major

---

Alexander the Great and the Battle at the Granicus River

Robert Rossen's *Alexander the Great* (1956) is full of the pomp and pageantry of ancient epics shot in the 1950s and 1960s. Unlike the more recent *Alexander*, this film includes a scene of the battle at the Granicus River. Unfortunately, however, despite the rich costuming of the combatants, the scene does little to illustrate the factors at work in the battle. The Macedonian and Persian cavalry stare at one another from across the river. Then Alexander (Richard Burton) leads his horses across the river and the Persians engage midstream. There are shots of more cavalry entering the river and then the scene devolves into masses of duelling horsemen with no clear formations and only their costumes to separate friend from foe. The sword blows appear tentative at best and many of the actors look like they are struggling to manage their horses and thus unable to put more energy into swordplay. Eventually the Persian cavalry flee, though not for any clear reason, and the audience is meant to understand that the battle has been won.

victory of the campaign, defeating the forces of the Persian regional governors. Thence he worked his way through Asia Minor subduing recalcitrant cities and tribes as needed. At the close of 333 BC, the Macedonian army had carved a path through to the southeastern edge of Asia Minor. There near the town of Issus, Alexander and his Macedonians clashed with a second, larger Persian army under the command of Darius himself.[22]

The Macedonians prevailed. Darius fled inland to regroup. Meanwhile, the Macedonian army worked down the Phoenician coastline, capturing Tyre and Gaza after substantial sieges. With these victories Alexander had seized the Mediterranean coastline of Asia and ended any threat to his supply lines. At the end of 332 BC, Alexander, thanks as always to his stalwart soldiers, came to Egypt. Here he was named Pharaoh of Egypt. He spent a few months there then another few months on the Phoenician coast stabilizing his conquests just a bit. Then he headed inland, northeast to Mesopotamia and, he hoped, a decisive battle against Darius. The army crossed first the Euphrates River, then the Tigris. They marched southeast down the east bank of the Tigris until scouts had located the Persian army by the end of September 331 BC. On 1 October, on the wide, flat, and dusty plains by the village of Gaugamela, the two armies met. It was to be both kings' decisive battle.[23]

Alexander's Battle of Gaugamela : Film Style

Aptly for a film crafted to capture the facets of Alexander's genius for command, the battle scene begins with a close-up of Alexander on horseback, surveying the arid, treeless plains of Gaugamela. Then the scene shifts to Alexander's tent and the review of the battle plan with his generals. He moves blocks representing units across the dirt and instructs his officers. 'Brave' Parmenio and his son Philotas will command the left wing and hold the line for an hour or two. 'Unbreakable' Antigonus along with Perdiccas, Leonatus, Clearchus, and Polyperchon, will command the phalanxes at the centre. Alexander finishes his assignments and reveals the grand plan for the battle:

> If you pin them on the walls of your sarissa's here in the centre, their cavalry will follow me out to the right. And when bold Cassander breaks, stretching their left a hole will open, and I and my cavalry, our revered Cleitus, Ptolemy and Hephaestion will strike through that gap and deal the death blow.

He punctuates his words by knocking over the block representing Darius and his guard.[24]

This segment of *Alexander* stands out among ancient battle scenes in most films for presenting a detailed view of the actual battle plan. Still, Stone takes some conscious historical liberties in the name of constructing a drama, mostly with the commanders. Though Stone places Philotas on the left with his father Parmenio, both Arrian and Diodorus agree that Philotas commanded the Companion cavalry on the right. The names of Perdiccas and Polyperchon appear in these sources' accounts as commanders of phalanx battalions. Leonatus, Antigonus, and Clearchus, however, are not named as phalanx commanders.[25] Ptolemy was not in a command position that day, but Stone includes him to reinforce continuity for the viewer, since Ptolemy is the narrator of the film. Cassander was neither present that day, nor particularly known for his command abilities. In this scene, however, he becomes a cavalry commander. Ultimately these represent changes in the historical record for the sake of the drama. According to Stone, these changes were made to enable audiences to form connections early on with certain key characters from the film. Clearly, though, another goal was to avoid confusing viewers with unnecessary complexities, such as the historically very complicated command structure of Alexander's army.[26]

Alexander, in the drama, gives a simple deployment and a simple directive for the officers that day. Phalanx on left, cavalry on right, and Hypaspists joining the two. Bait Darius into developing a gap in his line and strike at him directly through the gap. Of the battle itself audiences will only see a series of shots from the director that are meant as parts of the whole. If they are to understand that Alexander was a master tactician, the film needs to convey the critical tactical plan comprehensibly and in a short span of time. This scene achieves that. What is left out, however, is significant: how exactly the infantry on the left was to hold against an overwhelming Persian force was one of the most pressing tactical problems of that day. Estimates of Darius' forces that day range from a quarter of a million to a million soldiers. Taking the smaller estimates for sake of argument, Darius commanded, perhaps 250,000 infantry and 40,000 cavalry. Against this, Alexander could only field perhaps 40,000 infantry and 7,000 cavalry.[27] In sum, the Persians outnumbered the Macedonians more than five to one. Darius' best tactic in such advantageous circumstances is apparent even to modern eyes: use the overwhelming superiority in numbers to flank one or both sides of the Macedonian battle line and cause confusion and destruction. Indeed Darius selected the plains near Gaugamela precisely because he believed, perhaps rightly, the limited space for his forces to manoeuvre previously at Issus caused his defeat. Here in this literally level playing field there was plenty of room for him to deploy fully all his cavalry and his war-chariots.[28]

Historically Alexander's plan was to deploy so that he and his cavalry could catch King Darius himself – killing, capturing, or driving off the king would hammer a presumably irreparable dent in morale. It was a bold plan; some might say foolhardy. While he was off with his cavalry, the rest of his army faced the serious problem of encirclement. Alexander, in the historical sources, took several steps to counter this that are excluded from the cinematic account. First the main battle line was angled so that the left was farther away from the Persian line. This meant it would take longer to engage the Persians, optimal since the tactical plan was for Alexander's right wing to draw out Darius' left and cause a gap in the line. Next, he deployed a second line of infantry behind the main battle line.

Finally he positioned soldiers at each end of the main battle line, angled back from the main line. These flank soldiers would, if need be, swing back and join with the second line to perform a defensive rectangle if need be.[29]

The complexity of these technical details makes it that much easier to appreciate why Stone left them out rather than overwhelm or bore an audience not necessarily versed in things having to do with Alexander, antiquity, or planning and executing military campaigns. But the core of the plan is factual: the left held, the right pushed to open a gap in the centre, and Alexander and his cavalry headed straight for King Darius. Unlike most films where the tactical plan is ignored for a battle, indeed where it is difficult to understand what the larger army is doing at all, Stone's approach invites viewers to consider the audacity and brilliance of Alexander's tactics.

It is worth taking a moment to compare the complexity of the tactics in this scene with those in *Troy* and *300*. Neither the historical battles of those periods nor their representations in film suggest much was required in the way of special tactics. The armies of mostly infantry more or less massed together in a loose or orderly fashion and simply fought. A century and a half after the Persian Wars, however, Alexander commands an army consisting of different kinds of infantry, cavalry, and ranged units to engage in a complicated series of manoeuvres. Taken together, scenes from these three films illustrate well the significant changes in the size and complexity of battles in the Greek world.

The battle plan is simplified, but faithful to the critical historical points. The soldiers are, if anything, even more authentic. The core of the Macedonian army was its phalanxes of pikemen, the Foot Companions. To show the deployment on the morning of battle at Gaugamela, *Alexander* starts with a shot of pikes, the several hundred that made up a *syntagma*, bristling skyward over a small dusty slope. Slowly the soldiers bearing those pikes appear over the hill. Each carries a uniform, round shield, the *aspis*, much smaller than the shield of the classical Greek hoplite. Their helmets vary with the individuals in the phalanx. Some wear rounded helmets, others helmets that curve in the shape of a Phrygian cap. Most are open-faced though a few are closed Corinthian-type helmets. A few even have faceplates moulded with human features. Others have sweeping cheek pieces. As their helmets vary, so does their body armour. Corselets of stiffened linen or leather are most common, though some have metal muscled armour. They have greaves and wear white tunics. The shields are strapped to the soldiers' forearms, leaving hands free to manage the long pikes. Anyone impressed by the length of the *sarissas* in the film should note that, historically, those *sarissas* were even longer, 18ft instead of the 10–12 of the cinematic pikes. Stone himself points this out in the director's commentary; presumably the shorter pikes were used for practical purposes since he notes, 'these are long spears that require a lot of muscle control in the heat.' Stone also notes how proud he was of what his soldier re-enactors could achieve in such a short time. Indeed, it is helpful to remember that the Macedonians were professionals. These re-enactors, despite their modern military careers were no more than skilled amateurs in the ways of the *sarissa* phalanx. Still, the soldiers are highly authentic recreations of fourth century Macedonians.

No less authentic are the phalangites' formations. Each unit consists of 16 ranks and files of soldiers, matching the historical size of the *syntagma*. At the right of each unit is a horn player and a soldier carrying a red square standard, serving as a focal point about which the troops can manoeuvre. The standard bearer calls, 'phalanx, turn right', turns to the right, and we see the soldiers rotate quite smoothly in their positions, effectively executing a right face. Drums set the pace for all the manoeuvres. The phalangites look very well trained. And yet, Stone offers the following comment on this scene:

> The logistics of training these soldiers … was very difficult. In the time we had, the weeks we had, it was not possible to match the precision with which the real Macedonian phalanx must have done it [*i.e. marched and manoeuvred*] but these guys tried.[30]

And while it is true that the training of the Macedonians seems to have allowed them to execute turns and wheels near flawlessly, these reconstructed Macedonian warriors, played by volunteer military veterans from across Europe, present highly organized, unified bodies of troops. Imagining the historical troops manoeuvring in a more orderly fashion only serves to emphasize the visual point further: the Macedonian pikemen were highly trained and skilled professionals.

Though the camera does not show Alexander's Companion Cavalry until the army begins its advance, they are also clearly costumed with an eye toward authenticity. Riding without benefit of the stirrup, they are clad in muscled metal breastplates. Most wear the Boeotian-style helmet. Each carries a long spear. The Persian forces on the other hand, are varied in their levels of training, equipment, and battlefield functions. The infantry tend to have no body armour but carry either rectangular tower shields extending from their chins to the ground or slightly smaller oblong shields covering chin to knee. Those with tower shields carry spears, those with oblong shields, swords. If the Persian soldiers in *300* are caricatures, these look like the real deal. They wear head scarves to ward off the sun and sport immaculately curled beards in the style displayed on mosaics and sculptures throughout the empire.[31] The Persian cavalry on the left are *cataphracti*, well armoured riders that wear helmets, breastplates of scale mail, and guards for arm and thigh. They carry lances and are clearly meant to engage in close combat with the enemy. One documented force in the battle, war elephants, was left out of the scene because Stone wished to introduce them more dramatically later in the film.[32]

The establishing shots of these forces provide a useful contrast to those in *300*, illustrating important changes in Greek warfare. The Spartans and their allies at Thermopylae, embellishments and exaggerations aside, are shown as a small group of trained citizen soldiers equipped uniformly and fighting in a lethal, but uncomplicated, formation, the phalanx. Now, in *Alexander* the

Macedonian army is much larger. The force that the Greeks mustered at the Battle of Plataea – referenced at the end of *300* – was the largest that the Greeks had ever fielded, in the tens of thousands.[33] Before and after this conflict, Greek armies were normally only a few thousand hoplites. The Macedonian army was on the scale of the Greek force at Plataea, and the armies of Alexander's successors were normally in the tens, sometimes hundreds, of thousands.

This size became commonplace. In short, the armies of Alexander and his successors were orders of magnitude larger than the Greek armies of the early fifth century. To organize such a large force required a degree of professionalization achieved by Spartans perhaps in the fifth century, but no other Greeks at that time. The phalangites had to be well trained professionals, well organized into well led units. This required regular drills and excellent leadership. Of course not all the extra soldiers were phalangites. From the moment Alexander announced his battle plan, it is clear that this Macedonian army is an army of specialists, both infantry and cavalry.

Morale through Leadership and Organization

The establishing shots of the army and Alexander's address to his soldiers also casts light on another, equally important facet of Alexander's generalship: the care with which he tended to the morale of his officers and soldiers. During the strategy meeting the day before Gaugamela, the camera shows him praising and encouraging his officers: 'Brave' Parmenio, 'bold' Cassander, 'unbreakable' Antigonus, and so on. That night he walks around the camp, exchanging pleasantries with the men, joking, smiling, reinforcing what clearly are already strong bonds. On the morning of battle, Alexander rides slowly along the front of his troops, accompanied by some officers. As he surveys the army he singles out individual phalangites by name, noting their heroics in earlier campaigns, or achievements in the Olympics, praising their strength and courage.

He even makes note of those whose fathers served King Philip and shows he knows them and their brothers.

Now he enters that standard of Hollywood and ancient history, the battle speech. 'You've all honoured your country and your ancestors and now we come to this most distant place in Asia where across from us Darius has at last gathered a vast army ....' The film cuts to a close-up of an eagle as he wings across the battlefield and surveys the setup of the Persian forces. Stone's high level shot suggests tens of thousands of soldiers gathering together into formations. Alexander continues: 'But look again at this horde and ask yourselves, who is this great king who pays assassins in gold coins to murder my father, our king, in a most despicable and cowardly manner? Who is this great king Darius who enslaves his own men to fight? Who is this king but a king of air?' During this part of the speech, the camera closes in on the Persian army around Darius. Two-wheeled two-horse chariots are arrayed in front of cavalry, infantry with square shields and only clothing for body armour, and Greek-style hoplites. Some camel cavalry are revealed. The camera remains at longer range mostly and the shots of individual Persians are short. The impression is one of size – Darius has fielded a massive polyglot army with units from all the regions of the empire.

Alexander continues his speech. 'These men do not fight for their homes. They fight because this king tells them they must. And when they fight, they will melt away like the air, because they know no loyalty to a king of slaves!' Now the camera moves in closer to the Persian forces. Their mounted lieutenants call to them with short commands, more likely getting the men in line than offering any particular words of encouragement. The camera closes in on the Persian warriors' faces: serious, grim, and thoughtful.

'But we are not here today as slaves,' Alexander reminds his soldiers. 'We are here today ... as Macedonian *free men*! And all their arms, their numbers, their chariots and their fine horses will mean nothing in the hands of slaves.' On these notes of his speech the Macedonians erupt in cheers. The comparison to the Persian forces is deliberate: the film demonstrates that Alexander's pre-battle rituals have far more positive effects on Macedonian morale than those of the Persians. He is not done.

> Some of you, perhaps myself, will not live to see the sun set over these mountains today, for I will be in the very thick of battle with you. But remember this, the greatest honour a man can achieve is to live with great courage, and to die gloriously in battle for his home. I say to you what every warrior has known since the beginning of time: conquer your fear and I promise you, you will conquer death! Someday I promise you, your sons and grandsons will look into your eyes. And when they ask you why you fought so bravely at Gaugamela, you will answer, with all the strength of your great, *great* hearts: 'I was here this day at Gaugamela ... for the freedom ... and *glory* ... of Greece!' Zeus be with us!

He dons a golden helmet with the metal on top moulded into locks of hair, a high central crest with red horsehair and a feather to either side. Consummate performer that he is, he yells his final words and begins riding up and down the ranks, quickly building cheers from the crowd.

Did he give this speech? Probably not to the whole army: what use would it have been to most of the 40,000? Far more likely that he did what Arrian said, addressed his commanders with stirring words, and bade them each to talk to the soldiers under their command.[34] What these episodes, from the strategy meeting and the troop review to the speech, illustrate, however, is the great personal charisma Alexander used to motivate and move his men to face extraordinary dangers and toils. Above all, he led from the front, risking all the same dangers his men did, whether scaling a fortification wall or charging at the enemy. He had the wounds to prove he did not shirk his duty.[35] More than this, however, Alexander genuinely seems to have cared about his men and their welfare, to treat them as brothers-in-arms, not inferiors. An oft-quoted passage from Arrian reveals this so well:

At this point in my story I must not leave unrecorded one of the finest things Alexander ever did. Where it actually took place is uncertain ... The army was crossing a desert of sand; the sun was already blazing down upon them, but they were struggling on under the necessity of reaching water which was still far away. Alexander like everyone else, was tormented by thirst, but he was nonetheless marching on foot at the head of his men. It was all he could do to keep going, but he did so, and the result (as always) was that the men were better able to endure their misery when they saw that it was equally shared. As they toiled on, a party of light infantry which had gone off looking for water found some – just a wretched little trickle collected in a shallow gully. They scooped up with difficulty what they could and hurried back with their priceless treasure to Alexander; then just before they reached him they tipped the water into a helmet and gave it to him. Alexander, with a word of thanks for the gift, took the helmet and, in full view of his troops, poured the water on the ground. So extraordinary was the effect of this action that the water wasted by Alexander was as good as a drink for every man in the army.

Arrian, himself a commander, concluded that this laudable action was proof 'of his genius for leadership'.[36] Indeed Alexander seems to have had an affinity with his soldiers rarely seen among ancient or modern generals. He put this to use, calling for his men to endure all manner of hardship on the campaign.

The Course of Battle

Director Stone is determined to keep the main outlines of the battle as clear as possible for viewers, going so far as to use captions to identify the parts of the Macedonian battle line. From here to the end of the battle scene, the film constructs, through a series of shots, the plan in motion. The overall effect is impressive. Though the long shots taken from the vantage point of the eagle winging overhead provide an impossible perspective, they give audiences a better sense of the overall structure of the battle. The close-ups emphasize the experiences of the units and the individuals in them.[37]

Alexander ends his speech and rides to the right past his cheering soldiers. When he reaches the cavalry he calls, 'Cassander, four columns go!' and the cavalry begin their drive to the right. Watching from across the dusty plain, Darius wonders aloud where Alexander is going. Then he gives a simple order to Bessus: 'Envelop him.' Bessus stirs the Bactrian heavy cavalry to action, wheeling to the left to intercept Alexander. The dust rises from their horses' hooves, an excellent reminder of how much of this battle would be obscured to any witness. Meanwhile Alexander, more detachments of cavalry falling in behind him, passes another squad of cavalry and calls, 'Hephaistion, go!'

The camera cuts to the Macedonian centre, helpfully labelling it onscreen for viewers. Here in the centre the one-eyed Antigonus barks commands to the phalanx, the front rows lower their spears with a shout, and the centre shuffles forward, slowly, and in unison. Trumpets blare and the soldiers call out a cadence. Shots on the other side show Persians warriors chanting a rhythmic shout and clashing weapons on shields to bolster their courage.

And still Alexander rides, he and his cavalry in a desperate race to outpace Bessus and his squadrons. Or perhaps more accurately they raced to extend Bessus' cavalry so far left that the necessary gap opened in the Persian centre. Darius sees this push left and notes to a subordinate, 'He makes a mistake, Pharnakes.' Confident in his vast numerical superiority – and rightly so at this point – Darius orders his archers deployed in the centre with him to loose their arrows at the Macedonians. They release their bowstrings, and arrows fill the sky, heading for the Macedonian centre. The phalangites raise their shields as much as they are able. Unlike the *hoplon*, illustrated in *300*, which provided essentially full protection from arrows, the Macedonian shield offers far less protection and cannot be manipulated easily when its bearer is wielding a two-handed pike. Strictly speaking, the raised *sarissas* in the ranks farther back could serve as a screen for arrows, but that does not happen here.[38] A number of phalangites fall. Arrows, whistling, pierce Macedonian abdomens and limbs. The wounds are gruesome, but the phalanx continues its march. Now Darius orders light cavalry lancers and chariots to charge with infantry behind. The chariots have blades extending from the wheel hubs. Each has a driver and two archers. Again and again he sends units forward: camel cavalry, horse cavalry, infantry with hand axes, and so on. As these forces begin their charges, the camera shows Macedonian phalangites shouting their cadence and moving forward steadily.

Now the camera shifts to the Macedonian left, again helpfully labelled. There are soldiers here armed as Greek hoplites. Given the information provided by the film, it is not entirely clear who these soldiers are supposed to be. The Hypaspists, historically, were on the right side of the phalanx for this and most other battles. Perhaps they are the Greek mercenary hoplites that Arrian says occupied the second rank and were instructed to defend the left flank. This would fit with what is historically authentic, but these troops were left out of the tactical discussion in Alexander's tent. Whoever they are supposed to be, the officers tell the men to keep steady, 'Bend if you must, but never break, and keep watching the cavalry on the left.' Whether he means the allied cavalry or Persian, the point is clear. The task for the left is to hold and avoid encirclement at all costs.

The Macedonian officers call for their troops to hold steady as the Persian forces charge from a distance, dust clouds rising. The eagle again flies overhead from the Macedonian left to right. What is meant to be a literal bird's-eye view of the battlefield reveals the phalanxes organized in their square formations but not in a single straight line – the left wing is angled away from the Persians and the right bending towards it. This vantage point also illustrates the relative disorder of the Persian forces compared to the Macedonian. Both are important elements of the battle. Macedonian professionalism created outstanding unit cohesion and Alexander's risky but effective strategy of slanting the left of the line back contributed to the ultimate victory.

Again the camera shifts back to a dust-obscured Alexander, identifiable by his helmet, and riding with his cavalry to the right. Cut to Bessus momentarily urging his riders onward. The cavalry forces are still driving to the Macedonian right, each still, apparently, trying to outflank the other. Quick shots of Ptolemy and Cleitus follow as Alexander calls to all to ride faster and Bessus does the same with his cavalry.

Now the camera returns to the centre and the onslaught of the chariots. They are few in number and widely spaced, the whir of their scythed blades amplified for the audience. Antigonus yells an order to the troops in the centre: prepare to repel chariots. A close-up of the phalangites' legs follows. They side-step to create lanes in their formation, spaces through which the chariots can pass without harm. Those closest to the chariots and too slow to side-step, find their legs removed by the scything wheels, a bloody end indeed. Mostly, however, the chariots pass harmlessly and are caught by second line troops. One particularly authentic shot shows a chariot stop cold, its horses simply unwilling to charge into the second line's wall of pikes. This entire part of the scene comes directly from Diodorus Siculus' account of the battle:

> The scythed chariots swung into action at full gallop and created great alarm and terror among the Macedonians ... As the phalanx joined shields, however, all beat upon their shields with their spears as the king had commanded and a great din arose. As the horses shied off, most of the chariots were turned about and bore hard with irresistible impact against their own ranks. Others continued on against the Macedonian lines, but as the soldiers opened wide gaps in their ranks the chariots were channelled through these. In some instances the horses were killed by javelin casts and in others they rode through and escaped, but some of

them, using the full force of their momentum and applying their steel blades actively, wrought death among the Macedonians in many and various forms. Such was the keenness and the force of the scythes ingeniously contrived to do harm that they severed the arms of many, shields and all, and in no small number of cases they cut through necks and sent heads tumbling to the ground with the eyes still open and the expression of the countenance unchanged, and in other cases they sliced through ribs with mortal gashes and inflicted a quick death.[39]

Alexander makes it look easy. Too easy. It is not entirely clear whether this account should be believed. In particular if the Macedonian phalangites were already in close formation, packed tight, how exactly would they make way sufficiently to form wide lanes through which the chariots could pass? It is an unanswered question.[40]

Another high angle shot of the battle shows the Persian forces streaming in and the phalanxes losing a bit of their organization in the front ranks but still maintaining their basic formation. Now the camera tracks and pans back to the left. Slanted back as it was in the initial setup, the phalangites on the left are still unengaged, but now the Persian infantry close. The phalanx slowly advances, and light-armed infantry race forward in the small gaps between the units of phalangites. Such attacks, historically, at best increase the stress of attacking soldiers and injure or kill occasionally; they do not stop the attack. Now the charging Persian swordsmen engage the phalanx and we see the devastation of the Macedonian *sarissa* up close. Starting with a long shot, then a medium shot on a group of phalangites, the sequence ends with a shot of Persians impaled on the Macedonian *sarissas*. The pikes project some 8–10ft in front of the soldiers and the Persians must manoeuvre between them or be perforated with deadly result. Manoeuvring between them is, to say the least, extremely difficult. The later Greek historian Polybius commented on this in his comparison of the close-order Macedonian phalanx with the open Roman maniples of swordsmen:

One Roman must stand opposite two men in the first rank of the phalanx, so that he has to face and encounter ten pikes, and it is both impossible for a single man to cut through them all in time once they are at close quarters and by no means easy to force their points away, as the rear ranks can be of no help to the front rank either in thus forcing the pikes away or in the use of the sword. So it is easy to see that, as I said at the beginning, nothing can withstand the charge of the phalanx as long as it preserves its characteristic formation and force.[41]

Even were the Persians' infantry as closely packed as the Macedonians, which they do not seem to have been, the reach of their weapons would make it so that one Persian faced the points of five Macedonian *sarissas*. As Polybius says, nothing could stand up to a phalanx operating as designed. The level plains of Gaugamela provided the perfect terrain.

Finally, the moment has come; a gap has opened in Darius' line. Seizing the opportunity, Alexander commands a hard wheel to the left and the horses oblige, kicking up even more dust. The Hypaspists are close enough, apparently, to aid in the attack on the gap. He tells the Macedonian forces to drive for the hole, though surely none can hear him at this point. Meanwhile in the Macedonian centre, blinding dust obscures everything, and the camera must descend through it to see the struggle there. Things get a bit fanciful in order to emphasize the brutality of the battle. Antigonus and a number of phalangites have started to engage in hand-to-hand combat with swords and rocks. This counters the specialized purpose of the phalanx and obscures that important reality, a *sarissa*-armed phalanx could be in serious trouble if enemy infantry closed within sword range.[42]

The camera cuts to Parmenio and Philotas on the left, walking behind the engaged phalangites and giving orders. Parmenio sends a messenger to warn Alexander about the thin left flank. But things continue to degrade for the Macedonian left, which is steadily

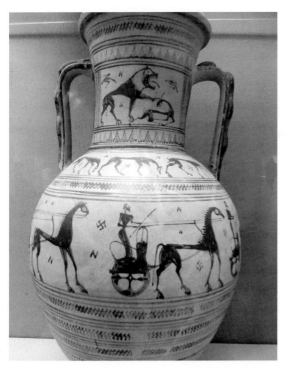

1. A depiction of the infantry soldier on the
Mycenaean Warrior Vase.

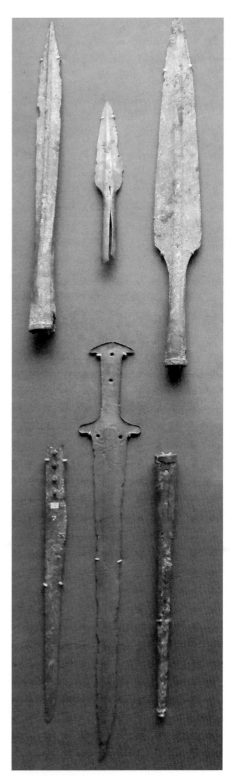

2. Athenian amphora depicting a chariot, c. 700 BC.

3. Mycenaean blades and spear heads
from graves at Ialysos, c. 1450–1100 BC.

4. Bronze Etruscan shield, second half of the 7th century BC. The shape is similar to a hoplite's shield though, unlike the hoplite shield, this has a central boss and handle.

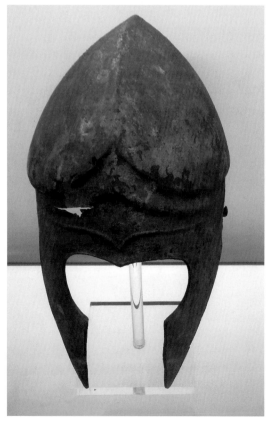

5. Chalcidian-style helmet. Apulia, c. 510 BC.

6. Bronze Corinthian style helmet, c. 650–570 century BC.

8. A Roman copy of a bust of Pericles showing the wearing of the Corinthian helmet outside of battle.

7. Bronze Corinthian style helmet.

9. Tomb of Kybernis showing a hoplite spear, shield, and
Corinthian-style helmet, c. 480 BC.

10. Corinthian-style Helmet
from Attica, 5th century BC.

11. Front of Laconian (Spartan) warrior figurine, 6th century BC. The warrior is depicted with helmet, shield, breastplate, and greaves.

12. Side of Laconian (Spartan) warrior figurine, 6th century BC.

13. The Macmillan Aryballos depicting warriors in hoplite gear, c. 7th century BC.

15. Bronze Montefortino type helmet of the style used by Roman legionaries in the Republic and early Empire. Apulia, c. 3rd century BC.

14. Bronze greaves of the type worn by hoplites. Southern Italy, 5th century BC.

16. A bronze votive figurine from Umbria, 5th century BC. Note the reinforced shoulder flaps that were characteristic of later Roman armour styles.

17. A bronze Roman figurine depicted in a *lorica segmentata*, 2nd century AD.

18. A gladius from Germany, c. 15 BC.

outflanked. Subsequently Parmenio sends Philotas himself to tell Alexander of the danger: 'And if he won't listen, then survive me and avenge this betrayal!' Historically, some of the Persian forces exploited a gap that appeared in the Macedonian line. Instead of using the opportunity to sever left from right and destroy the Macedonians the forces that broke through were driven by the promise of loot to move on to the baggage in the Macedonian camp. Somehow – exactly how is unclear – part of the second line in the Macedonian army rallied and turned against the would-be camp raiders from behind. Meanwhile the forces of the Persians placed tremendous pressure on the Macedonian left, but somehow the men under Parmenio's command held on.[43]

Alexander is in the thick of it, he and his companions plunged like a dagger into the now dangerously thinned centre of Darius' army. The horses are intermixed with each other and with infantry. The men duel from horseback, swords swinging. Alexander grabs a Persian by the shoulder and impales him on his sword. The man falls with Alex's sword lodged in his gut and Alexander dismounts to retrieve his weapon. A Persian clubs Alexander while he is intent on the sword. Before the Persian can deliver the killing stroke, however, Cleitus literally disarms him and admonishes Alexander to pay attention. Historically this episode happened years earlier at the Granicus River, Stone notes, but he wanted to illustrate the close relationship between Alexander and his officers. Alexander continues to fight on foot and we see other Macedonian infantry around him. Other Companion Cavalry dismount to fight, apparently thinking it more advantageous to be on foot now. It is an all-out brawl; close quarters slashing and stabbing and no lines. But then what should one expect from the fighting as the Macedonians and Alexander drove toward the centre, drove onward toward Darius? There was no way for the cavalry and support infantry to penetrate the thousands of soldiers in the Persian centre without losing at least some of their own cohesion as they worked their way into any gaps they could.

In the climactic shots of the battle scene, Alexander looks through the dust and sees that Darius is not too far off. He tells his two comrades to find their horses; certainly no easy task. Since the melee still continues, it is not clear exactly who accompanies Alexander in this last segment – perfectly authentic confusion for anyone watching through the dust, noise, combat, and confusion. Alexander grabs a javelin to throw at Darius and rides through what seems to be a relatively clear space with pairs of combatants here and there fighting. It is hard to imagine Darius would have such space in front of him and the space appears more likely to be the result of staging the shot for Alexander's desperate gambit. He rides up to the infantry in front of Darius, casts the spear unopposed, but misses. Now Darius' infantry challenge him and those of his companions who have just arrived – apparently Alexander launched this final attack essentially by himself and his troopers needed time to react to their leader's impetuosity. But Darius himself, fear openly on his face, has had enough. He flees the battle

The centre of the Persian army has collapsed with the assault of the Macedonians and the flight of the Persian king. Alexander sees Darius flee and tells the Companions they need to catch him before he reaches the mountains. Just then Philotas arrives. He reports that the left is crumbling and the Persians are attacking the Macedonian baggage. Alexander roars in frustrated anger. 'If you chase him you risk losing your army here,' Philotas cries. 'And if we capture him we gain an empire,' Alexander cries in return. The indecision is palpable but quick. Darius is left to flee and Alexander returns to tend to his left. The battle scene is over.

Alexander shows what a historically authentic cinematic view of ancient battle can look like. The film deftly mixes a variety of viewpoints to reconstruct the battle. The top level of strategy and tactics is provided in the planning session in Alexander's tent and the eagle-eye views of the battlefield. The close-ups of Macedonian phalanx and companion cavalry give us the face of battle: a brutal, bloody, and at Gaugamela, dusty affair. What is perhaps most striking about the whole battle scene in *Alexander* is that even with a preliminary strategy session and bird's-eye views, even with text appearing to label helpfully the Macedonian Left and Centre, it is still often not clear to the viewer exactly what is happening in any given shot and how the action of a shot fits into a grander narrative of the battle. This confusion reflects a reality that is often missing from battle studies. There simply is no position, no viewpoint from which one can capture the totality of a battle. The high level shot loses the actual struggles of the soldiers in the field. Close to see the actual fighting, however, and the general relationship of one unit to another and the states of the battle lines are lost. Stone's vision of Gaugamela paradoxically illustrates the futility of fully reconstructing such a battle by providing vignettes of the battle. Perhaps this is one place where one can declare that history has really joined drama in a way that does enough justice to both.

Taken together *Troy*, *300*, and *Alexander* illustrate the continuity and change in Greek combat over five centuries. With *Troy* we see a heroic culture at war and, unsurprisingly, the individual hero plays a large role. Though reinforced by his comrades, the hero leads the charge, fighting his rivals in the pockets of space between forces when not engaged in a formal battle-stopping duel. The moments where Achilles' Myrmidons cluster together to block arrows with their shields or the Trojans lock shields together and thrust back the Greek mob, however, point to the development of the phalanx illustrated in *300*. That splendid fantasy film does so much right in delivering the rhetoric of hoplite combat even though its battle scenes do not always support the rhetoric. It may be that the pull of a heroic aristeia is too much for filmmakers to ignore, and the camera in an epic film demands individual moments of glory. When *300* lapses into the vignettes of individual heroes, the film loses its value as a depiction of hoplite battle. But the grand moments when the focus is on the phalanx itself are instructive to behold. In those moments one can clearly see the transition from the more fluid and amorphous formations of Homeric warriors to the disciplined and orderly rank and file, the cohesive collaboration of the Spartan phalanx.

Alexander completes the set. At the dawn of the Hellenistic world the armies are massive. *Troy's* emphasis on hero-sized armies obscures this important point: Archaic Greek battles were small-scale affairs. The fighting in the Persian Wars was on a larger scale. The battles of the Macedonians and their successors were larger still. Size alone, however, was not the most important change in the face of battle. Most importantly armies came to be composed of a variety of unit types, each specialized in a particular type of combat. The phalanx of *300* became the phalanx of pikemen depicted in film. Unlike the Spartans, however, the phalanx no longer fought on its own. Light infantry and Hypaspists, archers and all manner of cavalry played their part in this time of large-scale battles between armies of specialists. The tent scene in *Alexander* illustrates the greater complexity well. Where the battle plan in *300* could be reduced to a simple 'stand and fight', *Alexander's* plan has a number of roles and manoeuvres. Taken with a critical eye to separate the inaccurate elements, then, these three films in their best moments depict the broad transformations in Greek warfare.

Chapter 4

The End of the Roman Republic

Though not without their share of problems, the three films discussed in the previous chapters, *Troy*, *300*, and *Alexander*, considered together, provide moments that can help one visualize how some ancient battles in the Greco-Macedonian world may have looked. When it comes to the armies of the Romans, however, there is a noticeable dearth of films. Very few modern movies treat of any period earlier than the Empire. The few exceptions portray armies in the late Republic, the first century BC. There are various retellings of the Spartacus Revolt of the 70s BC, of which we shall consider two: the classic *Spartacus* (1960) directed by Stanley Kubrick and a much more recent made-for-cable version by USA Films. For the very end of the Republic, HBO's series *Rome* depicts Caesar's Battle of Alesia (52 BC) and the Battle of Philippi (42 BC) between Caesar's assassins and successors.

To get a better understanding of Roman military developments in the late Republic, however, it is helpful to examine what Roman armies were like in the earlier stages of the Republic. But first a quick refresher on Roman political history will help contextualize the military developments. The city of Rome was founded at some point in the eighth century when a group of the people known as Latins united their village communities on several of the hills of Rome into one city. Rome was initially governed by a king, and under the kings the marketplaces, temples, and city walls were first constructed. By the end of the sixth century, however, a group of nobles, frustrated with the limits a monarchy placed on their quests for offices, honours, and prestige, overthrew the last king of Rome and established a political system called the Republic. The Republic developed slowly, as all ancient societies did, and it took several centuries, up to what is generally called the Middle Republic for it to gain its classic features. Essentially the administration of the Republic was handled by yearly elected magistrates from the elite of society. Long term guidance was provided by the senate, 300 former magistrates who handled the financial, diplomatic, and strategic decisions of the polity. A series of citizen assemblies ensured that even the poorer citizens at Rome had some say in their government's doings. These assemblies had functions ranging from electing magistrates to ratifying or rejecting proposed laws. As the Romans came to conquer first Italy, then the Mediterranean, political competition between members of the elite became more pronounced. By the late Republic, of the second and first centuries BC, murder and revolution became possible solutions to conflicts between politicians. Ultimately the Republic collapsed in what amounted to four civil wars, with intervals of peace, from 90–31 BC. At the end of this time a man named Octavian, the adopted son of the murdered dictator Julius Caesar, was essentially the last warlord standing. He received the honorific title, Augustus, from the senate and established what moderns call the Roman Empire. From Augustus' day until the collapse of the Empire in the fifth century AD, Rome and its empire were again ruled by a monarch, the emperor.

The Roman Army of the Middle and Late Republic

In the early Republic (sixth – fourth centuries BC), the Romans adopted the Greek-style phalanx, the cutting edge military innovation of the age. Men who could provide the minimum necessary equipment of shield spear and, perhaps, helmet, served in the phalanx. The wealthier men, however, could and did protect themselves with better equipment. Sometime no later than the early third century, the Romans transformed their phalanx into a more complicated and flexible system of fighters. The core tactical unit of this new army was the maniple, of which there were thirty in a legion. The front line fighters consisted of men in their fighting prime. The younger among these were called the *hastati*, those a bit older, the *principes*. Hastati were formed into 10 maniples of 120 men per maniple; the *principes* made up another 10 maniples, also at 120 men per maniple. The *triarii*, made up of veterans who were 45 or older, formed ten maniples of 60 men per maniple. The remainder of the infantry, the youngest and poorest troops, served as *velites*, light infantry with javelins. The citizen cavalry force of 300 brought the total size of a legion to the neighbourhood of 4,500 soldiers.

For defensive equipment the heavy infantry soldiers – *hastati*, *principes*, and *triarii* – carried that iconic legionary shield, the *scutum*. This large convex shield was oval-shaped in the Republic but transformed into a curved rectangular form during the early Empire, the first century AD.[1] According to the Greek author Polybius, at least in the Republic the legionary shields were made of thin layers of plywood glued together, topped with hide and bound round the edges with iron. The centre had a single metal boss with a horizontal handgrip on the inner side.[2] The few archaeological specimens of shields extant essentially corroborate Polybius' description while showing the great variety that was possible within that general form. A Roman shield found over a century ago in Egypt had no metal bindings and a wooden spine that ran vertically along the centre of the shield to reinforce it. This shield measured 4ft x 2ft and weighed over 20lbs – a heavy shield indeed.[3] The few other examples found suggest shields could be as light as 12lbs, have wooden or metal bosses, and come with or without metal binding. Presumably a *scutum* was meant to extend from a soldier's shoulder to knee at the least.[4]

In addition to their shields, the heavy infantry wore several different pieces of body armour. The bronze helmet was topped with a crest of feathers to make the soldier appear taller and more intimidating.[5] Greaves protected the legs. The type of body armour supplied depended on the wealth of the soldier. Those soldiers among the *hastati* and *principes* who had sufficient wealth wore a shirt of mail, while the poorer citizens wore only a small bronze breastplate, according to Polybius, about 9 inches[2] and designed primarily to protect the region of the heart.[6]

For weapons the *hastati* and *principes* carried a combination of a special javelin, the *pilum*, and the so-called 'Spanish sword' or *gladius hispaniensis*. The *pilum* was a specially designed javelin. Its iron head measured approximately 2 inches and was connected to a wooden shaft by means of a thin rod of iron. The primary function of the design was to enable the *pilum* to penetrate a shield and continue on into the shield-bearer's body. The pyramidal point most commonly found on the *pilum* head was a design that facilitated armour penetration, the weight of the device added penetrating power, and the low friction of the thin spit ensured that the javelin would continue on its course after penetrating the shield. Modern tests with reconstructed *pila* suggest one could be cast from 5 yards away, pierce a plywood shield ¾" thick, and continue its flight into the opponent's body. A helpful side effect of this design noted by ancient and modern authors, was that the thin metal rod attached to the head frequently bent on impact. This weakness made it likely for the *pilum* to bend as it punctured an enemy shield, weighing down the shield and making the *pilum* useless for a counter-attack.[7] Once the *pilum* was cast, the legionaries' main weapon was the *gladius hispaniensis*. This was a short sword with a sharp two-edged blade that ranged, judging from the various surviving examples, from 16–20 inches in length.[8] The blade ended in a sharp point, and thus a legionary could use it both to cut and stab his enemy (see plate 18).[9]

Though the precise details of the mechanics are lost to us, one key to the manipular legion's success was its flexibility. The army employed a mix of units, light infantry, cavalry, *pila*-armed *hastati* and *principes*, and even *triarii* who played a defensive role if the army was hard-pressed. A second key was its ability to rotate maniples in and out of the front lines as a battle progressed. The Roman historian Livy describes the rotation system,

When the battle formation of the army was completed, the hastati were the first to engage. If they failed to repulse the enemy, they slowly retired through the intervals between the companies of the principes, who then took up the fight, the hastati following in their rear. The triarii, meantime, were resting on one knee under their standards, their shields over their shoulders and their spears planted on the ground with the points upwards, giving them the appearance of a bristling palisade. If the principes were also unsuccessful, they slowly retired to the triarii, which has given rise to the proverbial saying, when people are in great difficulty 'matters have come down to the triarii'. When the triarii had admitted the hastati and principes through the intervals separating their companies they rose from their kneeling posture and instantly closing their companies up they blocked all passage through them and in one compact mass fell on the enemy as the last hope of the army. The enemy who had followed up the others as though they had defeated them, saw with dread a new and larger army rising apparently out of the earth.[10]

It is not at all clear how exactly this worked in practice. To give just one problem as an example: were the gaps between each maniple in a line maniple sized? If so, how did Roman soldiers with large maniple-sized gaps in their lines hold off enemies that had no gaps? The sources are clear it happened however, and historians have simply been left to speculate about the precise mechanics.[11]

Unfortunately, while some films have purported to deal with the period when Romans employed the manipular army, none offers a compelling cinematic depiction of the army in action. The majority fall under the category of 'sword and sandals films', low budget epics set in ancient Rome. Most were made by Italian directors and crews and their heyday was the 1960s.[12] They generally employ historical stock battle scenes focused on wild melees between Romans clad in imagined leather armour and their opponents. *Cabiria* is a notable example. Made in 1914, this silent film tells a tale of adventure set in the context of the Second Punic war against the Carthaginian Hannibal. The plot focuses on the Roman girl Cabiria, who along with her nurse Croessa is captured and sold to the Carthaginian High Priest. The priest plans to sacrifice Cabiria to the god Moloch, but she and her nurse are rescued by a Roman spy, Fulvius, and his slave Maciste. In the background of their adventures Hannibal's invasion of Rome and the Roman attack on Syracuse are depicted dramatically. This is an adventure romp, however, not a war film, and the soldiers are armed and equipped either as fantastically garbed generals in outlandish parade armour or as imperial legionaries in armour that did not come into use until the first century AD. Despite *Cabiria's* merits as an adventure film, it is typical of the genre and offers nothing for imagining Roman battles realistically.

Special mention should be made, however, of the 1937 Italian film *Scipio L'Africano*. The film itself consists of openly Fascist propaganda and, accordingly, dropped out of public favour quickly.[13] Leaving aside its dubious political pedigree, however, the film recreates a heroic Battle of Zama (202 BC) between the Roman forces of Scipio and the Carthaginian Forces of Hannibal. The scale is epic: hundreds if not thousands of actors were clearly employed to represent the battle scenes. The depiction of war wounds is realistic

---

Jupiter's Darling

Truly on the lighter side *Jupiter's Darling* of 1955 casts Hannibal's invasion of Italy as a musical starring star swimmer/actress Esther Williams and musical veteran Howard Keel. Amytis (Williams) is a Roman woman engaged to marry the dictator Fabius Maximus (George Sanders). Curious about Hannibal (Keel) who is marching against Rome, she sneaks out of the city and to the general's camp. Caught by Hannibal she is initially treated as a spy. Amytis and Hannibal fall in love, however, and after a series of misunderstandings characteristic of the romantic musical genre, decide to spend their lives together.

for the limited technologies of the time and the battle is depicted .
as a brutal affair. The attack of the Carthaginian elephants against
Roman *velites* is particularly notable as are the large scale cavalry
duel and the final clash of Roman and Carthaginian infantry. Still,
the battle scenes, while powerful, are not all that realistic. *Velites*
are distinguished from other legionaries but those legionaries are
all armed anachronistically with rectangular *scuta* and segmented
armour from centuries later. The legionaries all carry large thrusting
spears instead of *pila*. Most undermining, when the infantry
clash, which happens several times on film, they break formations
immediately and dissolve into mobs brawling.

Transformation of the Roman Manipular Army

The military demands of the Republic had grown steadily throughout
the second century. Rome acquired numerous new overseas provinces
after the Second Punic War, fought against Carthage and that oft-
praised general Hannibal. As the Republic took control of territory
in regions like Spain and northeast Italy, they came into conflict
with still more people. After winning many wars – not always easily
by any means – against these new neighbours, yet more territory
came under Roman influence, and so the Romans gained new sets of
frictions with peoples farther and farther away from Rome. And so
over the course of the second century, Rome came to dominate most
of the Mediterranean: Spain then the Balkans, followed by Asia
Minor and Tunisia, and so on. These new military commitments
were largely overseas. In the third century when Rome remained
mostly an Italian power, a year's service for a Roman usually meant
one spring and summer campaign, after which he could return to
his fields. And so when Polybius says each Roman was liable to serve
sixteen years in the infantry what he really meant was a maximum
of sixteen campaigns.[14] When military duties were exercised in a
far off province, however, those sixteen years could turn into actual
consecutive years, a very different proposition. Ordinarily the term

of continuous service seems to have been much less, but it still meant leaving home, family, and community for lengthy stretches.[15] Still, lengthy stints in the army led to increasingly well trained soldiers.

For centuries, in addition to age and physical fitness, the wealth of an individual Roman determined whether he would fight in the legion since each legionary was required to supply his own equipment. The late second century and early first century BC, however, brought a steady decrease and gradual elimination of property requirements for military service. Those the Romans termed *capite censi*, a term referring to the fact that the census only included them by a head count since they had no property, were normally not subject to conscription even as *velites*. Since at least the end of the third century, the Romans had levied *capite censi* to serve in the army during particularly grave military situations. Even so, the minimum property qualification for military service seems to have declined steadily over the second century. When exactly it was eliminated is unclear. In the late second century, when a Roman army had been unable to defeat rebels in Numidia (in north western Africa), the up-and-coming politician, Gaius Marius, was elected consul for 107 BC to conduct a swift campaign. One step he took in the name of expediency was to make an open call to *capite censi*, inviting them to volunteer for service. Apparently a number did. It is not clear that this was a permanent change in policy since, as was just noted, *capite censi* had been called upon to volunteer in crises for at least a century. What is clear is that by the time of Caesar's campaigns in Gaul (58 BCE), the property qualification for service no longer existed.[16]

In addition to extended terms of service and the elimination of property qualifications, other important changes may have been introduced during the Roman politician Marius' extraordinary series of military commands. While Marius was in North Africa campaigning against the Numidian King Jugurtha, a new military disaster erupted, this time near the Roman heartland. Two tribes, the Teutones and Cimbri made their way into southern Gaul in 105 BC, destroying a

Roman army in the process. The Roman people, fearing for their safety if the tribes should penetrate Italy, elected Marius to be consul in 104 while he was still in Africa. Marius returned to Europe and assumed command over the Roman army that had been levied. They seem to have had some breathing space, however, as the Cimbri and Teutones migrated away for a time and did not return to southern Gaul for several years. During that respite, Marius may have made some significant changes in his army. 'May have' because it is not entirely clear from the patchy Roman sources for the period whether Marius instituted these reforms or whether they simply occurred around the time he held the consulship. It appears Marius trained his army and built the stamina of his soldiers through a series of public works projects. He also reformed the supply system of the army. Instead of relying upon servants to carry core rations, Marius required each of his soldiers to carry an emergency food supply and the basic kit to cook it. Each soldier also had to carry an entrenching tool for constructing camps. It became the practice for soldiers to carry these and other necessary items slung on a pole carried on their shoulders. These actions greatly reduced the length and size of the supply train and increased the general strength and stamina of the soldiers. Marius also, perhaps, made the eagle standard the most important standard for the legion, the heart and pride of the legion, as it were.[17]

Several more developments transformed the Roman manipular army into the cohort army of the late Republic and early empire. One development was the tactical reform of the infantry. The cohort of 480 soldiers came to supersede the 60 to 120 soldier maniples as the core tactical unit of the army. Parallel to this development was the change in legionary equipment. The light armed *velites* were phased out and the distinction between *hastati*, *principes*, and *triarii* eliminated. By the end of the process in the late second – early first century BC each legionary in the cohorts used *pilum*, *gladius hispaniensis*, and *scutum*, in addition to head and body armour. These arms were now supplied by the state.[18] Additionally, though probably for different reasons, the *equites*, the Roman citizen cavalry, came to be replaced by cavalry levied from peoples allied to Rome.[19] In most respects the citizen legionaries who fought the escaped slave Spartacus in the 70s probably were indistinguishable from those who fought the Gauls at Alesia two decades later, and from those a decade after that who engaged in the civil war that destroyed the Republic. They fought in cohorts composed of centuries each with relatively uniformly equipped comrades.

Spartacus

Stanley Kubrick and Kurt Douglas' *Spartacus* is a Hollywood classic produced in 1959 and based on Howard Fast's novel. It details the rise and ultimate destruction of thousands of slaves who rebelled against their Roman masters and formed an army that roamed Italy for several years in the late 70s. A Thracian gladiator named Spartacus led the rebel army to victory over several Roman forces. At last, the rebels were decisively defeated by an army under the command of Marcus Licinius Crassus.[20] Thousands of survivors from the slave army were crucified along the side of the Appian Way, an object lesson in the dangers of defying Rome.

Unfortunately, *Spartacus*, in its current form has almost none of the original battle scenes that were shot, save only the final showdown with the army of Crassus. The rest was left on the cutting room floor. There were two concerns at work in the editing process. While concerns about the total length of the film were an issue, there was also a political controversy about how Spartacus' victories should be interpreted. Filmed at a time when many Americans feared Communist plots, some felt emphasizing Spartacus' victories would seem too much like endorsing class warfare and revolution.[21] Most of the cut footage was subsequently lost. Though the 1991 Restored Criterion Collection version of the film includes some previously deleted footage, little of that has anything of note for our purposes. And so the only significant battle scene occurs toward the end of the film between Spartacus' and Crassus' forces.

The scene begins with the camera surveying the rebel army, positioned along a hilltop. The soldiers of Spartacus' army wear a wide variety of arms and armour, reflecting their need to scavenge for equipment over the past few years. Several of the cut victories over Roman forces are alluded to, however, by the number of fighters who wear Roman armour. All seem to be armed with thrusting spears. The old and young, men and women, are all in arms. After surveying the slave army, the camera shifts to the forces of Crassus across the plain on a hillside marching forward in orderly lines. This is the cohort army of the late Republic in its glory. A shot of Crassus and two officers shows the men in leather muscled-armour with ornate golden decorations. Behind all three are the legionary standards. The camera shifts back to the slave army's view and the articulation of the Roman army into cohorts can be seen in the distance. A shift to a position behind Crassus and his officers shows the legionaries marching by.

Ten thousand Spanish soldiers were recruited for this scene.[22] The shot is magnificent insofar as in an age before CGI enhancements, it gives a hint of what it must have been like for an enemy of Rome to see such a large and extremely disciplined army. Their approach was captured on cameras about half a mile away that were set on 100ft high cranes.[23] What the viewer sees is two legions, each of ten cohorts, each occupying four lines for battle: first two cohorts with a cohort sized gap in between each, then three cohorts, then two, then three more. As with the manipular army, the cohorts in a legion fought in formations that were designed to allow the units at the front lines of battle to be replaced as needed by fresh ones, and, as with the manipular army, we are not entirely clear how that worked.[24] Still, this scene gets the flavour of that organization but clearly errs in the details. The actual formation of cohorts in the first legion filmed looks something like this.

Front

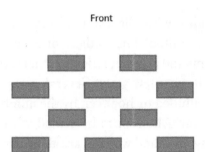

Rear

Something's not quite right, however. Most commonly the cohorts were arranged in the *triplex acies*, the threefold battle line in which, so far as is known, cohorts were distributed in staggered lines, first three then four then three; from this position they could transform into solid lines as needed.[25] What is even odder is that official movie promotional material that discusses the cohort legion gets the pattern right with only three lines.[26] The problems compound when the legions have finished their approach over the nearby hills. They halt. Slowly the first two cohorts widen their front to form one battle line like so:

Front

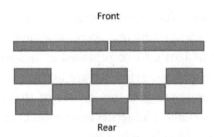

Rear

Then the four cohorts on the wings of the formation move in to form a hollow rectangle:

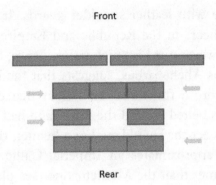

Finally the front line, unsupported by the rear ranks, marches up the slope to attack, alone. It appears that all *Spartacus* has shown authentically in this scene is that the legionaries march in formation and those formations change shape. Beyond that, though, it is difficult to perceive a historical logic to this simulated formation change.

Nor is this the only significant problem with the battle scene. The legionaries' equipment has a number of problems, starting with their weapons. Each wears a *gladius* at the hip but carries a spear of uniform width, clearly meant for thrusting and equally clearly not a *pilum*. There are also problems with the legionary shield, or *scutum*. Spartacus' legionaries are equipped with flat, rectangular *scuta*, not a curve in sight. The legionary *scutum*, so far as we know, was always curved and did not take its rectangular curved form until the early Empire.[27] Furthermore, instead of the central boss with a handgrip, the shields in Spartacus are attached by a strap at the elbow and a handgrip. Using these attachments places the forearm parallel with the long edge of the shield. Such a system not only causes the *scutum* to be worn differently, it requires the actor-fighters to hold the shield with the long edge parallel to the ground, not perpendicular as it was used historically, and therefore sacrificing much of its ability to shield the body.

The body armour is equally problematic. The soldiers are in standardized leather armour of some sort that is sculpted to look like musculature with leather shoulder guards. It may have been the case that officers in the Republic and Empire wore muscled-breastplates. However our best pictorial evidence, the first century altar of Domitius Ahenobarbus, suggests that the legionary of the late Republic wore a functional mail shirt that extended to the upper thigh, was belted around the waist, and had additional wide mail flaps to protect the shoulders. For a helmet, the soldiers wear something that approximates an Imperial-Gallic type helmet, a more ornate helmet than the Montefortino (see plate 15) that was not in use until the early empire.[28] Leather *pteruges*, much like those of a Greek hoplite, cover the soldiers' abdomens and thighs. Overall, their equipment is a mash-up of different types of armour from different periods.

The slave army waits atop the hill as the first line of legionaries approaches, four deep. When the enemy is close, the rebel army resorts to the tactic of rolling flaming logs down the hill. Each has two handlers holding a chain on each side to keep the log rolling. These crash into and burn unwary legionaries. It's a seemingly clever ploy, but there simply is no historical evidence for the rebels using this tactic.[29]

Hot on the trail, as it were, of the flaming logs, the slave army charges collectively down the hill as a single mob. The men manoeuvring the flaming logs continue to chase the routing front line of Roman soldiers. The waves of slaves dispatch any legionaries left behind by the logs.

Then the slave army and legion engage in hand-to-hand combat. The Roman soldiers are in disarray, duelling with the slaves. Suddenly, Spartacus sees Roman reinforcements approaching in the distance, Pompey's troops, arriving on his left flank. Spartacus then leads his cavalry into the melee at the bottom of the hill – not, it should be noted, a particularly good tactic when one is about to be outflanked.

The battle is nothing more than clumps of men fighting, each spaced out significantly from the others. Here and there are some spaces that might indicate formations of soldiers, but certainly not orderly ones. Overall, the scene suffers from a lack of any clear battle order or distinction between infantry and cavalry formations. For example, after Spartacus rides into the melee, a Roman rider and horse appear conveniently to duel him, though no Roman cavalry has been seen in the mix before this. It's a problem of positioning. The Romans and Spartacus certainly had cavalry, but these were normally stationed along the wings, not mixed in the centre with the infantry. From the flanks they could harass and disrupt infantry formations. As the film has it, however, there are no formations once the fighting begins and combat consists of simply pouring more and more men, sometimes on horses, into the central brawl. By the time Pompey's army arrives, they too are little more than a mob poured into the mix. This is not a Roman battle; it's a street fight.

So how exactly did the battle transpire? Unfortunately, our evidence is very sparse for the exploits of Spartacus and his army. The ancient sources do note that he won a number of battles against the Romans. The final battle is not narrated in any detail, however. All that the sources seem to agree upon is that Spartacus died in the fighting.[30] Spartacus' first battles were against relatively untrained local militias, but he went on to defeat both consuls and their armies.[31] This would be difficult to explain if he used the mob tactics depicted in the film. Far more reasonable to suppose that the slave-soldiers had adopted rudimentary infantry and cavalry formations sufficient to challenge the Romans: a simple mob would just have been cut to pieces.

Strictly speaking, then, as a representation of Roman battle the scene in *Spartacus* lacks authenticity. Beyond the fearsome survey of cohorts marching from a distance, there is little in this battle sequence that can help visualize a battlefield from the first century. One would take away an inaccurate view of equipment, formations, and tactics, almost everything for practical purposes. Unfortunately, more recent cinematic efforts to capitalize on the story of Spartacus have done little to improve upon the flawed vision of the Roman

Leather Armour

Despite its lack of historical authenticity, Roman soldiers with leather armour are something of a standard in many films. Historians Sekunda and Simkins explain how leather came on to the scene. 'This misconception arose very largely from the apparently common Roman habit of painting on to sculptures parts that were tedious to portray with a chisel ... By the time the artists of the Renaissance began to portray the classical warrior, most or all of the painted or plastered parts had weathered away, leaving the mail shirts looking smooth and very like leather jerkins.' (Sekunda *et al.*, *Caesar's Legions*, 109) Leather, they note, was simply not strong enough to make effective body armour against cuts and thrusts, but the artistic impression crystallized in many films.

army presented in the 1959 film. USA Network Pictures released another *Spartacus* in 2004, this one made-for-cable. Though the scale of the final battle is much smaller than that achieved by Kubrick, at first glance it appears that the equipment is more authentic: the infantry's *scuta* are curved at least. That impression vanishes upon closer scrutiny. The legionaries, as in the 1959 *Spartacus*, are equipped in segmented armour and helmets whose style belong over a century later in the early Empire. Well, sort of belong. While the legionaries in the later first century AD wore metal helmets and segmented armour, the film has constructed its legionaries' armour wholly out of leather. Perhaps this is a cost saving measure for the film, but it adds insult to anachronism, as it were. For weapons, all the legionaries carry thrusting spears, decidedly not *pila*. There are gaps between the units, but it is not at all clear what these units represent: they are too small to be cohorts. Spartacus' army, as in the Kubrick version, is a mass of people, a crowd more than an army.

Crassus bellows, 'For Rome ... Time to die' and Spartacus, on foot shouts, 'Freedom!' as his mob army surges forward. The Roman army has archer units on its flanks and they launch arrows at the slave army. Clad in purple with leather armour and helmets, they likely

The Many Lives of Spartacus

Spartacus is pretty much the perennially favourite subject for films set in the Roman world. In addition to the classic 1959 version and the version from USA films mentioned in the text, there are no fewer than six earlier renditions of Spartacus. Four alone were shot in the years 1909 to 1919!

Most recently Spartacus has been the heroic subject of a series on the STARZ network. So far the focus of the episodes has been on heroic duels and romance, however, not representations of battle.

represent auxiliary units – units levied from foreign peoples subject to the Romans – but their equipment does not clearly distinguish them. The orderly Romans then countercharge and sacrifice their order, pulling apart in the rush to contact. The two armies, Roman and slave, intermingle into a mob. At this point the scene devolves, as did its predecessor, into a series of individual combats, a brawl. And while it makes sense that slaves might not fight exactly as Romans, there is still no reason for the Romans' complete lack of order. Still, the lack of discipline that historically would have cost the Romans the battle does not harm them in the film. The legionaries slowly vanquish their foes. Spartacus' trusted comrades die, one after the other. Meanwhile Spartacus slowly fights his way toward Crassus. Their gazes lock. Spartacus is coming to extract vengeance. The mass of legionaries in his way, however, overwhelm him and he falls melodramatically with his eyes skyward, a noble sacrifice. The legionaries pile around the spot where he fell, stabbing a now hidden Spartacus over and over.

To be fair, this depiction of the dramatic end of Spartacus is not wholly without the support of the ancient sources. Plutarch gives a similar account: 'Pushing his way towards Crassus himself through many flying weapons and wounded men, [Spartacus] did not indeed reach him, but slew two centurions who fell upon him together. Finally, after his companions had taken to flight, he stood alone, surrounded by a multitude of foes, and was still defending himself when he was cut down.'[32] Regardless of whether Spartacus met his end this way, the mechanics of the battle itself are far-fetched.

The Spartacus movies, whatever their merits as dramatic epics, are of little use for imagining the Roman army of the late Republic. When it comes to depictions of the Caesarian legion, HBO's *Rome* series gets off to a far better start. Throughout the series the legionaries, indeed all the characters, are equipped with impressive attention to accuracy. The legionaries are equipped more or less uniformly. They wear Montefortino-style helmets of bronze (see plate 15 for an example), mail shirts, military tunics and sandals. They carry large oblong or rectangular curved shields and are armed with *pila* and short swords. Like most of the military props and scenery in the series, looking at these soldiers gives one a reasonably authentic glimpse into the past. There are only two scenes in the two-season series, however, that actually show the legionaries in battle to any significant extent. The very first episode takes us to Alesia in Gaul where Caesar crushed a Gallic rebellion in 52 BC. The sixth episode of the second season depicts elements of Philippi, the decisive battle in 42 BC between Caesar's successors, Octavian and Marcus Antonius, and his assassins, Brutus and Cassius.

The scene at Alesia is dramatic without appearing over the top and has an air of authenticity. Grim, determined centurion Lucius Vorenus (Kevin McKidd) looks ahead and waits for the Gauls to arrive. Similar determination shows on the faces of the legionaries nearby who await his command. The centurion Vorenus commands stands in organized files four soldiers deep. From the hillock in front of them, a series of figures approach. They carry axes, swords, spears, clearly whatever was available to them. Some wear helmets; most have no protection other than their long-sleeve shirts and trousers. There are a number of them, but they advance as individuals rather than as units, a stark contrast to the orderly lines of the Romans. As the Gallic warriors approach, the centurion brings a whistle to his lips and blows a signal note. The legionaries, who have essentially been standing ready but at ease up to this point all lift their shields and hunker into fighting positions behind them, shield-side leg in front. Column by column, each soldier grabs hold of the soldier in front of him the better to preserve the orderly formation, an interesting interpretation though one that really cannot be substantiated by the evidence. They hold their ground, professionals all the way.

A spear-wielding Gaul closes with the centurion, still in formation beside his comrades. He stabs with a two-handed grip, but the centurion has anticipated the attack. He crouches into a ready pose, catches and pushes the spear up and away with his shield, and stabs the Gaul's vulnerable leg with his sword. Centurion Vorenus has won this encounter and still holds the line. The camera pulls back to show legionaries in the second and third ranks standing firm, standing together. The front line soldiers all fight like Vorenus, as they have been trained. Indeed their fighting style recalls the admonition of the late imperial writer, Vegetius, who noted that Roman recruits were trained to stab with the sword, a more efficient and deadly attack than a swing.[33] The Romans parry with their shields and stab. Above all, however, they stay in formation, disciplined and deadly. A particularly heroic Gaul leaps over the front line of shields but is cut down by Romans in the rear ranks. And still the Romans maintain their position against the accumulating mass of Gallic warriors hacking and slashing at their heavy shields.

The centurion blows his whistle again, and something incredible happens. The camera rises to look straight down at the legionaries, and we see the front rank of soldiers shuffle in profile to the back while the second man in each file occupies the front. In other words, the legionaries have rotated in fresh troops while maintaining the integrity of their battle line. The rhythm continues. Legionaries block or divert spears, axes, swords, and return with a thrust at their attackers. Again a whistle blow and fresh troops rotate to the front. This time legionary Titus Pullo (Ray Stevenson), another series protagonist, comes to the front. Both strong of limb and headstrong, Pullo uses his *scutum* as a weapon, slamming into a kneeling enemy, driving another back. Unlike his better reserved comrades, however Pullo moves out in front of his line and wades into the mass of Gauls, parting them with his *scutum* as he trades blows with his enemies. Centurion Vorenus stabs another enemy and reprimands his subordinate for his unsanctioned progress. 'Pullo, formation,' he calls. Pullo will not or cannot hear and continues his individual attack on the Gauls. 'Pullo, single formation!' Vorenus growls with even more conviction, but Pullo fights on as before. Unwilling to sacrifice the integrity of his formation for this imbecile, he gives another order: 'Shields on me!' and the front rank moves forward on Vorenus' command. As the front line advances, it loses the morale and physical support of its second line and some of its integrity, and a series of individual duels erupt. Vorenus' helmet is knocked from his head, and he dispatches the assailant. Now in reach of Pullo, he grabs the wilful legionary by his shoulder straps and orders again, 'Get back in formation, you drunken fool!' Pullo takes a swing at Vorenus; Vorenus floors Pullo with his shield. A pair of legionaries drag Pullo to the rear. Vorenus calls out, 'Re-form!' and blows his whistle again.

This has all the makings of a military morality tale: obedient and disciplined is how a legionary must be. Indeed Vorenus turns the scene into an object lesson for the legion. The scene shifts to Caesar's camp. The battle has been won, but Pullo is chained to posts and whipped as Vorenus lectures to watching soldiers: 'Legionary Titus Pullo is a hero of the Thirteenth Legion. But look at him now. Justice knows every man's number. He has committed a terrible sacrilege. And he will pay for it with his life.' As Vorenus continues the camera shifts here and there showing the mostly uncomfortable faces of legionaries. 'As will any man here, who breaks the law. Brawlers and drunkards will be flogged. Thieves will be strangled. Deserters will be crucified.' Pullo is untied and dragged off.

How does this fare as a model of battle at the very end of the Republic? To start, some important historical details are lost in *Rome's* depiction of Alesia. One of the most important is the type of battle depicted between Caesar's soldiers and the Gauls at Alesia. The final battle is depicted as set in the forest, army against army. Historically, Alesia was a town where Vercingetorix and his Gallic armies were trapped and besieged by Caesar's legions. The Roman army made an impressive set of siege-works, a wall and ditch to hem in the Gauls at Alesia, and a larger fortification around that so that the Roman besiegers could defend themselves against any Gallic forces that hoped to relieve the besieged. Certainly they had to defend their fortifications, but they did not engage in any normal field battles. The scene of the century in action misrepresents the kind of actions occurring at Alesia.[34]

A second inaccuracy is the portrayal of the protagonists. There really were a Titus Pullio and Lucius Varenus; *Rome* has simply changed the names ever so slightly. The story Caesar tells of them is different, but one no less impressive in its display of Roman courage. In Caesar's commentary on the Gallic Wars, these two soldiers are both centurions as it happens, both distinguished for their courage, and both competing to be promoted to the highest rank of centurion. The tribe of the Nervi attacked the winter quarters of one of Caesar's legions, giving the two another opportunity to compete in valour. This is the account Caesar gives:

> When the fight was going on most vigorously before the fortifications, Pullio, one of them, says, 'Why do you hesitate, Varenus? What [better] opportunity of signalizing your valour do you seek? This very day shall decide our disputes.' When he had uttered these words, he proceeds beyond the fortifications, and rushes on that part of the enemy which appeared the thickest. Nor does Varenus remain within the rampart, but respecting the high opinion of all, follows close after. Then, when an inconsiderable space intervened, Pullio throws his javelin at the enemy, and pierces one of the multitude who was running up, and while the latter was wounded and slain, the enemy cover him with their shields, and all throw their weapons

at the other and afford him no opportunity of retreating. The shield of Pullio is pierced and a javelin is caught in his belt. This circumstance turns aside his scabbard and obstructs his right hand when attempting to draw his sword: the enemy crowd around him when [thus] hampered. His rival runs up to him and aids him in this emergency. Immediately the whole host turn from Pullio to him, supposing the other to be pierced through by the javelin. Varenus rushes on briskly with his sword and carries on the combat hand to hand, and having slain one man, for a short time drove back the rest: while he urges on too eagerly, slipping into a hollow, he fell. To him, in his turn, when surrounded, Pullio brings relief; and both having slain a great number, retreat into the fortifications amidst the highest applause. Fortune so dealt with both in this rivalry and conflict, that the one competitor was a helper and a safeguard to the other, nor could it be determined which of the two appeared worthy of being preferred to the other.[35]

The contrast between the disciplined Vorenus and the brave but insubordinate Pullio did not exist for Caesar. Rather both centurions found an opportunity for bravery that apparently met with the satisfaction not only of the surrounding soldiers but of Caesar himself who included this episode in his narrative.

Leaving aside these changes to the historical narrative, how does this recreation of legionaries fighting Gauls fare? Again, the legionary equipment is impeccably modelled. The legionaries have chain mail shirts with the extra shoulder protection. They wear helmets of the Montefortino type, again to be expected from Roman soldiers of this period. Their shields are rectangular and curved, reasonably consistent with what is known of the very late Republic. Strictly speaking curved rectangular shields were not definitively in use for another forty years, but it is not known when they began to be adopted.[36] They have swords that are short, powerful weapons made for thrusting. Visually, with one exception that will be dealt with shortly, they are highly authentic. They stand out in comparison to the strange varieties of leather armour found in the Spartacus films.

The depiction of the Gauls is, however, a bit stereotyped. The Gallic warriors are depicted as ill-armed, and ill-organized, the classic barbarian mob. Caesar himself in his account of the Gallic wars, describes a different set of foes. Vercingetorix is presented as using mixed unit tactics – cavalry and light infantry, cavalry and archers – making sound strategic decisions, and generally ably leading the Gauls. Caesar writes with respect about the Gallic armies, refers even to some forming phalanxes.[37] It is reasonable to suppose the Gauls lacked the depth of organization and training possessed by Roman legionaries, now veterans after years of constant war, but this does not mean that they cast themselves against their enemy without formation or plan.

Other than the less plausible arrangements of the Gallic infantry, the depiction of the combat lacks one important detail: the *pila* volley. The legionaries simply wait for the Gauls to close to sword range. An initial *pila* volley, however, seems to have been the standard way for Caesar's soldiers – and perhaps all Roman soldiers of the period – to demoralize and injure their enemies before closing to short-sword range.[38] This particular passage from Caesar's memoirs describes the damage the *pila* could do:

[Caesar's] soldiers, hurling their [pila] from the higher ground, easily broke the enemy's phalanx. That being dispersed, they made a charge on them with drawn swords. It was a great hindrance to the Gauls in fighting, that, when several of their bucklers had been by one stroke of the (Roman) javelins pierced through and pinned fast together, as the point of the iron had bent itself, they could neither pluck it out, nor, with their left hand entangled, fight with sufficient ease; so that many, after having long tossed their arm about, chose rather to cast away the buckler from their hand, and to fight with their person unprotected. At length, worn out with wounds, they began to give way.[39]

This is one of several references to an initial *pila* volley, and elsewhere Caesar writes about these episodes as if they were standard procedure.[40] Indeed Caesar takes care to mention one occasion where the legionaries were too close to their enemies to throw *pila* and had to advance with swords only.[41] The legionaries under Vorenus' command, however, do not throw their *pila* at the Gauls; indeed in this first episode encounter they do not even carry *pila*.

What this cinematic vision captures that is so very striking, however, is a model of how the legion preserved its all-important formations, a view of the mechanics in action. We have seen how ancient sources described the manipular and cohort armies as having multiple lines of units that could relieve those in the front line. But these were systems for replacing one unit with another, not individual soldiers. Rome offers a suggestion of how, at the level of a century, fresh soldiers would replace tired ones within the same unit and maintain their formation. The soldiers in each rear rank hold on to the hauberk of the man directly in front of them. At regular intervals the centurion sounds his whistle. Upon the signal, each man fighting in the front rank shuffles sideways back through the narrow spaces between the columns while the next in line takes his place at the front. The transition is seamless as depicted in the film, a tactic that could only have been executed by highly drilled troops, but then, that is exactly what Caesar's legionaries were at this point.

A few historians have suggested that the legions employed a system like this, in which fresh troops within a unit replaced fatigued ones at the front.[42] In part this system is designed to resolve the issue of why infantry units were normally deployed several lines deep. Others have countered that the primary purpose of having multiple lines of men in a unit after the first is to provide moral support to the front row.[43] Clearly these possibilities are not mutually exclusive: one can readily imagine that the back rows provided both moral support and fresh soldiers should those in the front become incapacitated by wounds or exhaustion. Still there is no evidence that the Roman legionaries of Caesar's day, or any other day, rotated men in and out of a unit's front line in so regular a fashion as depicted by *Rome*. One can imagine a number of reasons why not. First of all, the condition of each soldier in the front line of a unit must have varied widely moment to moment; rotating all soldiers out after a half minute would make little sense if some front rankers were still fresh and ready to go. Secondly a line of soldiers each holding the belt of the one in front would restrict the freedom of movement of the front soldiers, perhaps dangerously so. On the other hand, it is reasonable to suppose a fresh second ranker would, if possible, relieve an exhausted or injured file leader. And so it may be that a more informal individual system was used that partially resembled that shown in *Rome*, but it is unlikely the system as depicted was put into place. In most respects, then, the scene of the century engaged at Alesia is noteworthy in its representation of battle mechanics, but it emphasizes this untestified tactic. It is one thing to offer a cinematic interpretation of how cohorts cycled in and out of battle. It is quite another to invent a systemized routine of whistle blowing and the rotation of the front line in a unit.

Rome: The Battle of Philippi

Following hot on the heels of Caesar's conquest of Gaul, the very Republic itself collapsed, and *Rome* chronicles this collapse through the eyes of its chosen characters. Caesar and his enemies in the senate, the most powerful of whom was Gnaeus Pompeius Magnus, Pompey as moderns call him, reached a level of political hostility that could only be resolved, they believed, through war. Caesar made the decision to march against his enemies in Rome at the beginning of 49 BC. By the end of the next year he had decisively defeated his enemies in battles ranging from Macedonia and Spain, to Africa. Or at least he seems to have thought so. At Rome Caesar had himself declared dictator first for five years and later, for life. Soon after Caesar received this unprecedented power of permanent dictator, some senators came to the conclusion that murder was the only way to remove Caesar and restore the normal offices of the Republic. And so that fateful day, the ides of March 44 BC, Gaius Cassius Longinus, Marcus Junius Brutus, and a number of other conspirators surrounded Caesar when he entered the senate and stabbed him – twenty-three times no less.[44]

When Caesar died, the Republic did not spring back into operation as the conspirators seemed to have hoped it would. Rather a handful of powerful Romans began to joust politically to take the dominant place that Caesar had held in the past five years. Caesar's lieutenant, Antony, and his posthumously adopted teenage son, Octavian, both claimed the right to succeed to Caesar's position. Both gathered armies of veterans and were prepared to battle to a decision. The veteran soldiers, however, had once fought together under Caesar's command and were not willing to spill one another's blood to settle a political dispute between Caesar's successors. And so Octavian and Antony were forced, temporarily, to make a pact. Once they did, they set their sights on their remaining rivals, Cassius and Brutus. These assassins, or liberators as they preferred to term it, fled Italy in 44 BC and travelled to the Greek east, gathering money and supporters. Octavian had the senate, packed with supporters, declare Cassius and Brutus to be outlaws for murdering Caesar. By the end of 42 BC Octavian and Antony had crossed with their armies to Macedonia and found Cassius and Brutus outside the city of Philippi.

The scene of Philippi expands dramatically on the model of combat shown at Alesia. Now audiences are treated to a view of a full battle, ostensibly involving tens of thousands of Roman soldiers. The camera looks down from a high angle panning perpendicularly across the multitude of legions; this battle in a hot and dry plain will mean the death of thousands of Romans. The enemy today is no foreign foe; Roman will kill Roman to decide who will determine the empire's destiny: Antonius and Octavian or Brutus and Cassius. A low angle close-up of the liberators' legionaries shows each standing at the ready, *scutum* resting on the ground and hands on their swords. Then the camera runs from the front to the back of the ranks where Brutus and Cassius sit atop their horses in full gear, open faced helmets with plumes and muscled breastplates. The two engage in trivially aristocratic banter, a decision of the writers, perhaps, to make them appear more out of touch with realities.

Then the camera switches to Antony and Octavian's legions. The soldiers are equipped just as their foes, expressions on faces just as grave. Shifting to Antonius and Octavian the camera shows Antonius quip to his much younger partner, 'If you need to urinate, now would be the time.' Octavian, stony-faced, assures him he does not. 'You sure?' spars Antonius. 'I'm fine, thank you', Octavian replies, barely holding his anger in check at this jest. Unable to resist, Antonius asks one last time, then begins the battle with a wave of his arm, the sign for a subordinate to yell, 'ADVANCE!' Starting with the front ranks, the army moves forward in unison, steps measured, each soldier's *pilum* resting on his shoulder and *scutum* hanging low to his side.

After another vacuously polite exchange between the liberators about who should get the honour to give the order, Cassius commands the advance. Close-ups of legs and feet show the slow orderly cadence of the legionaries. The camera pulls back to a position between the closing armies, whose battle lines are so long that they fade away into the distance. Then the camera slowly closes to show the clash of the lines. Shield strikes shield; a few legionaries grab their *scutum* with both hands and jab it forward at their foes – one may well wonder what these Romans had done with their swords. The men remain in formation except for a bit of inevitable confusion at the front. As a sequence for a developing battle, this part of the scene is effective. Things start to get appropriately jumbled from here as one would expect in battle. The camera dances about. Here, a second ranker holds on to the file leader's sword belt to maintain the formation. There, a *pilum* goes straight through a shield into a man's face. If there is any way to determine which army is which, it is mostly lost on the viewer. A centurion blows a whistle and a high shot shows the rotation of ranks in what must be the conspirators' army, judging from the colour of the standard. The view from above reveals that each legionary in a file holds on to the back of the legionary in front of him to maintain the formation. Despite the order of the legionaries, the killing zone is chaotic. A downed soldier is slaughtered. Another uses his low position to stab up and into his foe. Blood flows everywhere: swords pierce mail and bite deep: here into a shoulder, there into the back of a foe. Time passes and the shot dissolves into a position high and to the rear of one army. The impression is of organized chaos.

The camera shifts to Antonius, eyeing the battle with the interest of a football fan, and picking at a loaf of bread. Octavian asks what is happening in the battle and Antonius flippantly returns, 'No idea.' He casts his bread aside nonchalantly, draws his sword and speaks to the riders beside him. 'On my command, follow me.' Octavian asks where he is going, and Antonius replies, 'when in doubt .... ATTACK!' The order given, he and his squad of cavalry ride off. The audience does not see them again. The cavalry's role in this battle is simply ignored.

Meanwhile the cohesion of both armies' front ranks is fast dissolving and individuals are duelling. Fresh soldiers, when they arrive, however, restore order to the front and drive soldiers on the other side to retreat. A messenger tells Cassius that Antonius' troops have broken the right side of their line. Cassius moves forward with a unit of foot soldiers. Arrows fly into their midst and he orders the *testudo* to be formed. The soldiers kneel and form a shield wall in front of them and a shield roof overhead. A shot of the huddled soldiers under shields shows arrows puncturing the shields, one going through the metal boss and through its bearer's wrist, which was highly unlikely historically. Another receives an arrow in the cheek. Most are unharmed. When the sound of the arrows stops, Cassius orders his unit to reform and move forward. He is with them every step of the way. The legionaries close and Cassius is cut down almost immediately. A new shot shows clouds and smoke. Cassius is brought by stretcher to Brutus, coughing, blood staining his tunic. Brutus watches and sees the rout, his soldiers fleeing the field. When he looks again, Cassius is dead. Staring ahead, Brutus sees the enemy soldiers marching toward him in organized ranks. He comes to a decision. He looks at the officers and soldiers around him. 'It has been an honour and a pleasure leading you,' he says, 'and I am sorry we could not do better. But you must look to yourselves now. Save your skins.' Brutus asks his trusted lieutenant to say something 'suitable' to his mother. With that he takes a sword from a nearby centurion, looks again at the advancing forces, his own vanished. He walks toward the enemy, cutting the straps of his breastplate and discarding the armour as he walks. His first attempt to provoke the victorious soldiers is unsuccessful but soon he inflicts a grievous leg wound on one and a series of men pierce Brutus with their swords, some in the front, others from behind. The director clearly hopes to invoke the spectre of Julius Caesar's murder, for the soldiers continue to stab Brutus long after he is done for and falls to the ground.

As with the depiction of fighting at Alesia in the first season, this battle of Philippi plays fast and loose with the actual events. There were actually two battles at Philippi between Brutus and Cassius, and Antony and Octavian. Several ancient sources recount the battles, and while they have their differences, their similarities are sufficient to reconstruct a historical outline of events. On the first day of battle, Octavian was sick and may well have missed the battle.[45] On that first day Brutus, whose forces occupied the left wing of the line, drove off Octavian's legionaries and managed to plunder his and Antony's base camp. On the right, however, Cassius' troops were soundly defeated by Antony's men. Cassius, unaware of Brutus' victory and despairing because of his own defeat, killed himself. Brutus, likely very demoralized by his comrade's premature death, refused to give battle for a number of days, instead maintaining his fortified position on a hill. Several days later, probably due to the plunging morale of his soldiers, Brutus committed to a second battle at Philippi. Octavian and Antony's forces routed those of Brutus. He, in despair, followed Cassius' in death, ending his own life.[46] *Rome* selects elements from this narrative and conflates them into something very different from the ancient testimony. In *Rome* there will be only one battle. Cassius is reluctant to commit to battle, but Brutus insists on it. The two command together from the centre against Octavian and Antony who also command together. Cassius' forces are routed first and Cassius is mortally wounded attempting to shore up the flank. He is carried back to Brutus who watches him die, sees that the entire army has been scattered and provokes the approaching enemy legionaries to kill him.

Once again, though, there is more to an authentic depiction of battle than the historical context, though that is certainly not insignificant. How effectively does the battle scene at Philippi represent the mechanics of the Caesarian legions at war? The legionaries, as at Alesia, maintain their formations as they approach, marching in unison column by column, row by row, and this is authentic enough. When the camera captures both battle lines fading into the distance, the soldiers are grouped in distinct units. Each unit has a depth of four soldiers and the battle line appears to be four or five units deep. This is deeper than the standard *triplex acies*, but not out of the realm of the possible when such large armies clashed.

The *pila* volleys have been ignored again, however, the soldiers immediately closing to short sword range instead. Right before the clash, the order of the infantry degrades just a bit as each soldier chooses when to charge the remaining few feet to his enemy. This is a good take on human behaviour in battle – despite their high discipline, they are men, not machines. Shields are held up high and legionaries mostly stab economically with swords held in overhand grips, continuing to practise the doctrine to thrust rather than to cut.[47] The confusion in battle is represented through the jumping camera. A centurion drops to his knees, dead. Another centurion looks around quickly, then blows his whistle. His soldiers follow their training and relieve the first line fighters through the rotation system demonstrated at the battle of Alesia, an unfortunate ripple in an otherwise authentic looking battle scene. Soldiers continue to stab at each other in the front lines and shove with their shields. The rear ranks continue to hold on to their comrades in front, clinging to keep formation. In this close-up, however, there are six ranks of soldiers each holding on the man in front and it is not clear how the original formation morphed into this.

There is space at the front as soldiers die, enough for one man to stab a grounded enemy then lose his hand at the forearm in turn. Another grounded soldier stabs his enemy's groin. A dramatic touch to the brutality: a wounded soldier with no helmet stares around in a daze at the slaughter. He is quickly dispatched with a stab to the back. It is safe to say that the battle line in this section has disintegrated to a fair extent, the soldiers of each side intermingling and killing. When the camera pulls back and up, one can still see the remnants of a formation – the soldiers are not simply off on their own duelling – but the strains of battle have clearly caused the orderly formations in the killing zone at the front to dissolve.

Of the many noises emanating from the battlefield, however, one is a bit puzzling. The neighing and galloping of horses can clearly be heard, but there are no depictions of cavalry. Indeed Antony rides in leading a cavalry charge, but we never see the results. This is not surprising, however, given the series' choice to focus on the small unit's experience in battle, not the experience of the whole or the use of strategy. It is also arguably more expensive and difficult to capture believable shots of cavalry in action, and requires the use of trained horses and riders.

The Middle and Late Republics are still wide open for serious cinematic treatments of battle. Despite the array of adventure films set in the period, HBO's *Rome* series shoulders the burden single-handedly of depicting battles, and here only for the very end of the

Republic. At the level of the century, *Rome* provides a fair glimpse into the brutal business of fighting, the stab and block of sword and shield, the generation of entropy. There are problems: the cavalry are ignored and no serious treatment is given to the positioning of armies. Still the series does an admirable job with what it does show. Unfortunately for Roman history buffs, the series ended with the second season and so ended the possibility to see more battles during the years in which Augustus came to power. For the period of the Roman Empire, however, the field of films spreads somewhat more widely and it is to the Empire we now turn.

Chapter 5

Imperial Rome

At the height of its power, the Roman Empire was vast, stretching from the deserts of Africa to the borders of northern England. Over one quarter of the world's population lived and died under the rule of the Caesars. In the winter of AD 180 Emperor Marcus Aurelius' twelve-year campaign against the barbarian tribes in Germania was drawing to an end. One final stronghold stands in the way of Roman victory and the promise of peace throughout the Empire.

With this Ridley Scott's *Gladiator* (2000) begins. To represent the Roman General Maximus' (Russell Crowe) memories of his beloved Spanish fields, the camera offers a close-up tracking shot of his left hand gliding gently over heads of wheat as he walks. Then the scene shifts to a markedly overcast and grey battlefield. General Maximus wears his hair short and his beard cropped close. His breastplate is made of overlapping plates of iron, and he wears it over a tunic of red wool. As the camera pulls back Maximus is revealed to be standing in the torched clearing of a forest. Woods lie in the near distance beyond hillocks and smoking stumps. 'GERMANIA' appears on screen to provide a location. If anything it is a scene of destruction.

As Maximus fades into the distance, striding contemplatively across the charred fields, a squad of legionary cavalry rides past in the foreground. They are clad in segmented armour, red cloaks, and the iconic lobster-tailed helmets and flags representing the honours won by the legions. They take the road up a gentle hill where the Roman camp is revealed. The cavalry pass by the bearers of the standards, one pole with medallions and trophies, the other bearing

the banner Felix XIII, for 'The Lucky Thirteenth' Legion. Higher
up the hill on which the encampment was constructed, infantry of
all sorts march by, moving into various positions. The legionary
infantry are armed with helmets, weapons, and armour and carry
the iconic red shield with eagle wings and lightning bolts in yellow.
The camera pans up and to the right to capture the outskirts of the
camp. A row of soldiers is behind a short earthen wall, and behind
them a palisade of sharpened stakes points outward on slightly
higher ground. Everything is dead, blackened, uprooted. The view
shifts to a nearby hill where the emperor, Marcus Aurelius (Richard
Harris), sits aside his horse, waiting. His is a look of patient concern.
Wearing armour of leather decorated with gold and clad in a hooded
cloak of purple, the emperor is surrounded by soldiers. These men
are much cleaner than the legionaries and garbed in imperial purple.
There is no mistaking the personal bodyguard of the emperor, the
Praetorian Guard.

The camera returns to Maximus. He begins his review, walking
up to the first line of defence in front of the sharpened stakes that
surround the Roman camp. His men bow in deference or salute.
Maximus strolls the lines of men in his gathered army, pats some on
the shoulder, smiles at others.

The camp buzzes with preparations, as the soldiers ready for
battle. Two hours prior, scouts were dispatched to locate the enemy
position. Maximus learns from his lieutenant that they have not
returned. The lieutenant asks a simple question whose answer will
decide their fate: 'Will they fight, sir?' Maximus' reply: 'We shall
know soon enough.'

Gladiator is one of a number of films set in the Roman Empire.
Arguably the film single-handedly revived the genre of the ancient
epic film and demonstrated its commercial viability for a new
generation. For the student of Roman military history, however,
the opening battle scene in *Gladiator* offers one of the few visual
depictions of the Roman Imperial Army at work. Beyond *Gladiator*
there are two major films from the past decade that have a significant

scene modelling Roman combat: *Centurion* (2010) and the *The Eagle* (2011). Neither spends long on the subject but together the three films present images of the Roman army in very different scenarios. In *Gladiator*, the army fights a pitched battle against a Germanic foe. In the *The Eagle* a small squad of Romans skirmishes outside its fort with a Briton war band. Finally, in *Centurion*, the ambush of the mighty Ninth Legion in Britain is reconstructed on film. Together the battle scenes in these films illustrate well the strengths and weaknesses of the Roman Imperial Army.

The Army of the Roman Empire

The army of the Roman Empire, for several centuries, continued along the principles that had developed at the end of the Republic. For equipment, the legionaries had discarded their varied panoplies from the Republic and became uniformly armed at the state's expense. In the waning days of the Republic and through the early Empire, legionaries wore a corselet of scale or chain mail reinforced with mail flaps across the shoulders. In the middle of the first century CE however, quite probably under the direction

---

Anachronistic Armour

The *lorica segmentata* only came into use in the first century AD. The association of Roman armies with this type of armour is so strong that a number of films set well before the first century (incorrectly) show soldiers wearing it:

Cabiria (1914)
Scipio L'Africano (1937)
Spartacus (1959)
Spartacus (2004)

Most of these films add to the inaccuracy by using leather versions of segmented armour, not metal as was historical.

of the Emperor Claudius, the archetypal segmented armour was adopted – the armour dubbed *lorica segmentata* by modern writers, though we do not know what the Romans called it.[1] It consisted of multiple bands of iron that wrapped around the torso connected by straps and hinges. The shoulders, as was the case with earlier armour types, were protected with additional armour, in this case by a series of overlapping bands covering the shoulders.[2] Legionaries wore undergarments and a cloth tied around the neck to prevent the armour from chafing.[3] Roman legionary tunics, essentially two rectangles of fabric sewn together on three sides with holes for neck and arms, were worn short by gathering excess material at the belt, leaving the legs bare from below the knee. Indeed the shortened tunic was a sign of military position. Somehow the idea that the tunics of legionaries must have been red has rooted itself in costume designers' heads. In fact it is not clear that military tunics were of any fixed colour at all, let alone red.[4] Though officers wore a type of closed-toe boot, the *calceus*, regulars wore the *caliga*, a soldier's sandal with thick soles, and leather fasteners that wrapped across the leg and were secured in the middle of the shin. Socks added to the comfort of the footwear.[5] Generally speaking, trousers were considered effeminate, barbaric, or both, and only soldiers whose duties took them to colder climes wore them. As far as helmets, the Montefortino helmet was gradually replaced by a style modern experts have dubbed Imperial Gallic. This combined a metal skull cap with a guard at the brow line, sizeable hinged cheek-pieces, and a neck-guard that fanned to the rear not unlike a lobster's tail.[6] *Gladiator*'s soldiers follow suit, looking for all the world like infantry straight from the second century.

The legion was generally subdivided into 10 cohorts of 480 men each on paper. Six centuries of eighty men each, again on paper, made up a cohort. The actual numbers of troops in the field could vary substantially. Each century had its own lead officer, a centurion, and several sub officers, including a standard bearer, the *signifer*. Each legion also had a 1,200 trooper squad of cavalry attached to it, the *equites*. Sometime in the late Republic, the legionary cavalry ceased to be used as primary battle cavalry and instead served as scouts, while larger auxiliary cavalry forces served as shock cavalry.[7]

Of course, the armies of the Empire did not consist only of heavy infantry. Far from it. The Roman army, like Alexander's centuries before, recruited foreign specialists to complement their existing strength in heavy infantry. Foreign – *i.e.* non-citizen – recruits joined the *auxilia*, the supplemental forces that regularly accompanied the legion into battle. The Romans had auxiliary infantry and cavalry, archers and slingers, and light infantry. The evidence suggest that, though their equipment was somewhat different, functionally many *auxilia* infantry not uncommonly fought as heavy infantry in close order, just like the legionaries.[8]

How the legionaries and *auxilia* were deployed for battle clearly varied depending on the commander, the geography, and the immediate tactical needs. There were some common features to most ancient armies, such as a heavy infantry deployed in the centre and cavalry on the wings. It was the Roman standard custom to deploy its soldiers in multiple battle lines. With very rare exception – one is noted in the sources – armies deployed in two lines of cohorts or most commonly three lines – the *triplex acies*. The standard tactics of the infantry continued to include launching of *pila* then closing in an organized fashion to use short swords.[9] The developments in the organization and tactics of the army of the late Republic survived well into the Empire. What the Romans did in the Empire, however, was create the terms for a truly professional army. Legionaries were recruited for a standard term of twenty years. They were trained, paid, equipped, and sheltered by the Imperial government.[10]

Gladiator

Let's apply this information about the Roman army to the battle scene opening *Gladiator*. The Roman commander, Maximus, has prepared his army to battle its enemies in Germania one final time.

According to the film's introduction, it is winter of AD 180 and this Roman army is under the authority of Emperor Marcus Aurelius. Ostensibly, Maximus as general is the agent of the emperor, who watches the battlefield from the safety of a hill near the Roman camp. Although no stronghold can be seen, the introduction insists that one last stronghold and one last army are all that is left of Germanic resistance in the region

The problems of historical setting are easily noted first. Before diving in, however, it is worth noting that unlike *Alexander*, a film where director and historical consultant worked closely together, the historical consultant for *Gladiator* noted that few of her suggestions for historical accuracy were accepted. This led to a movie that historians treat with ambivalence, thankful that it revived interest in the Roman Empire while disturbed by its misrepresentations of the Romans. Certainly the setting of the introductory battle scene is largely fabricated. There was no final battle with Germanic peoples on the day of Aurelius' death. Indeed there was no final battle at all; when the emperor died he was busy planning yet another attack on Germanic tribes from the other side of the Danube River.[11]

But it is, as we have seen, possible for a film to have authentic elements in its model of battle alongside grave inaccuracies. And since the scene in *Gladiator* provides the largest scale and most detailed cinematic reconstruction of a battle in the Roman Empire, it is reasonable to ask: how authentic is its reconstruction? During Maximus' review of the troops, audiences see a superior reproduction of the physical components of the army: troop types, equipment, and weaponry. To the extent that can be judged without seeing the replica equipment up close, *Gladiator* recreates the equipment of the legionaries skilfully. Legionaries are equipped with the Imperial Gallic-style helmet and wear *lorica segmentata*. They are, however, also clad in arm bracers, something not regularly found historically. For protection against chafing armour, each soldier wears a cloth tied around his neck. Tunics are red and sleeves are long, and while the sleeve length is certainly not standard, it is certainly the case that clothing choices varied according to the climate and this, after all, is the German winter. Shields are rectangular and convex with metal edge bindings and a central boss. *Pila* are constructed of metal spit and wooden shaft. These re-enactors essentially look the part.

After Maximus finishes reviewing his legionaries, shouts erupt from the forest. The warband, it seems, has arrived. The white horse of a Roman scout trots across the charred and uneven ground to the Roman camp, its rider now headless. A warrior appears in the distance, head of said scout in hand. He wears trousers and boots, has a bear pelt over his tunic, and carries a war maul in his hand. He shouts defiantly. Behind him, through the trees – which must be said have remarkably little undergrowth – the warband approaches. They have come for a fight and carry a variety of equipment. Some carry swords, others spears, other axes. Some wear helmets with horns, other's conical helmets, still others are bare-headed. Some wear leather jerkins, most just clothing. The shields are of all sorts. They shout and clamour at the instigation of their head-toting leader.

In general, this fits what we know about Rome's Germanic foes. The basic political unit in early Germanic culture was the clan, and a number of clans grouped together to form a tribe. Each clan was politically organized, so far as we know, so that a chief and high nobles led, but an assembly of free men dominated by warriors provided some form of voice to those of lower status. In this it was not unlike the noble warbands of Homer. Each noble formed the nucleus of what the Romans termed a *comitatus*, a band of warriors whom the noble supported and who fought under his leadership as a consequence. The *comitatus* was a band that relied heavily on concepts of loyalty, honour, and reciprocity. The warriors expected regular rewards of land and loot from their noble and gave their loyalty in return. The need for a steady flow of loot to the warband made raiding neighbours a time-honoured custom in Germanic society.

The nobles and their personal warbands were the core of any Germanic army, which would be mustered by decision of the assembly, under the command of a particularly charismatic chief, especially one from a royal lineage. These armies consisted mostly, if not completely, of infantry, cavalry being used by only a few tribes at all. Mustering such a force took time, however, and the Romans often did not encounter any significant force until they withdrew from their punitive expeditions, responses to raids into Roman territory.[12]

The depiction of the German army is reasonable in broad brush strokes. Such armies, when they did muster, organized according to *comitatus* and clan. Such organization was of a basic sort, however, and Germanic armies were not, it seems, capable of sophisticated formations and manoeuvres, certainly nothing of the sort the legions regularly did. And so, the basic tactic of such armies was to find suitably open and flat terrain upon which to unleash its warbands. Roman authors, like Tacitus, who described the Germanic armies tended to emphasize the fear-inducing size of particular warriors. Tacitus describes their arms in the first century as consisting mostly of short spears, with the occasional sword.[13] For protection they carried shields coloured however they chose, and a very few had some armour or helmet. The archaeological evidence seems to confirm this broad outline. This is certainly a fair enough description of the host the Romans face at the beginning of *Gladiator*, although the battle axes are essentially absent from the testimony. It is not clear what formations the warriors adopted, but the various accounts suggest they offered dense lines of fighters, presumably with the better armed at the front. En masse they would charge enemies.[14] When it comes to looks, the props and actors in *Gladiator* provide convincing enough representations of Roman and Germanic soldiers from the second century.

The Commander's Speech

Once they have exchanged a final review of plans, Maximus bids Quintus, 'Strength and honour,' and Quintus returns the benediction, Maximus rides off and his dog – fictitiously and perhaps with intentional irony a German Shepherd – insists on joining him.[15] Quintus, meanwhile shouts orders: 'Load the catapults,' 'Infantry form up for advance,' 'Archers ready.'

When Maximus reaches his cavalry squad deployed far to the side of the battle lines he addresses them as '*Patres*' (a term, which it must be said makes no sense, meaning 'fathers' and when not referring to factual fathers was used in the Republic as an address of nobility). Having their attention, he makes a short speech.

> Three weeks from now, I will be harvesting my crops. Imagine where you will be, and it will be so. Hold the line! Stay with me! If you find yourself alone, riding in the green fields with the sun on your face, do not be troubled. For you are in Elysium, and you're already dead!

The cavalry troopers laugh and Maximus closes with the exhortation, 'Brothers, what we do in life … echoes in eternity.' It is a striking display of fraternity between general and soldier, but wholly within the norms, as we have seen. Roman generals in the Empire were just as capable and willing to form bonds of trust and affection with their soldiers as leaders from other cultures.[16]

The Infantry Battle

Back with the infantry, catapults and *ballistae* are loaded. A line of oil or pitch is lit in front of the auxiliary archers so that they may ignite their arrows. A large pot is placed in a catapult and its rag is lit.

The Roman soldiers are grim, determined, professional. They have clearly done this before. The camera shifts back to the cavalry, where Maximus dons an ornate open-faced helmet with a plume. He gives his order with a nod, and an archer stationed with the cavalry lights and launches an arrow, the signal for the attack to begin. The signal in the air, the officer gives the command to the archers to ignite their arrows. In unison the archers lower their arrows to the fire trench. They draw and fire as the catapults launch incendiary pots. The clay pots shatter against the trees and spread flame along the German ranks. Warriors are pierced by fire arrows or ignited from the flames of the firepots as they retreat to a safer distance. A *ballista* bolt passes through two warriors in a row, pinning them together.

It is an interesting question whether the Germans would have stood within range of the artillery from a fixed camp or whether this is simply the stereotype of the dumb barbarian. Certainly, artillery was normally used for sieges against fixed defences, but it actually could be used against infantry formations. Tacitus provides an example from the civil wars of the late first century AD:

> Antonius had meanwhile called up the guards to reinforce his wavering line. Taking up the fight, they repulsed the enemy, only to be repulsed in their turn. For the Vitellian artillery, which had at first been scattered all along the line, and had been discharged upon the bushes without hurting the enemy, was now massed upon the high-road, and swept the open space in front. One immense engine in particular, which belonged to the Fifteenth, mowed down the Flavian line with huge stones. The slaughter thus caused would have been enormous, had not two of the Flavian soldiers performed a memorable exploit. Concealing their identity by snatching up shields from among the enemy's dead, they cut the ropes which suspended the weights of the engine. They fell immediately, riddled with wounds, and so their names have perished. But of their deed there is no doubt.[17]

This episode does not include flaming artillery, however, and it seems highly unlikely the Romans would have found it desirable to torch a forest they currently occupied. Indeed it was not common to support a legion with artillery, at least in the armies at the very end of the Republic.[18] However the case may have been in historical standoffs, those Germans in the film who are unscathed by the flaming barrage shout their defiance.

Interspersed with shots of the missile volleys, Maximus and his cavalry nudge their horses forward into position in the woods. They adopt a wide formation. When the missiles cease and the infantry starts its approach to the Germans' position, they begin their gallop. Shots of cavalry and infantry are spliced together. As the legionaries march, archers and catapults continue to fire – the infantry appear to be at least a hundred yards away from their foes and so in no danger of being hurt by friendly fire. The camera pulls back and pans at a high angle across behind the Roman line, surveying the battle from left to right. Cavalry race, archers fire, and infantry determinedly trudge; the camera shifts between the three.

The organization of the Roman infantry becomes clear. They march in three battle lines, each line two men deep. Shields are held up, emblazoned with the eagle wings, and *pila* are thrust forward. The Germans give another war cry, the lead man waving at the Romans defiantly to 'come get some'. The noise of the Germans contrasts sharply with the quiet of the Romans, whose only sound is the orders to march. Now that the legionaries are close, the German archers use their bows – and one cannot help but wonder if the German bow was really so inferior in range to the Roman. The second rank of soldiers in each Roman line lifts their shields to form a roof protecting themselves and the men in front of them. They stop moving forward to receive the arrows, which harmlessly miss or embed in shields. Now the Germanic warriors charge en masse, not unlike the warriors in *Troy*. They are together but not organized in any way. Then the impact. The Germanic warriors attempt to work their way between the shields to get at the Romans with varying degrees of success.

But what about the width and depth of the Roman infantry's battle line? Is it authentic? Setting the width and depth of an infantry formation required managing several problems. First came the problem of marching in an organized manner. Marching in a straight line across any sort of terrain is an extremely difficult proposition at best, and so one should expect to see legionaries moving in an orderly, but by no means mechanical fashion, toward their enemy. In general, the wider a formation of infantry, the more difficult for the soldiers in it to keep a straight line as they marched. Formations that were deeper than they were wide were often used to manage better soldiers who were not sufficiently trained to march in cadence. Were the only goal to address that of orderly marching, the Romans, and indeed all other commanders of pre-modern soldiers, would simply have deployed their legionaries in columns, narrow and deep.

Deep formations, however, were rendered ineffective because of the short reach of the legionaries' weapons. *Pila* volleys aside, the primary legionary weapon was the *gladius*, and it, as has been noted, measured perhaps 2ft at most. A column formation would have kept most legionaries from using their weapons at all, placed too far back from the melee as they would have been. So the trick was to have as wide a formation as possible while not so wide that the soldiers could not keep an orderly formation. The third problem for any formation came from the morale of the soldiers. It is generally understood by modern historians of ancient battle that the ranks beyond the first rank in an infantry formation provided critical moral support to the front, beyond any function they would have had to replace the injured and slain in the front ranks. With the physical and psychological proximity of one's comrades came an increased sense of security, an increased will to fight or, at the very least, not to flee. This was one of the main reasons the phalanxes of Classical Greece deployed their hoplites in four or eight ranks, or in extreme circumstances, such as the Theban battle line at Leuctra (371) fifty![19]

So, what sorts of formation depths did the Romans choose to adopt for their infantry? The number of ranks in which a cohort was deployed varies with the source. Some deployments testified to in the Roman sources are three ranks, others four ranks, and some six, eight, and ten. When the evidence is weighed and sorted, it appears that three to four ranks of soldiers was a common deployment for a cohort, with deeper formations used for more skittish soldiers, or against enemy cavalry.[21] The Roman force in *Gladiator* shows three battle lines, each line two men deep. This may be within the parameters suggested by ancient testimony, but it all depends on what those lines on film represent: a single unit six rows deep with gaps after every two rows, or three separate units each two men deep.

The Cavalry Charge

The cavalry charge, shots of which are spliced between shots of the infantry approach, is a note worthy rendition. The straight line of cavalry quickly begins to warp due to the different speeds of the horses. Although a skilled cavalry force would likely pace its mounts to remain in formation, the natural differences in horses' speed is definitely a factor in the maintenance of a line formation, so those shots offer some authenticity. The final destination and the whole of the battle plan is revealed after the infantry engage. Maximus yells 'Roma Victor', a Latin phrase whose meaning in English is clear enough. The cavalry has outflanked the Germans and now approaches from behind the warband. The German warriors look back and some break off to fight against the cavalry. Here is a cinematic moment whose authenticity is laudable. The cavalry have charged home into the enemy, but there is no physical impact of horses and foot soldiers. In recent decades, ever since the notable work of military historian John Keegan, historians have stressed that the result of a cavalry charge under normal circumstances was not a collision. It would have been inconceivable to the Romans to sacrifice expensive horses and trained men intentionally in some mass impact. Rather, well-formed cavalry would attempt to drive off their foes on foot. Barring that, the skilled horsemen would work their way into the enemy infantry at something far slower than a charge, hacking and stabbing with weapons, and using horses to muscle the infantry about.[21] This is what Maximus and his cavalry force do, work their horses into the loose enemy formations, slashing as they go and causing a great deal of disruption in the German ranks.

The authenticity of the cavalry charge, however, soon gives way to a pile of implausibilities. Things are getting chaotic; formations have disintegrated. A warrior with a pole-axe begins swinging it around in a space, dealing death to legionaries nearby. The Roman soldiers have lost all unit cohesion. Those engaged are no longer in any recognizable formation. Instead they are fighting simply as individuals duelling with their adversaries. Close-ups of stabs, screams and blood follow. A shot appears of a legionary moving alone *behind* Maximus' horse – in other words the film suggests there are infantry who have made their way through and past where the cavalry attacked the German formation. Shots like this make clear that either the filmmakers planned to depict that the Roman infantry lines have disintegrated completely or it simply has not occurred to them that the troops should be in formation if they followed their training.

Now cavalry and infantry engage in personal combats. Granted, pockets did seem to open up in land battles historically, but there is simply too much space in which to move here. Maximus takes advantage of the space to ride forward and rescue a threatened legionary by cutting down the warrior astride him. Maximus' horse is cut down. He falls beside a dead warrior and several legionaries. Maximus displays sword-work most clever as he fights and gets back on his feet – though it is difficult to understand why a second century Roman general would put himself in this kind of danger in the first place. If anything the fighting resembles the massing and disintegrating of pockets of warriors described by Van Wees' vision of Homeric battles. Friend and foe, infantry and cavalry, all are mixed. Maximus is knocked down and a rider comes by, killing the German before he slays Maximus. Then there is his trusty dog, still alive and bringing down enemies.

Scott clearly sought to make things feel chaotic. A sweeping camera, shifting from one brief shot to the next, blurriness, and interspersed slow motion and real time are indicative of the director's vision. In a moment of likely unintended irony, two standards are stuck in the ground with no bearers and with absolutely no formation around them – the whole purpose of a standard. The brawl sputters out with a blurry wrap-up scene of stabbing and dying, amidst the groaning faces of wounded and dying. A number of downed enemies are stabbed while completely vulnerable, turning the end of the battle into a butcher's work. The camera returns to Maximus standing between two standards. He finally declares 'Roma Victor', and scattered legionaries cheer. There is a clump of perhaps ten legionaries near him, cheering, but there are no more formations.

So how, theoretically, should this battle have looked? First off, presumably the legionaries and especially their officers would have made more effort to keep in their formations start to finish. It was by no means an easy thing for heavy infantry to remain in strict formation, front line cohesive throughout their advance. The horrible stress of anticipation made a slow pace difficult. Nevertheless the importance of keeping a close, orderly formation is stressed by Roman authors and seems to have been achieved by Roman legionaries. The slow march kept the troops together until they closed the gap with the enemy. Keeping the soldiers calm and organized during this approach must have been a difficult task, one mitigated by extensive legionary training and reinforced by officers tasked with keeping soldiers in formation.[22] While a *pilum* might have an effective maximum range of 30 yards, it was best at a range much closer to 5 yards and that meant the Roman soldiers had to get very close even when it meant walking through fields of arrows.[23]

Once the sides closed within javelin range, the *pila* volley was executed together on command, or at least that was the plan. As noted previously, *pila* would not uncommonly penetrate shields, rendering them largely useless for the coming battle. Of course, this was a secondary function and the primary purpose of the *pila* throw was to wound or kill enemy soldiers.[24] It would be difficult to overestimate the blow to morale suffered by those standing on the hostile end of a legionary army which, having cast armour piercing javelins into their midst, uttered a war cry and began to charge. Certainly such an advance was enough in some cases to cause the enemy to flee, their formations melting before the Roman onslaught; on this point the ancients testify.[25]

Assuming that, like these German warriors, the enemy did not flee, the charge of Romans and countercharge of the enemy led to a clash. The initial goal of some men on each side was to knock their opponents to the ground, and a collision of shields and bodies must have been a regular affair. In this context a *scutum* was quite useful, for its central grip and iron boss made it a useful bludgeoning tool. Assuming, however, that the Roman legionaries did not immediately smash their enemies into submission, the melee contest began in earnest. The Roman sword was useful for both cut and thrust, but the proximity of one's comrades in the formation probably made it inadvisable to engage in wide slashes but rather in overhand slashes close to the body. Still the stab was a more dangerous attack. Vegetius, a fourth century writer who drew heavily from works centuries before him, insists that Roman soldiers were trained to stab as part of their normal drill:

> [The Romans] were likewise taught not to cut but to thrust with their swords. For the Romans not only made a jest of those who fought with the edge of that weapon, but always found them an easy conquest. A stroke with the edges, though made with ever so much force, seldom kills, as the vital parts of the body are defended both by the bones and armour. On the contrary, a stab, though it penetrates but two inches, is generally fatal. Besides in the attitude of striking, it is impossible to avoid exposing the right arm and side; but on the other hand, the body

is covered while a thrust is given, and the adversary receives the point before he sees the sword. This was the method of fighting principally used by the Romans, and their reason for exercising recruits with arms of such a weight at first was, that when they came to carry the common ones so much lighter, the greater difference might enable them to act with greater security and alacrity in time of action.[26]

The Roman infantry sword, however, was clearly made to be as effective at cutting as stabbing and cutting. Visual evidence from monuments such as Trajan's column corroborates this, showing Romans cutting as well as thrusting.[27] Through their training process a soldier would learn to stand with left foot forward and the plane of the shield somewhat perpendicular to the shoulders to keep the body well protected by the shield on the left hand that extended from lower face to mid-thigh. From this position the legionary would assay to land cuts and thrusts on the enemy. There is also testimony to suggest that a Roman soldier might combine a shield-bash followed up with a sword stroke.[28]

It is a mistake to assume that the legionaries were mechanical, willing and able to execute commands perfectly at all times, and thus able to stay in perfect formation at all times. At the same time, they were very well trained professionals and their training included an emphasis on staying in position. The line officers, centurions and *optiones*, indeed were tasked with keeping the men in formation.[29] *Gladiator*, unfortunately, ignores these considerations and turns a Roman battle into an orderly approach followed by a mixed up brawl.

The Eagle

The Eagle (2012) does a better job illustrating the role of discipline in a Roman army, though it does so in a skirmish scene rather than a pitched battle. The film takes up the story of the Ninth Legion, a legion that seems to have mysteriously disappeared in the northlands of Britannia. An adventure story at its core, *The Eagle* chronicles the journey of one Roman officer, Marcus Flavius Aquila, into the wilds of northern Britannia on a quest to regain the eagle standard the Ninth lost under the command of his father. The film provides the back-story like so:

> In AD 120 the Ninth Legion of the Roman Army marched into the unconquered territory of northern Britain. They were never seen again. All 5,000 men vanished, together with their treasured standard – *The Eagle* (Title).
>
> Shamed by this great loss, the emperor Hadrian ordered the construction of a giant wall to cut off the north of Britain forever. Hadrian's Wall marked the end of the known world.

With this introduction the film begins, '20 years later [in] Roman occupied southern Britain,' setting this scene somewhere in the 140s. A river boat is poled along, carrying new recruits for the legion. The banks are obscured with trees and brush. The scene shifts to the recruits marching to the fort in a large plain surrounded by wooded hills. A close-up on their legs shows military sandals and trousers that stop just below the knee. The camera shifts up and each carries a pole over his soldier, laden with gear. The new commander of the fort, Marcus Flavius Aquila (Channing Tatum) – a pun since 'Aquila' means 'eagle' – rides beside the recruits on a horse without stirrups. Unlike the legionaries who are wearing segmented armour, Aquila, an officer, wears a muscled cuirass of shaped leather with reinforced shoulder flaps. The men in the camp are clad in red military tunics, and don segmented armour when on duty.

The commander of the garrison has left before his replacement Aquila arrives, and the second in command, Salinator, informs Aquila that the garrison is too small even to warrant a dedicated paymaster. Aquila assays to raise the morale and effectiveness by combatting idleness and assigning a series of chores. The fort is

Roman Forts

The Roman fort in *The Eagle* consists of a sloping dirt mound topped with a wooden palisade. The whole of the defensive wall is perhaps 12ft high. At the bottom of the mound a ditch has been dug and filled with stakes to discourage any who might climb the walls. When Aquila institutes a rehabilitation of the fort, the soldiers dig a new ditch around the base of the mound and pour tar over the stakes to hold them in place. The basic construction of the fortifications in the film matches the standard Roman plan. The *fossa*, a broad ditch, is dug first. The earth from the *fossa* is piled up to serve as a mound or *agger*. Atop the *agger* a wooden wall or *vallum* is constructed. (le Bohec 157, plate XXVI 19.) The film does not provide enough shots of the interior to judge whether it met the layout of a Roman military camp. The Romans had a standard plan for laying out their camps. Two main avenues were surveyed and where they intersected at a right angle marked the centre of the camp. From there everything was laid out along a grid of streets. Infantry and cavalry, auxiliaries and legionaries, all had their standard place in the fort plan. (le Bohec 156–61)

repaired. Rather than passively await attack, a patrol is dispatched to look for the lost grain shipment. Each soldier carries two spears with a mallet across to form a cross; a bag and what seems to be some form of metal cooking gear are suspended from it.

Enemies attack the walls at night. Practically speaking, it is impossible to evaluate the accuracy of such a fight scene. Anything known about formations and training goes out the window when each soldier is caught in a state of surprise and has to fight for his life. Such things did happen on the frontiers and a night brawl may well have looked like this. Still, there are clearly fanciful elements. Perhaps the most visible of these is Aquila's use of two swords at once, a scene surely straight out of fantasy. Roman soldiers were trained to use a sword and a shield; fighting well with two weapons – and Aquila seems to be an expert – is not the sort of skill a Roman would normally ever find place to put to use.

> **They make a desert and call it peace**
>
> Unfortunately, the leader's accusations in the *Eagle* are probably accurate. The Roman author Tacitus once attributed a saying to the British chieftain Calgacus: 'To ravage, to slaughter, to usurp under false titles, they call empire; and where they make a desert, they call it peace.' (Tacitus Agricola 30; Birley trans.)
>
> Romans, like most ancient peoples, did not believe conquered enemies deserved any mercy, any human dignity. Raping, killing, and enslaving defeated enemies was not an uncommon result of a Roman victory.

The next day, the patrol returns as captives of a British clan in the region. The Britons are depicted in various states of dress: trousers and no shirt for some, tunics and trousers for others. Their equipment is eclectic, to say the least. Some carry axes, others swords, still others, spears. Some carry shields, tiny bucklers for the most part. The leader is bare-chested with a sleeved robe over his arms. He has a wild look about him and his long, straight, gray hair wisps about in the wind. Both men and women from the clan accompany him. Indeed it appears as if the whole clan is on hand to watch the public execution of the captured scouts. The chieftain shouts in Gaelic to his clan, 'Our gods will bring us victory today.' He forces the captive members of the patrol to kneel and yells again in his tongue, 'You have stolen our lands and killed our sons. You have defiled our daughters. I curse you!' So saying he has one kneeling captive dragged forward and slays him.

In response Aquila orders fifty soldiers mustered at the gate. It seems a nice round number, but really it might have been difficult to arrive at quickly: a century was eighty to one hundred soldiers and the basic mess unit, the *contubernium*, was eight; neither readily converts into fifty. Be that as it may, they wear segmented armour made of leather, a type that perpetuates a mistake about Roman armour that filmmakers have made for a century.[30] Aquila prays

quietly to Mithras before the battle: 'Mithras, lord of light, father of
our fathers, let me not bring misfortune to my legion. Mithras, lord
of light, father of our fathers, accept whatever sacrifice that I may not
bring misfortune to my legion.' A nice touch, this, since Mithras,
historically, was a very popular deity with Roman soldiers.[31]

The film does an excellent job at this point illustrating the
tension between fear and the discipline instilled by training. A
scan of the Roman soldiers' faces shows some apprehension, a little
fear, but acceptance of the task. Aquila addresses the squadron.
'On my command, we form testudo.' A frightened soldier vomits,
heightening the sense of fear the soldiers radiate. The gates open
and Aquila barks, 'double time, march!' The soldiers trot in three
columns with Aquila at the head, shields at their sides and hands on
their swords. As far as the eye can see, none carry a *pilum*; apparently
this task requires sword-work, though an initial *pila* volley might
drive back the Britons very effectively. The legionaries trot in
unison, well ordered, organized. Their training and Aquila's steady
leadership counter the fear.

As the squad approaches, the Britons give a war cry and rush
forward, a stereotype of the warband with no particular order.
Indeed the shifting shots between legionaries and Britons seem
designed to emphasize the contrast. The faster warriors in the band
begin to outpace their comrades and whatever there was of a battle-
line comes apart. The Romans move more slowly, but in unison, an
effective illustration of the difference between a controlled advance
and an uncontrolled charge. There are many more Britons than
Romans making one wonder why Aquila selected only fifty soldiers.
The answer the director clearly gives through this scene is that the
superior training and discipline of the legionaries will bring them
through. As the charging Britons approach, Aquilus orders the
testudo to form. The legionaries slow their pace, those in the centre
raise their shields overhead and the *testudo*, or 'tortoise' is formed.
The Britons assault the *testudo*, launching themselves on top and
trying to stab down into the men at the centre of this formation, or

attacking the legionaries on the sides. We see several warriors on top looking for gaps in the shields to hack down into. From inside we see Romans stabbing up from their improvised fortress. Two centurions order a move forward and the group does so. It is not an easy advance and it is not flawless, but it is organized and orderly in the front row. As they shuffle forward, Aquila and the others seize opportunities to stab with their short swords in a way suggestive of Vegetius' drill.[32]

This rather dramatic defensive formation, the *testudo*, is discussed by several ancient authors. When describing the campaign of Marcus Antonius against the Persians, the historian Cassius Dio provides an excellent description of the formation:

> … One day, when [the Romans] fell into an ambush and were being struck by dense showers of arrows, they suddenly formed the *testudo* by joining their shields, and rested their left knees on the ground. The barbarians, who had never seen anything of the kind before, thought that they had fallen from their wounds and needed only one finishing blow; so they threw aside their bows, leaped from their horses, and drawing their daggers, came up close to put an end to them. At this the Romans sprang to their feet, extended their battle-line at the word of command, and confronting the foe face to face, fell upon them, each one upon the man nearest him, and cut down great numbers, since they were contending in full armour against unprotected men, men prepared against men off their guard, heavy infantry against archers, Romans against barbarians. All the survivors immediately retired and no one followed them thereafter.[33]

It is important to note that Antonius' men in this account go down on one knee and are defending themselves against missiles, neither of which is the case in the *The Eagle*. Next Dio goes on to describe the formation of the *testudo* in more detail:

This testudo and the way in which it is formed are as follows. The baggage animals, the light-armed troops, and the cavalry are placed in the centre of the army. The heavy-armed troops who use the oblong, curved, and cylindrical shields are drawn up around the outside, making a rectangular figure; and, facing outward and holding their arms at the ready, they enclose the rest. The others, who have flat shields, form a compact body in the centre and raise their shields over the heads of all the others, so that nothing but shields can be seen in every part of the phalanx alike and all the men by the density of the formation are under shelter from missiles. Indeed, it is so marvellously strong that men can walk upon it, and whenever they come to a narrow ravine, even horses and vehicles can be driven over it. Such is the plan of this formation, and for this reason it has received the name testudo, with reference both to its strength and to the excellent shelter it affords. They use it in two ways: either they approach some fort to assault it, often even enabling men to scale the very walls, or sometimes, when they are surrounded by archers, they all crouch together – even the horses being taught to kneel or lie down – and thereby cause the foe to think that they are exhausted; then, when the enemy draws near, they suddenly rise and throw them into consternation.[34]

The *testudo* for Dio, is a formation the Romans used to defend against missiles or as a platform from which short defensive structures might be scaled. Dio's testimony is corroborated by other examples from the ancient sources.[35] Together they suggest that Aquila's legionaries could form a *testudo* and having formed it could support the weight of Britons jumping on it. It is critical to note, however, that none of these sources refer to the *testudo* used for anything other than defence against missiles or for gaining height. In the case of Aquila's sortie, the choice is unlikely, but then so is this particular mission.

Next, after reaching the Roman prisoners, Aquila orders the soldiers to form a defensive circle with the prisoners at the centre. The

Roman's follow drill and continue to use their shields to great effect, warding off the blows of the British melee weapons. The discipline of the Roman legionaries continues to shine forth in marked contrast to the Britons. The Romans are not engaging in personal duels; following the prescriptions of Vegetius they do not stab and slash wildly.[36] Instead each maintains his place in the defensive formation, shield up. Each holds his sword at the ready for a precise stab or cut here or there. Organized and united, they provide a force that the Britons cannot easily overcome, despite their larger numbers.

But then a horn sounds from behind the Britons. War chariots arrive with scythes on their wheel hubs. Two men occupy each, one the driver, the other a spearman. Aquila gives the order to fall back. Ignoring or casting aside their training, the Roman squad quickly shifts from falling back to running at Aquila's command. The clear implication is that the scythed chariots cannot be withstood. This offers an excellent contrast to the war chariots in Alexander. In those sequences the chariots faced a large force of orderly heavy infantry, a losing proposition so long as the infantry maintained their formation. In this scene a small handful of scattered Roman soldiers are pursued by the war chariots. Lacking any formation or order to counter the chariots or intimidate the horses into breaking their charge, the infantry are extremely vulnerable. It is worth noting, however that Aquila gave the order to run. This was the worst possible counter for a man on foot to make against a chariot and up to this point, Aquila has shown himself to be a skilled commander. It's not that a Roman soldier would automatically stand against such an enemy, it's that a skilled commander, presumably, would be trained to keep the soldiers together for protection. Scattered and running, individual Romans are scythed down by the chariots.

Then, as seems to be the case in every one of the films, there comes the leader's *aristeia*, his display of heroic qualities. Aquila turns as his men continue to flee, steels his resolve, grabs a spear, and trots toward the leader's chariot. He casts a spear, kills the charioteer, upends the chariot and is gravely wounded as the wreckage of the chariot crashes into him. The battle is over.

The collapse of order toward the end of the battle notwithstanding, *The Eagle* shows soldiers with a more authentic level of discipline and training than *Gladiator*. Though one cannot extrapolate too far with the limited skirmishing *The Eagle* shows, it is difficult to imagine the trained soldiers modelled by the film fighting in such a disorganized and haphazard way as they do in *Gladiator*.

The Roman Army Ambushed – *Centurion*

The Romans in *Gladiator* prevail despite their abandonment of Roman discipline; the squad in *The Eagle* prevails because of its discipline. The Roman army in *Centurion* (2010) fares less well than either. Set in the early second century, the film is primarily an adventure story about a Roman centurion who escapes captivity in the north of Britain and returns safely to his fort. The film plays on the historical disappearance of the Ninth Legion: though the evidence for the disappearance of the legion is spotty, some have argued that the Ninth met its end in northern Britain.[37] Whatever the truth is, the film sets up a hypothetical ambush by the Picts, a Celtic tribe.

The Ninth Legion

Both *Centurion* and *The Eagle* refer to the destruction of the Ninth Legion. In the traditional version of the story, the Ninth was sent to the north of Britannia to crush a revolt. From there they disappeared, seemingly taken unawares by native rebels and slaughtered.

Verifying this episode is difficult. Some argue that the Ninth was never destroyed in Britain but simply transferred off the island. An inscription from York in AD 108, however, says that the Ninth rebuilt a fort there in stone. Certainly the Romans did lose a significant number of forces in second-century Britain. This plus the fact that the Sixth Legion occupied the fort the Ninth had rebuilt suggests that the Ninth may have suffered extreme losses.

(http://www.bbc.co.uk/news/magazine-12752497)

The Governor of Britain, Agricola, has tasked the Ninth to eliminate the threat of the Picts. Accordingly, the legion, under the command of general Titus Flavius Virilus, marches into the northern wilderness, seeking to engage the forces of the Picts in a decisive encounter. The legion marches in a column three soldiers wide. Two standard bearers lead carrying the eagle and the unit standard. Most of the soldiers wear segmented armour and imperial Gallic helmets, appropriate for the period. Some of the soldiers, most notably the centurion from the title, Quintas Dias, and the general Flavius wear other types of armour, mail for the centurion and for the general a combination of muscled cuirass with the shoulder guards of segmented armour. The general's armour is probably fanciful, but the presentation of legionaries wearing different forms of armour is not. Officers are depicted with crests running crosswise on their helmets, a nice touch of authenticity. The main problem with equipment, however, is posed by the legionary weapons. As they march, the short iron heads of spears are evident, when the soldiers should be carrying *pila*. Details like changing a thrown weapon to a thrusting weapon are a small matter in films; historically it would have dramatically changed how the Romans fought.

The Ninth rescues the fugitive centurion, and, despite warnings that the Picts are near, marches forward into danger rather obliviously. In doing so the film sets up the timeless stereotype of the massive conventional force, the Romans in this case, trying and failing to provoke the guerilla warriors, here the Picts, to a set battle. The Ninth has come looking for a fight. They march in all their glory, a show of strength that would deter most would-be challengers from offering a pitched battle. But there will be no such battle. Instead the mighty Romans will walk straight into an ambush. The Picts occupy the high ground to each side of the forest path. The warriors wear trousers and carry swords axes, and small shields. There are men and women in their warband. Some have war paint of red and blue on their faces. They watch from safety as the Romans march on. Then a tree falls, a massive trunk that blocks the legion's progress. An officer shouts orders to the legionaries to form up. The soldiers spring into action, orderly, trained, and efficient. The units form rectangles with shields outward, one man deep. They kneel down behind the shields so that only their heads show. It is the junior officers who give the commands, like 'Steady boys' and 'Shields'. One named Septus reassures them: 'Whatever comes out of that mist lads, you will hold the line.' It is a scene that illustrates the ideal of the well-trained professional legionary. These troops are well trained and they have the solid presence of the veteran officers to support them.

Unfortunately for these cinematic Romans, their training and officers will not save them. Before long the forested hills rising to each side of the road erupt in shouts and the blowing of horns. General Virilus orders Quintus Dias to ride to the rear and tell centurion Remus to pull back, but it is already too late. Fireballs, each 6 or 7ft in diameter and presumably constructed of burning wood and underbrush, roll down the wooded hills – conveniently enough the hillside is open enough for these weapons to roll freely. They smash into soldiers with enough force to drive them back and inflict serious burns on the unfortunates in their path.

Once the fireballs have taken effect, scaring and stunning the legionaries, the Picts charge. They flow down the hills on either side of the path, individually and in packs. As they come, the Picts

---

Fireworks

Logs or brushwood spheres set aflame is something of a recurring theme in cinematic ancient battles. *Spartacus* (1960), *Troy* (2007), and *Centurion* (2010) all show an attack involving flaming objects rolling toward the enemy. While the lack of evidence for such tactics cannot prove they were not employed, we should be quite sceptical of these cinematic flights of fancy. The logistics alone of setting alight such objects and using them effectively, argue against their regular use. They make, however, for a great picture – likely the reason why several directors have included them in battle scenes.

scream war cries, disdaining any orderly approach. The Romans must engage in a rather haphazard melee. The effect is similar to that in *Gladiator*: a series of shots focus on individuals and small groups mixing it up. Here unlike *Gladiator*, however, there is logical reason for the mash-up – the road was narrow and the fireballs disruptive of the Roman formations. Here and there, a Pict archer takes an opportune shot. The focus of this part of the scene is on the dealing of brutal wounds, and the camera records a fair number of decapitations. Ultimately the legion is destroyed, the corpses left in a natural trench.

The fireballs stretch common sense, but Roman armies ambushed in the forests was a real enough historical phenomenon, and it was a way for less numerous and poorly armed combatants to humble the Romans. Livy gives a detailed account of a forest ambush with an unusual technique during the war against Hannibal:

It was reported that L. Postumius, the consul elect, and his army had been annihilated in Gaul. There was a wild forest called by the Gauls Litana, and through this the consul was to conduct his army. The Gauls cut through the trees on both sides of the road in such a way that they remained standing as long as they were undisturbed, but a slight pressure would make them fall. Postumius had two Roman legions, and he had also levied a force from the country bordering on the Upper Sea, sufficiently large to bring the force with which he entered the hostile territory up to 25,000 men. The Gauls had posted themselves round the outskirts of the forest, and as soon as the Roman army entered they pushed the sawn trees on the outside, these fell upon those next to them, which were tottering and hardly able to stand upright, until the whole mass fell in on both sides and buried in one common ruin arms and men and horses. Hardly ten men escaped, for when most of them had been crushed to death by the trunks or broken branches of the trees, the remainder, panic-struck at the unexpected disaster, were killed by the Gauls who surrounded the forest. Out of the whole number only very few were made prisoners, and these, whilst trying to reach a bridge over the river, were intercepted by the Gauls who had already seized it. It was there that Postumius fell whilst fighting most desperately to avoid capture. The Boii stripped the body of its spoils and cut off the head, and bore them in triumph to the most sacred of their temples. According to their custom they cleaned out the skull and covered the scalp with beaten gold; it was then used as a vessel for libations and also as a drinking cup for the priest and ministers of the temple.[38]

Or to take an example from imperial history, one need go no further that the destruction of three legions in AD 9, under the command of Varus. Here the Roman writer Velleius Paterculus describes the disaster:

An army unexcelled in bravery, the first of Roman armies in discipline, in energy, and in experience in the field, through the negligence of its general, the perfidy of the enemy, and the unkindness of fortune was surrounded, nor was as much opportunity as they had wished given to the soldiers either of fighting or of extricating themselves, except against heavy odds; nay, some were even heavily chastised for using the arms and showing the spirit of Romans. Hemmed in by forests and marshes and ambuscades, it was exterminated almost to a man by the very enemy whom it had always slaughtered like cattle, whose life or death had depended solely upon the wrath or the pity of the Romans. The general had more courage to die than to fight, for, following the example of his father and grandfather, he ran himself through with his sword. Of the two prefects of the camp, Lucius Eggius furnished a precedent as noble as that of Ceionius was base, who, after the greater part of the army had perished, proposed its surrender, preferring to die by torture at the hands of the enemy than in battle. Vala

Numonius, lieutenant of Varus, who, in the rest of his life, had been an inoffensive and an honourable man, also set a fearful example in that he left the infantry unprotected by the cavalry and in flight tried to reach the Rhine with his squadrons of horse. But fortune avenged his act, for he did not survive those whom he had abandoned, but died in the act of deserting them. The body of Varus, partially burned, was mangled by the enemy in their barbarity; his head was cut off and taken to Maroboduus and was sent by him to Caesar; but in spite of the disaster it was honoured by burial in the tomb of his family.[39]

Though the details of the defeat are not clear, it would appear that these legions fell prey to an ambush. In both cases armies that generally did not fare well against the Romans in pitched battle, Gauls and Germans, instead used their local forest terrain to their advantage. *Centurion* models its combat scene on a sound principle: if the Romans are surprised and caught in a tight spot so that they cannot adopt their normal organization, they are much easier to defeat.

Between them, *Gladiator*, *The Eagle*, and *Centurion* show the Roman army in operation in three different capacities: in a pitched battle against Germanic foes, a small-scale skirmish against a Britannic tribe, and under ambush by a force of Picts. In each case the level of attention paid to equipment and weaponry is impressive. The segmented armour is made of metal as it should be, *scuta* are curved rectangles, and *pila* are carried, not spears. The list could go on. When it comes to actual depictions of battle, *The Eagle* and *Centurion* attempt much less ambitious scenes and correspondingly fare reasonably well. In part this is due to our ignorance. Small unit actions are rarely if ever described by our sources in detail nor are the actual mechanics of an ambush. The most ambitious of the films, *Gladiator*, oddly offers the most inaccurate view. Its attention to detail in camp construction and soldier equipment is impressive.

In the end though the film represents the actual action of a battle as a disorganized brawl between forces, one only made worse by the influx of cavalry. All three fail to show auxiliary infantry in battle to any extent, with the exception of the archers in *Gladiator*'s Roman army. This is a significant drawback since auxiliaries made up half to two-thirds of the forces in any given Roman army.

Pitched battles were not the only type of warfare in which the Romans engaged. Indeed a significant number of Roman military operations were sieges of fixed settlements, forts, and towns. Accordingly, in the last chapter we will consider Roman siege-craft and the film *Masada*.

Chapter 6

Roman Sieges and *Masada*

T he made-for-American-television mini-series *Masada* (1981; later released as a two hour feature film outside the United States), begins with an aerial view of that imposing mount rising from the valley gorges in southern Israel. The narrator begins: 'Masada, the Hebrew word meaning fortress' and tells of the grip Masada still has on the imagination as thousands of visitors come to see its ruins, its mighty walls, its cisterns. The views are impressive, to say the least. Then the scene shifts to the plains where the remnant of one of the Roman camps lies and a convoy of trucks bears Israeli army recruits. They will venture to the top of Masada and swear their military oaths, a final ceremony marking the completion of their training phase. Part of the ceremony, the narrator explains, includes recounting 'that moment in history which still echoes resoundingly today, the stand of 960 Hebrew men, women and children against the 5,000 men of the Roman 10th Legion.'

As the Israeli soldiers climb the rugged path, the formidable slopes of Masada are revealed by the camera. It is not insurmountable by individuals, but the treacherous path will not suffer an army such as the one the Romans fielded in AD 73 to ascend it. The camera continues to follow the soldiers at the top, who are now preparing for the induction ceremony. The narrator intones that any young recruit who comes to Masada cannot help but remember the past ...

He knows that along with so much of the world the Roman Empire had also conquered Palestine in the first century BC. And he knows that finally the Jews had rebelled against the Roman oppression. The soldier has been taught since childhood that it took four years, the full military might of Rome and 600,000 Jewish dead before Jerusalem would fall and the Romans could claim that the rebellion was at an end. But he knows too that for the incredible events that took place on this mountain, that was only a beginning.

The scene shifts to 'Jerusalem AD 70'. The camera spies Roman soldiers standing outside the city wall as the Temple burns within. Then the shot shifts to residents of Jerusalem in the dark streets, running and screaming, buildings in flames around them. The Romans have breached the final walls of the great city and the inhabitants are panicked. Cavalry troopers ride by; one kicks a man off a bridge. Others stab and kill indiscriminately. Many civilians are dead, but some still hope for shelter. The scene is limited in its graphic violence as things were on American television in the 80s, but still illustrative of a horrific scene: the sacking of a city.

Eleazar (Peter Strauss), soon-to-be leader of the Jewish resistance at Masada, enters the scene. The man beside him dies, transfixed by a spear; Eleazar leaps out to challenge the Roman horseman who cast it. Swords ring; Eleazar pulls the trooper from his horse and dispatches him with a sword stroke. We see the start of the stroke and hear the Roman shout in pain. Eleazar returns to his house where his wife and child remain waiting with another family. 'They're at the Temple,' he says, referring to the Romans. 'It won't be easy, but if you keep to the back streets we'll try to meet where we planned.' The families embrace and split up. Eleazar sends his wife and their children ahead as a soldier breaks into the house with a torch, another scene custom-made to demonstrate his skill as a warrior. This time he takes on the Roman soldier unarmed, managing to disarm his opponent and slay him with his own sword.

Back on the streets death, fire, and destruction reign. Eleazar and his family hide in the shadows and see the mighty *menorah* of the Temple carried off by a group of soldiers. The camera shifts to refugees gathering outside the city walls. In the background the city heights are aflame. Eleazar muses aloud: after two years resisting the Romans and fending off starvation, this is how it ends. Another refugee joins the group, bearing news of friends and family who have been slain that bloody night. 'It's finished!' says one, but Eleazar replies with grim conviction, 'No. No, it's not finished.' He helps his son up and begins the walk towards Masada.

And so, the audience is prepared for a cinematic version of the siege of Masada, that imposing Judaean fortress where a little under 1,000 Jewish men, women, and children made their last stand against the 10th Legion and its auxiliaries, some 10,000 men. With the skill and steady pace of craftsmen, the Romans methodically circumvallated the mountain fort, constructed a siege ramp along a natural spur up the mountain, and brought a siege tower with a ram up the ramp. The fortress wall crumbled under the blows of the ram. The defenders scrambled and built a second wooden and earth wall behind the stone walls, one that could absorb the strikes of the ram. Undaunted, the Romans set fire to the second wall. At this point the defenders apparently collectively committed suicide rather than wait for their inevitable slaughter or enslavement. When the Romans entered the fortress on the next day, they found all the defenders drained of blood and life. Only a pair of women and five children, who did not share the zeal of the defenders, hid and survived to tell the Romans about the mass suicide. The film weaves a tale of honour on both sides, an account that unfortunately, does not accord fully with the evidence. Though the characterization of the combatants is embellished and softened in the cinematic telling, and liberties are taken with the historical evidence, the film nevertheless provides in reasonable detail the components of a Roman siege, albeit one in particularly rough terrain. It also illustrates how a spare narrative in ancient sources requires that the dramatic filmmaker fill gaps, but not necessarily in ways that fit the historical evidence.

Roman Siege Warfare

The account of the calamitous Jewish war against the Romans, comes essentially from Flavius Josephus. Born Joseph, son of

Matthathyahu, he was a member of the priestly elite of Judaea when that province revolted against Roman rule in AD 66. The task fell to him of commanding the Jewish forces of Jotapata, the main city in Galilee. He ultimately failed at this task, however, and surrendered to the Roman commander, Vespasian. Vespasian was soon to enter a Roman civil war for the imperial succession and become emperor. After he did, he granted Josephus his freedom. Josephus stayed in Judaea for a while with the emperor's son Titus as he besieged Jerusalem. Then he travelled to Rome and wrote four different works over the next decades. Crucially, his is the only complete surviving account of the Jewish war against the Romans.[1]

According to Josephus, the Romans crushed the rebellion of Judaea through a series of sieges. The Judaeans fortified a number of cities including Jotapata, Joffa, Gamala, and Jerusalem. One by one the Romans, sometimes at great cost, reduced these strongholds and subjugated or slew their inhabitants. The course of these campaigns illustrates the skill of Roman siege-craft. What is not as often appreciated, however, is how these sieges were part of a long historical process by which the Roman legionary shifted transformed from front line combatant to combat engineer. To them fell the work of moving earth, stone, and timber to build mighty siegeworks and siege engines. Increasingly it fell to the auxiliary forces to serve as the main troops in pitched battles. Historian J.E. Lendon notes this change. In Caesar's day it was the centurions, citizen soldiers like Vorenus and Pullio about whom tales of valour were told. In Josephus' accounts, however, pride of place in the melee belonged to the auxiliaries, no longer to the citizen soldiers. This trend, seen in the changes from Caesar to Josephus is further demonstrated in Trajan's column, a celebration of that emperor's conquest of Dacia in the early second century.[2] At the front of the battle narrated on the column stand the auxiliaries, engaged directly in the fight. To the rear the legionaries construct defences, man *ballistas*, and, significantly, stay out of the front line fighting. This division is punctuated by a scene higher up the column. Here the auxiliaries occupy the enemy wall and fight the defenders directly while the legionaries with them gnaw at the wall with their picks. This pattern continues throughout showing, as Lendon notes, 'legionaries parade, march, and work – and non-legionaries fight.'[3]

Roman military equipment corroborates what the column reveals. The legionary of the first century wore armour with added shoulder protection in the form of large bands of mail or metal sheet arching over his shoulders. His helmet acquired the lobster tail neck guard that fans out from the back of the helmet. The legionary armour in the first century was increasingly designed to protect the wearer from enemies above – those one encountered when laying siege. This shift to combat engineering did not turn the legionaries into spiritless workers, however. Constructing fortifications and siegeworks became an arena of competition for legionaries in itself, just as exploits in pitched battle had once been. Records and literary texts tell of competitions, praise, and awards for soldiers who built fast and well. Construction on a large scale was facilitated through building contests between units. The Roman legionaries competed in their discipline, their ability to excel in training and in building. None of this is to suggest that legionaries no longer used their weapons in pitched battle or auxiliaries their picks and shovels. Rather there was a shift in emphasis in the main tasks assigned a legionary and auxiliaries.[4]

Looking at more detailed siege accounts, like those for Jotapata and Jerusalem gives the sense of Roman skill in siegecraft needed to evaluate *Masada*'s version of a siege. When it came to Jotapata, the Roman army was very much the irresistible force. The road to the city was too rugged for cavalry, so Vespasian simply ordered a detachment of troops to level the approach. The army reached the city and proceeded to deploy on all sides in order to hem the defenders in and stop them from resupplying. Built on high ground with valleys on three sides, Jotapata could only be approached easily from the north. And so Vespasian ordered his soldiers to construct an earthen bank against the northern wall.[5] The entire army set to work scavenging the needed materials: wood, earth, and stone. Under cover of defensive screens, the soldiers built the earthen ramp. As they laboured, Vespasian deployed *ballistae* and archers to prevent the city defenders from harassing the builders. The defenders made counter defences, tried a trick or two, and even sallied out to strike at the Roman siege works. Through these efforts they managed to prolong their defence of the city. Despite the fierce Jewish defence, however, Vespasian's soldiers managed to complete the ramp and position a battering ram against the wall. The ram penetrated the wall, and still the defenders fought fiercely, desperately, to hold the Romans off. Ultimately a defector informed Vespasian of the exhausted states of Jotapata's night guards; the city could now be taken by stealth. Armed with this intelligence, Vespasian's son Titus led a night sortie to scale the walls, slay the guards, and occupy the citadel. After so much effort, the city, like so many others, fell not through the blunt force of siege weapons, but the precision cut of betrayal.[6]

Josephus himself commanded the defence at Jotapata, and so it is not clear how much we can trust his reports of the defenders' ingenuity. Regardless, his account reveals a standard Roman plan for sieges. The Romans built embankments against a shorter or otherwise weaker segment of the enemy wall. The embankments allowed them to position siege towers and ladders to scale the wall, or battering rams to break them. If, during these labours, the defenders succumbed to thirst and hunger and surrendered, so much the better. If not, once the wall was breached, the Romans launched an assault to gain access to the city interior. Sometimes, as in the case of Jotapata, that was still not enough to secure the Romans victory. There as in many other sieges, treachery provided by far the most effective way to seize an enemy stronghold.

As formidable a siege as Jotapata was, the siege of Jerusalem taxed the Romans further.[7] At this point, Josephus was an advisor to the emperor's son Titus. As such he had an excellent vantage point from which to observe the Roman siege. Jerusalem was a mightily fortified city with high walls, sturdy towers, and rugged ascents from the valleys around. Vespasian, pressed to enter the civil war that would ultimately put the Empire in his hand, left the task of taking Jerusalem to his son, Titus. Titus targeted a wall on the northwest side of the city which was weaker than the rest. His soldiers dutifully applied themselves to building an embankment against that wall. Once the siegeworks were completed, a task that took five days, battering rams were brought up to the wall. The rams breached the wall with ease, and the Romans progressed to the second wall – Jerusalem was well fortified. Five more days of fierce fighting and laborious building, and the rams climbed a second set of earthworks to breach the second wall. This left the Romans the task of taking the fortified Upper City, which included the Temple. Or rather it would have left them with only this task, except that a ferocious Jewish counterattack from the Upper City drove the Romans back behind the second wall again. Three more days of fierce street fighting enabled the Romans to regain their positions outside the Upper City walls.

Again the Romans built earthworks and used them to position battering rams against the stone walls. The defenders, now desperately in need of food, still put up a fight. Rather than risk the casualties of an all-out assault, Titus switched tactics for a moment and ordered his soldiers to circumvallate the city. The troops built a wall over five miles long – with thirteen towers no less – to keep the defenders in the city and assistance out. It took them only three days, striking testimony to Roman building skills. Still, the defenders held on.

When the wall was complete and the city isolated from the outside world, the troops returned to the task of breaching the final walls. When they broke through to the upper city, however, they found the defenders had built a new, makeshift wall in their path. One can only imagine the dismay the Roman soldiers felt. At this point Titus offered a peace deal to the remaining defenders holed up in the Temple – one of several offers over the past months. They scorned any offers of peace. And so with the predictability of clockwork, the

Romans built a final set of embankments for their rams. The task was completed when Titus, now out of patience, gave the orders for the wall to be scaled. The soldiers tasked with this duty, however, were driven back by the stalwart defenders. Then Titus ordered the gates of the Temple area put to the torch. In the next round of fighting, the Temple itself was lit ablaze. Josephus makes a point of saying this was against Titus' express orders.[8] He may simply have been politic; who can say? Either way this ended the Jewish resistance. As a capstone to the grim task, the weary and frustrated Roman soldiers, under Titus' orders, sacked the city.[9]

The first insight to glean from this account is certainly the heroic, desperate fight of the Jewish defenders. All told, it took the Romans five months to capture mighty Jerusalem. The episode also illustrates several important points about Roman siegecraft. First, the tactic of building earthworks against a wall in order to bring rams up to topple it was a standard practice. Second, the Romans were superior logisticians. Each ramp they built required them to seek materials from further and further away. Even when the supply chains ran to twelve miles – a distance ox carts took five hours to travel – they steadily supplied the builders with the needed stone and wood. The Roman army's logistical experts and siege masters, combined with a trained soldiery, brought even an imposing target like Jerusalem within their reach.

Masada

According to the film, tax collection is the spark that initiates the final encounter at Masada. In a sense this is authentic: when it came to provincial administration, the Romans were indeed concerned mostly with maintaining peace and the collecting of imperial taxes that peace facilitated. Indeed Josephus notes the negative economic effects of the Sicarii raiders on the Judaean countryside:

There was a fortress of very great strength not far from Jerusalem, which had been built by our ancient kings, both as a repository for their effects in the hazards of war, and for the preservation of their bodies at the same time. It was called Masada. Those that were called Sicarii had taken possession of it formerly, but at this time they overran the neighbouring countries, aiming only to procure to themselves necessaries; for the fear they were then in prevented their further ravages. But when once they were informed that the Roman army lay still, and that the Jews were divided between sedition and tyranny, they boldly undertook greater matters; and at the feast of unleavened bread, which the Jews celebrate in memory of their deliverance from the Egyptian bondage, when they were sent back into the country of their forefathers, they came down by night, without being discovered by those that could have prevented them, and overran a certain small city called Engaddi, in which expedition they prevented those citizens that could have stopped them, before they could arm themselves, and fight them. They also dispersed them, and cast them out of the city. As for such as could not run away, being women and children, they slew of them above 700. Afterward, when they had carried everything out of their houses, and had seized upon all the fruits that were in a flourishing condition, they brought them into Masada. And indeed these men laid all the villages that were about the fortress waste, and made the whole country desolate; while there came to them every day, from all parts, not a few men as corrupt as themselves. At that time all the other regions of Judea that had hitherto been at rest were in motion, by means of the robbers.[10]

The film's chronology on this point is vague however. Josephus places the raiding in the period when Vespasian was still in command in Judaea and Jerusalem still standing, but the film places the Sicarii's raiding in the period after Jerusalem fell, Vespasian was emperor in Rome, and Flavius Silva commanded the army – a difference of about four years. Collapsing these helped the filmmakers create a narrative about the Roman commander, Flavius Silva (Peter O'Toole), as a general weary of war and reluctant to exterminate the rebels. Early in the film when Flavius believes – incorrectly as it happens – that he will be relieved of his command, he notes to his successor, 'What Rome wants is money. There's money to be found here alright, but you must give [the Jews] a chance to let the crops grow and that means keeping the peace. Can you do it with 5,000 homesick policemen?' The scene continues, allowing Flavius to wax on how tired he is of his post and all that comes with it.

Flavius is portrayed as a sympathetic pragmatist throughout the film. The Romans want taxes. Farmers need time to get harvests in to pay taxes. He reprimands a centurion at Hebron who destroys farm houses in retaliation for a zealot raid. Flavius points out caustically that destroying the farmers' houses will do nothing to get the tax situation stabilized. Flavius even meets clandestinely with Eleazar – a meeting without any support in the sources – and attempts to arrange a permanent peace. The negotiation between Eleazar and Flavius is fictitious, but certainly achieves the dramatist's goal: illustrating how reasonable Flavius is, a point to which we will return later. In this fictitious meeting, they agree upon equally fictitious terms: the Romans will suspend taxes in Judaea for one year, and allow Judaea to be independently ruled by a Jewish king allied with the Romans. Flavius agrees to withdraw the 10th Legion to Jericho and suspend taxation in the region, while Eleazar and his band wait at Masada until their peace arrangement can be approved by Vespasian. Ultimately though, political intrigue at Rome undermines any hope of Flavius confirming this sort of peace. The zealots must be destroyed. Flavius is forced to do his duty and crush any resistance at Masada.

This is all fantasy. The dramatic urge to make the characters sympathetic and complicated has constructed an Eleazar and a Flavius without support from the evidence. What little is known about the commander Flavius Silva comes from Josephus' references. He spares few words, and no dramatic flair, for the commander:

> When Bassus was dead in Judea, Flavius Silva succeeded him as procurator there; who, when he saw that all the rest of the country was subdued in this war, and that there was but one only stronghold that was still in rebellion, he got all his army together that lay in different places, and made an expedition against it.[11]

Josephus mentions Silva a handful more times, but only to record what the Roman army did at Masada: 'Silva ordered ...', 'Silva built a wall', etc. His character is not mentioned. Josephus likely gained all his information about the siege from the Roman officer reports, however, and it is not really surprising that he felt no need to delve into the inner workings of a Roman who did not merit even a chapter in his work.

Eleazar is softened in the film also. Here there may be more cause. Certainly Josephus spares no kind word for Eleazar or his followers:

> It was one Eleazar, a potent man, and the commander of these Sicarii, that had seized [Masada] ... The Sicarii got together against those that were willing to submit to the Romans, and treated them in all respects as if they had been their enemies, both by plundering them of what they had, by driving away their cattle, and by setting fire to their houses; for they said that they differed not at all from foreigners, by betraying, in so cowardly a manner, that freedom which Jews thought worthy to be contended for to the utmost, and by owning that they preferred slavery under the Romans before such a contention. Now this was in reality no better than a pretense and a cloak for the barbarity which was made use of by them, and to colour over their own avarice.[12]

The vehemence of Josephus' words warns historians to handle his account cautiously. Any even mildly even-handed treatment from the film would skew greatly from the account. But what is striking is not so much that the film treats Eleazar more sympathetically. Going further he is portrayed as a hard man who undergoes a spiritual journey. The agnostic Eleazar in film increasingly comes to believe in his god, ending the film as a person of deep faith. None of this is in the evidence. Josephus consistently refers to Eleazar in less than admirable terms, though he does attribute to him sermons about the Jewish God delivered as the defenders contemplated their end. While we should not accept his testimony at face value, we should not construct a more personable figure with a more interesting character arc in the absence of evidence to support it.

Josephus covers the course of the Roman siege at Masada briefly compared to the detailed accounts of Jotapata and Jerusalem:

Since therefore the Roman commander Silva had now built a wall on the outside, round about this whole place ... and had thereby made a most accurate provision to prevent any one of the besieged running away, he undertook the siege itself, though he found but one single place that would admit of the banks he was to raise; for behind that tower which secured the road that led to the palace ... there was a certain eminency of the rock, very broad and very prominent, but three hundred cubits beneath the highest part of Masada; it was called the White Promontory. Accordingly, he got upon that part of the rock, and ordered the army to bring earth; and when they fell to that work with alacrity, an abundance of them together, the bank was raised, and became solid for two hundred cubits in height. Yet was not this bank thought sufficiently high for the use of the engines that were to be set upon it; but still another elevated work of great stones compacted together was raised upon that bank; this was fifty cubits, both in breadth and height. The other machines that were now got ready were like to those that had been first devised by Vespasian, and afterwards by Titus, for sieges. There was also a tower made of the height of sixty cubits, and all over plated with iron, out of which the Romans threw darts and stones from the engines, and soon made those that fought from the walls of the place to retire, and would not let them lift up their heads above the works. At the same time Silva ordered that great battering ram which he had made to be brought thither, and to be set against the wall, and to make frequent batteries against it, which with some difficulty broke down a part of the wall, and quite overthrew it.[13]

Josephus' account tells of a group of defenders, huddled together on a mountain top and unable to offer serious resistance to the Roman siege efforts. Efforts to shoot missiles at the Roman tower from their walls were ultimately foiled. As for the Romans, Josephus narrates a pretty matter-of-fact campaign. Supplies, especially water, had to be brought in from a distance, and the paths up the mountain were treacherous, to be sure. Still, the Romans had a great advantage in their siege works. The existing spur, the White Promontory, simply needed more earth to turn it into a proper ramp for a siege tower. A great deal of earth, but far less than what would have been required without the spur.

The film elaborates this sequence of construction as indeed it must in order to run more than six hours long. Where Josephus' account has left out essentially all the details of life occurring in the context of the siege, the film presents the full investment of Masada as a formal affair. At the start Flavius Silva rides along in front of his soldiers, the army standing at attention. There are legionaries and auxiliary archer units standing side by side. The camera moves back to capture the long lines of men. In the era before computer graphic modifications, however, it is clear that this is meant to represent a large force but equally clear that nothing close to 10,000 or even 5,000 soldiers are present. All the Roman officers stare at Masada in the hot sun. Flavius gestures, the *cornifer* plays his horn and the soldiers march forward in orderly lines. The lines split, each heading to a different side of the plateau's base. Rubrius Gallus, the siege expert, surveys the plateau. Then the camera retreats to a long distance, high angle shot of units, perhaps 10 in all, each consisting of about 120 men. A pan to the left reveals a few more. It is an impressive scene but still not as impressive as thousands of soldiers must have been.

Once the initial deployment of soldiers has finished, Flavius and Rubrius confer about the mountain fortress:

F: Impressive.
R: Impossible.
F: Exactly. That is why I sent for you.
R: Nobody can do the impossible, that's what the word means.
F: I've seen you do it.
R: We'll see.

Now the formal proceedings begin. 'Let's make it official,' Flavius mutters and Roman trumpeteers play a stirring Hollywood-style Roman tune. The zealots cock their catapults and launch bags of manure at the musicians. Rubrius notes that they are within the zealots' catapult range. The Romans do not return fire because the steep angle makes it difficult for their catapults to hit and they also risk giving ammunition to the zealots by tossing their own stones at the fortress.

Flavius shouts an ultimatum from Rome and Eleazar shouts back one from God. 'The formalities are over, let's get to work,' snaps Flavius and the Romans begin the hard work of besieging Masada. The first step is to construct the camps. A centurion reads off orders to illustrate the difficulties of the siege. Soldiers are to wear full armour and maintain 'maximum military discipline'. This seems plausible enough. Though wearing armour in the Judaean heat must have been brutal, Trajan's column depicts legionaries in armour engaging in the labours of siegework.[14] The tents they pitch are on the actual remains of the historical Roman camps adding to the authenticity of the scene. There is no mention that the historical

Romans surround the mountain fortress with a wall to keep supplies out and prevent the zealots from escaping.[15] This is probably because simulating a circumvallation wall would be quite a monumental task for the film crew. In any event, the film does note that the Romans hem the zealots in; indeed, Eleazar jokes to a comrade that no one was going to try to escape anyway.

Masada asserts that the siege was a colossal construction task. At the start of the siege, Rubrius sketches the mountain and a ramp to go up. 'There's only one way to do this,' he says to Silva showing the map, 'we have to build an assault ramp up this western side. ... See that ridge over there?' he gestures. 'We have to bring a large part of that over here and up against that,' gesturing again to the face of Masada. Silva wishes to know if this task can be accomplished in the six months he has been allotted by Vespasian. With luck, Rubrius notes. Silva calls for the priests and heads off to check the omens. The next scene shows Silva with an audience of soldiers about to drive a spike into a stone held by priests, the symbolic first piece of the siege ramp. Then the soldiers begin their work in earnest. They pound rocks into gravel with hammers and wedges. Donkeys pulling carts haul the gravel to the emerging ramp and soldiers push the carts as the animals pull. The camera follows one donkey, cart laden with stone, walking past large catapults, and more soldiers moving earth and gravel. Now the shot shifts to Rubrius as he makes sight lines with the Roman surveying instrument called a *groma* – though that was normally used for laying out the intersecting main roads in a city. He has soldiers holding poles along the route of the ramp as he surveys.

The actual siege took far less time, but clearly the six months are used to give more space to the constructed drama. In that time span, the film suggests, the defenders taunted and tortured the Romans in the heat. As the soldiers continue their labours throughout the hot months, Eleazar and his defenders harass them steadily. When the Romans have moved carts and materials within catapult range, the defenders launch stones and break up the works. For added drama in this desert land, one of the defenders' catapults destroys a water depot, smashing the clay pots and freeing the water. It is hard to suspend disbelief here. The idea that the Romans, weeks into the siege, would be so unaware of enemy catapult ranges that they put their water supplies in danger is nonsensical. Yet this allows for another point of drama. Flavius has the people of the local towns gathered and forced to carry earth to the ramp. Eleazar is thwarted, for he is not willing to harm the innocents working on the ramp. Instead the defenders torment the thirsty, sun-baked Romans by taking baths in Masada's copious water supplies where the Roman observers on a distant hillside can see. A soldier collapses from heat and is sent to a tent where others lie similarly prostrate from the sun. Eleazar taunts the Romans about the heat. Still the work continues and steps are taken to construct the tower and ram. Then a near disaster strikes the Romans, still racing in the film to meet the fictional six month deadline. Rubrius is busily sketching and planning when he suddenly realizes an error in his calculations. Raising the ram 3m on the tower would allow the ramp to be 3m lower, saving valuable time in construction. Rubrius goes to the ramp personally to measure and is shot dead by a zealot arrow. As he dies he dictates the rest of the instructions for modifying the ramp. Nor is this the end of the fabricated intrigues and tensions by far, none of which are in Josephus' account. Ultimately, after most of the six months have passed and the Romans have expended incredible efforts, the siege ramp and tower are complete.

Certainly viewers' imaginations can readily appreciate why the siege of such a dramatically remote rock in the middle of a desert could have been a horrible experience for the Romans, a task that stretched their abilities to the breaking point. One cannot help but be impressed by the Roman camps and siegeworks, especially the mighty ramp for the siege tower, all still present today. But was the siege of Masada really that difficult, really that extraordinary?

It is something of an open question. The archaeological evidence suggests Masada was besieged by one legion and its accompanying auxiliary forces. There were eight camps at Masada, each consisting of rows of *triclinia*, stone foundations upon which tents were erected to serve as the basic dwellings for the *contubernia*, the group of eight legionaries who bunked together and shared meals. Judging from the number of *triclinia*, the Roman camps at Masada housed somewhere between 7,000 and 9,000 soldiers. This figure is sufficient to cover a legion along with auxiliary units of cavalry and infantry, supplied, presumably by Syrians. The army would require the support of noncombatants servile and corvee. These would perhaps have numbered another 5,000. All told, the legion and its accompanying support at Masada would have numbered some 13,000, a figure that is consistent with ancient testimonies. Though we cannot be certain, there are clues in the archaeological remains that suggest the siege was not lengthy by Roman standards. The lack of defensive ditches around the camps, the absence of cooking pottery and metalware and abundance of local pottery for storing food, all suggest that the Romans did not plan to be in that devilishly dry and sunburnt place for long.[16]

The siege wall circumvallating Masada was almost 3 miles long, about 5ft thick, and 10ft high. Though this is certainly an impressive set of siege works, the amount of time required for the Romans to build these structures and a road system for supplies is estimated at about three weeks. It is worth noting as a comparative check on this estimate that the four legions besieging Jerusalem, according to Josephus, were able to circumvallate Jerusalem in three days. Historian Jonathan Roth noted that the wall itself was, strictly speaking, unnecessary, a single legion being more than enough to prevent escapees from fleeing the mountain fortress. Perhaps then, he suggested, the purpose of the wall was more to give the soldiers something to do as they attempted to wait out the Jews. The siege ramp that climbs from the valley floor to the walls of Masada is the most striking and probably most debated feature of the whole site. How long did it take to construct? First of all, it is critical to remember that a natural spur ran to a high point along

Masada's cliffs and the ramp was built on top of that spur. This means that a great deal of earth was already present to form the basis of the ramp, a fact that would have saved the Roman engineers considerable time. Geologist Dan Gil studied the natural spur and the earth massed atop it for the ramp, concluding that the ramp could have been constructed in 16 days with 2,400 men working in continuous 8 hour shifts of 800 men. Comparison with other siege ramps attested in the literary sources suggests that this estimate may not be far from the reality.[17]

So where does this leave us? Quite simply, the insistence cinematic Silva makes about having only six months to complete his siege, and the assertion that the construction took that long are both fabrications intended, presumably, to heighten the drama. The siege at Masada, while challenging, was not a unique endeavour for veteran Roman engineers. It seems likely to have taken perhaps seven or eight weeks, not the six months emphasized in the film.[18] And while the terrain posed some uncommon challenges, this was, by no means, the hardest siege the Romans had ever undertaken.

But the representation of the work stages is quite well done. Soldiers and conscripts from the surrounding territory labour steadily. Some are breaking rocks. Others carry baskets of excavated earth and gravel to the site of the ramp. Still others tamp down the material with special tools for the task. Every so often, specialists are shown as are the siege weapons of the Romans, authentic wooden catapults and *ballistae*. These scenes of labour punctuate the dramatic episodes interspersed through the film, contributing to the impression that audiences are witnessing a mighty feat of construction. In the fourth episode, the dramatic climax, special attention is paid to the siege tower. Fashioned out of timber, it stands perhaps 50ft high and is pulled by teams of conscripted labourers using cables. There are four stories. Archers occupy the top level. The next has a ram suspended from the ceiling by ropes and a gangplank to allow soldiers to exploit any breach opened by the ram. The ram itself is a massive timber topped with a mighty metal head, forged into the shape of a ram's head. It looks reminiscent of the one Josephus described at Jotapata:

> This battering ram is a vast beam of wood like the mast of a ship, its forepart is armed with a thick piece of iron at the head of it, which is so carved as to be like the head of a ram, whence its name is taken. This ram is slung in the air by ropes passing over its middle, and is hung like the balance in a pair of scales from another beam, and braced by strong beams that pass on both sides of it, in the nature of a cross. When this ram is pulled backward by a great number of men with united force, and then thrust forward by the same men, with a mighty noise, it batters the walls with that iron part which is prominent.[19]

The two lowest two stories are protected by iron plates to allow soldiers to climb up to gangplank level in safety.

The scene of workers hauling the tower to the base of the ramp is made more dramatic by trumpeted music, and indeed the defenders are terrified when they first see this mighty engine of war. In Josephus' account the ram swiftly breaks through the fortress wall. Then,

> The Sicarii made haste, and presently built another wall within that, which should not be liable to the same misfortune from the machines with the other; it was made soft and yielding, and so was capable of avoiding the terrible blows that affected the other. It was framed after the following manner: They laid together great beams of wood lengthways, one close to the end of another, and the same way in which they were cut: there were two of these rows parallel to one another, and laid at such a distance from each other as the breadth of the wall required, and earth was put into the space between those rows. Now, that the earth might not fall away upon the elevation of this bank to a greater height, they further laid other beams over cross them,

and thereby bound those beams together that lay lengthways. This work of theirs was like a real edifice; and when the machines were applied, the blows were weakened by its yielding; and as the materials by such concussion were shaken closer together, the pile by that means became firmer than before. When Silva saw this, he thought it best to endeavor the taking of this wall by setting fire to it; so he gave order that the soldiers should throw a great number of burning torches upon it: accordingly, as it was chiefly made of wood, it soon took fire; and when it was once set on fire, its hollowness made that fire spread to a mighty flame. Now, at the very beginning of this fire, a north wind that then blew proved terrible to the Romans; for by bringing the flame downward, it drove it upon them, and they were almost in despair of success, as fearing their machines would be burnt: but after this, on a sudden the wind changed into the south, ... and blew strongly the contrary way, and carried the flame, and drove it against the wall, which was now on fire through its entire thickness. So the Romans ... returned to their camp with joy, and resolved to attack their enemies the very next day; on which occasion they set their watch more carefully that night, lest any of the Jews should run away from them without being discovered.[20]

This was the end of any hope for a serious defence of the fortress.

The inherent drama of this historical episode as Josephus described it is apparently sufficient to be included almost 'as-is'. The only elaboration is that necessary to transform spare narrative into a cinematic scene. Eleazar sees the ram and is dismayed – it will destroy the wall. His friend Ezra notes that the wall could be made stronger. After a few moments of thought, Eleazar says, 'No, not stronger; softer. We must build an inner wall that will absorb the blows of the ram.' He gives the necessary orders, and the defenders scatter to prepare the wall. The camera shows the wall built essentially in the way Josephus describes. Vertical timbers the height of the defensive wall are placed side by side. The first wooden wall of timbers is followed by a second spaced several feet back. The space in between is filled with dirt and gravel, then tamped down. When the Roman ram is put into action, the defenders stand in silence listening, waiting. The casemate wall is penetrated and the ram continues to the inner wall. When it hits the wooden wall, however, it is thwarted. The blows of the ram only compact the filler material between the timbers. Here is an instance where the film may do better service to historical reality than Josephus. He says the Romans destroyed the wall section first and then the defenders built a wooden wall. It is difficult to understand, however, how this could have been the case. Once the wall was breached Roman troops could surely have exploited the breach before the defenders had time to build a counter wall. In the film version, this is solved, perhaps correctly, by having the defenders build the wooden inner wall before the ram is first used.

In any case, the fire noted by Josephus provides dramatic tension for the film. Rather than sending the Romans over the top of the wall four or five at a time, Silva opts to set fire to the wooden wall. The danger of course is that the flames might shift on to the tower, which of course they do. But the shifting winds will not last. The Roman tower is not destroyed, but within the span of the night the wooden wall is. Silva gives the word: 'We'll take it in the morning.'

The End and the Roman Sacking of Cities

The Sicarii did not try to escape, as it turned out, nor did they plan to resist the Romans the next morning. Instead they made the weighty decision to end their own lives rather than be captured by the Romans. Lots were drawn. Ten Sicarii assisted anyone who could not do the deed themselves. Men, women, and children all died. Finally one of the ten assisted his comrades before plunging a sword into his chest. When the Romans entered the breech the next morning, they found the dead. As it happened, however, two women and five children hid as the Sicarii executed the mass suicide. They revealed themselves when the Roman soldiers arrived and told the tale. Josephus closes this episode by noting the Roman soldiers,

> came within the palace, and so met with the multitude of the slain, but could take no pleasure in the fact, though it were done to their enemies. Nor could they do other than wonder at the courage of their resolution, and the immovable contempt of death which so great a number of them had shown, when they went through with such an action as that was.

Silva established a garrison on Masada; the opposition to Roman rule had been thoroughly crushed.[21]

It comes as no surprise that this decision to take their own lives is a poignant episode in the drama. Accordingly, Eleazar delivers a lengthy speech as he works to persuade his comrades that death is better than the inevitable defeat. He closes with these words:

> The choice is yours. I've made mine. You can choose to fight them in the morning. They'll kill you or enslave you. You can choose to hide from them. They'll find you. Or you can choose to take their victory from them. They will remember you.

And of course, almost two millennia later, we do. It's a touching moment, the zealots disarming and hugging their loved ones, preparing for their ends. The congregation says its final farewells after so great a journey together. The sacred scriptures are buried. Eleazar and his wife Miriam have a tender exchange. Sadness is tinged with horror for the viewer as Eleazar clasps the knife behind his back. Miriam says, 'There is plenty of time,' but Eleazar sadly shakes his head no, and Miriam removes their son's head garb to prepare for self-sacrifice. The slightest trace of a loving smile is on his son's face as Eleazar moves close. We see a close-up of his knife hand behind his back. He draws the knife forward and the scene goes black. It is a dramatic and personal moment of the kind that cinema conveys so very well.

The next day, of course, the Romans find nothing but the dead. Disturbed by the silence as the Romans enter the breach in the wall, Silva climbs up through the tower to see for himself. He wanders the scenes of slaughter in increasing dismay. He is stunned, and dismisses the tribune Curio so he can be alone. When he finds Eleazar and his family, he admonishes the corpse in even tones. 'This is stupidity itself. I made the novice's mistake: I overestimated you … I waited too long putting the proposition.' Here Silva refers to another unattested meeting at night between Silva and Eleazar before the tower began its assault. Silva offered a final chance at surrender; the opportunity was declined. Silva continues, his voice raising:

> 'What in the name of common sense does a thing like this prove,' his voice raising, 'you thought I was a liar. What did you tell them? they'd be tortured? … You felt you were cornered. I overestimated you. A leader must know not only who his enemy is but also who his friend is… I would never have let this happen to you. You did this yourself. You blamed Rome for it. I should have put the proposition sooner; you'd be alive now. You'd be halfway to Rome now … With us, you had a chance to build something good here. Without us, this is how you always end, killing one another, killing yourselves, no foresight, no sense of reality. I should have put the proposition sooner. An error in tactics on my part, but it doesn't prove that the system is wrong. In fact it proves just the opposite.'

Drained of strength, his voice empty, Silva concludes, 'Nobody is listening anymore.'

This speech offers an excellent example of how film can modernize a story and make it appeal to modern sensibilities, while presenting a misleading picture of the past. The tale the filmmakers clearly wish to tell is about two admirable leaders, both of whom are hardened by war, hard-nosed when need be, but who both essentially follow their duty despite their misgivings. In a word, they are admirable. And while historians, unlike filmmakers, have an obligation not to moralize in their works, it needs to be said that a speech like the one above substantially misrepresents Roman attitudes toward war and conquest. Flavius mourns the loss of the Jewish defenders, wishes openly that they would have trusted him. Submission to Roman government would have ushered in peace and prosperity, Flavius believed, both for the zealots and for the legion.

Certainly, the Romans did, on the whole, believe they brought peace and order, civilization, to others. The Pax Romana, 'Roman Peace,' they called it. As for the idea that the defenders would be allowed to live in peace, that Flavius would not torture them, that Eleazar would have been brought honourably to Rome to help build a new Pax Romana in Judaea, it is nonsense. The Roman record of treating defeated Judaeans speaks for itself. In Jaffa all the men were slaughtered in various parts of the siege, and Josephus reported, 'There were no males now remaining, besides infants, which, with the women, were carried as slaves into captivity.'[22] When the high ground of Jotapata, betrayed, was secured by the Romans, they engaged in an indiscriminate slaughter of the defenders. Josephus, an eyewitness says,

> [The Romans] so well remembered what they had suffered during the siege, that they spared none, nor pitied any, but drove the people down the precipice from the citadel, and slew them as they drove them down; at which time the difficulties of the place hindered those that were still able to fight from defending themselves; for as they were distressed in the narrow streets, and could not keep their feet sure along the precipice, they were overpowered with the crowd of those that came fighting them down from the citadel. This provoked a great many ... to kill themselves with their own hands; for when they saw that they could kill none of the Romans, they resolved to prevent being killed by the Romans, and got together in great numbers in the utmost parts of the city, and killed themselves.[23]

The seafarers of Joppa took to the sea rather than resist the Romans, but the winds and waves were against them. When their ships were grounded the Romans slaughtered them.[24] Taricheae is a particularly apt parallel to Masada. The inhabitants of the city did not wish to fight the Romans. Those dwelling in the hinterlands, did, and seized control of the city. Titus, according to Josephus, apparently knew this and still the Romans slaughtered the unresisting city dwellers along with the rebellious outsiders.[25] Thousands were slain after the capture of Jerusalem; Josephus says 110,000 slaughtered. Those that were spared were enslaved, almost 100,000 by Josephus' estimate, some to work in mines, others to adorn Titus' triumphal parade back in Rome.[26]

The 'laws of war' according to the Romans, and the Greeks before them, authorized victors to do absolutely anything they willed to the vanquished. Commonly this meant all property could be seized and destroyed, all inhabitants could be slain, raped, or enslaved. The Romans did not always engage in these behaviours. Indeed there was a recognized virtue of *clementia*, clemency, and it was possible for the conquered to be spared.[27] Here's the thing: the treatment of the Jews in the years before Masada had involved no clemency to speak of, there is *no historical evidence* to suggest that Flavius Silva was gentler than his superiors, and no reason to suppose that the defenders of Masada would be spared if they held the fort until the Romans breached the walls. It is not that Silva could not have acted differently, but that there is no historical reason to expect he did from the spare references to him in Josephus' narrative.

And so *Masada* like the rest, has strengths and weaknesses in what one takes away from the film. Certainly the film does not overcome the Hollywood reliance on leather segmented armour. These sorts of details aside, when it comes to depicting the labour and effort expended on a Roman siege, the film does well, though it significantly overestimates the time the historical siege took. Camp life, ritual prayers, construction tools, many of the incidentals of the siege camp are shown giving life to what in Josephus' work is a spare narrative. The characters are misrepresented in the film, becoming more heroic, honourable, and even kinder than the evidence warrants.

Conclusion

A t the close of our exploration it is worth considering in general what cinematic depictions of ancient battle have to offer those interested in the subject. Clearly, film is multimedia and can communicate in text, sight, and sound, the combination of which can be very powerful. How do filmmakers use these assets when it comes to portraying ancient battle? In what ways can film help us imagine historical ancient battles? In what ways do they contribute to our misunderstandings?

Let's start with the misunderstandings. Of course trying to cite all the inaccurate details in each of these films would take a book longer than this. Understanding this, what are some major areas where inaccuracies become part of the core version of the battle a film portrays? First, while many of the films considered here do a fine job replicating the arms and armour of the period, there are notable exceptions. In the case of *300* the Spartans' lack of body armour is surely the result of the director's conscious choice to heighten the heroic look of the warriors. A number of films make substantial errors in representing equipment, however, without any particular dramatic motive. Equipping the legionaries of the middle and late Republic, for example, stands out as a task most filmmakers fail to get right. From *Cabiria* in 1914 to the 2004 *Spartacus*, films depicting Romans of the Republic have a penchant for leather versions of armour that never existed in leather and did not even exist in metal until centuries after the period depicted. As for weapons, Romans are regularly portrayed with thrusting spears nothing at all like the armour piercing *pila* that Romans cast at their enemies. Some of this is a matter of the film's age: the makers of epic films of the 1950s and 1960s were simply less concerned with portraying equipment in faithful detail. One cannot help but wonder, too, how many films, particularly older ones, continued to use inaccurate armour because that was what was available from their studio's prop department.

Another problem in many of the films is the portrayal of actual formations. It is not always clear what kind of units are represented onscreen and how those units are meant to be deployed. *Alexander* stands out as a model of authenticity when it comes to almost every aspect of ancient battle, and this is certainly true in the matter of formations. Director Stone goes so far as to make sure the Macedonian *syntagma* have the requisite 256 soldiers. Other films pay less regard to that kind of accuracy. In *Rome* centuries appear to be represented insofar as the centurions are the chief officers shown, but it is not entirely clear to watchers that this is the case. *Gladiator* depicts three lines of two soldiers per line, but it is not clear whether these are centuries or cohorts. Kubrick's *Spartacus* shows cohorts, though the manoeuvres it makes these cohorts perform wreck any sense of authenticity.

These are certainly important details, but one could easily descend into nitpicking. A more substantial concern is how some of the films represent melee: the hand-to-hand infantry combat that was the core of battle in the classical world. Well over a century ago, a French colonel, Charles Ardant du Picq, made the following observations:

The word mêlée employed by the ancients ... meant a crossing of arms, not a confusion of men ... In pursuit it was possible to plunge into the midst of the fugitives, but in combat everyone had too much need for the next man, for his neighbour, who was guarding his flanks and his back, to let himself be killed out of sheer wantonness by a sure blow from within the ranks of the enemy. In the confusion of a real mêlée, Caesar at Pharsalus, and Hannibal at Cannae, would have been conquered. Their shallow ranks, penetrated by the enemy, would have had to fight two against one ... With the confusion and medley of combatants, there might be a mutual extermination, but there would not be any victors. How would they recognize each other? Can you conceive two mixed masses of men or groups, where everyone occupied in front can be struck with impunity from the side or from behind? That is mutual extermination, where victory belongs only to survivors; for in the mix-up and confusion, no one can flee, no one knows where to flee.[1]

Du Picq contributed a number of important insights to our understanding of ancient battle, not least of all the critical role of morale in determining an army's success or failure. In this particular case though, he noted that when Greco-Roman soldiers with melee weapons engaged, their units did not intermingle, did not disappear replaced by an all-out brawl with friends and foes in all directions. Armies, effective armies anyway, kept their formations in the melee and did not dissolve on contact with their enemies.

Yet this dissolution and confusion of soldiers is exactly what is depicted in a number of films. This is particularly a hallmark of films from the mid twentieth century. In 1956's *Alexander* and 1959's *Spartacus*, the major battle scenes devolve into a series of individual duels with no effort to approximate battle lines or formations. Unfortunately, even *Gladiator* with the benefit of CGI makes the same mistakes. The whole point of Greco-Roman infantry organization from the Archaic phalanx to the Imperial legions was to maintain an orderly formation. In doing so soldiers gained protection and morale from their comrades and could present a far more formidable face to their, often more disorganized, opponents.

Some of the films do illustrate the physical and psychological benefits of close-order infantry formations in Greco-Roman armies. In *Rome* the value of the formation reaches the level of a morality play when the very first episode shows Varenus bellowing at Pullo to keep in line. The phalanxes in *300* and *Alexander* show the effectiveness of such organization against far less orderly troops. Both films show Persian enemies that fight in more open order and with shorter weapons. The effects are murderous for them. Interestingly enough, Petersen's *Troy* also illustrates the brutal effectiveness of an orderly force that remains in formation, although in this case it is the organized Trojans that push back the disorderly Greeks. Even *The Eagle* represents this well for while the soldiers are not in a particularly historical unit or formation, they maintain their positions in their formation and in doing so, are able to rescue their comrades from their far less organized foes.

There are still other facets of ancient battle that this corpus of films illustrate well. Let's start with the sights and sounds. These films aim for the dramatic, and in the twenty-first century, even the gruesome. Almost across the board, the best of these films capture the horrors of battle in the ways they portray wounding. The brutality of close combat should not be underestimated and the films of the past fifteen years mostly do not underestimate it. For the most part killing in these battles is restricted to a zone the length of a hand-held weapon, in most cases a few feet. This means most warriors are close enough to look in the eyes of the person that they kill, or is about to kill them. That would be brutal enough, but swords and spears do terrible things to human bodies. The filmmakers often do their best to capture that. At times it seems pure spectacle: weapons penetrate heads and bodies, arms are severed, skulls split, and sometimes heads removed. The sights and sounds are gruesome, but the reality could hardly have been different. The poets tell of the horrible wounds that the weapons of the Greco-Roman world inflicted. Encouraging young warriors to remain in the fight, the seventh-century poet general, Tyrtaios notes,

For 'tis a foul thing, truly, for an elder to fall in the front and lie before the younger, his head white and his beard hoary, breathing forth his stout soul in the dust, with his entrails all bloody in his hands, a sight so foul to see and fraught with such ill to the seer, and his flesh also all naked.[2]

And Homer's *Iliad* is preoccupied by deadly wounds that make those in the movies seem far tamer. These are just three out of hundreds of such descriptions:

> Meriones killed Phereclus... Meriones caught him quickly, running him down hard and speared him low in the right buttock – the point pounding under the pelvis, jabbed and pierced the bladder – he dropped to his knees, screaming, death swirling round him.

> Meges killed Pedaeus... Closing, Meges gave him some close attention ... the famous spearman struck behind his skull, just at the neck-cord, the razor spear slicing straight up through the jaws, cutting away the tongue – he sank in the dust, teeth clenching the cold bronze.

> Euaemon's son Eurypylus cut down brave Hypsenor, ... Eurypylus, chasing Hypsenor fleeing on before him, flailed with a sword, slashed the Trojan's shoulder and lopped away the massive bulk of Hypsenor's arm ... the bloody arm dropped to the earth, and red death came plunging down his eyes, and the strong force of fate.[3]

Though Homer and Tyrtaios range to the graphic side, there are numerous references to the horrible wounds that blades cause on flesh in the corpus of Greco-Roman texts that we have, not least of all in the ancient medical literature.[4] This should not be surprising, but it is not always emphasized in modern written accounts of battle. Most of the films in this list rectify this imbalance, to say the least, displaying in all manners the gruesome sights of battle.

These sights come with all manner of sounds. Victor Hanson's comments on the sounds of Greek hoplite battle hold true for all Greco-Roman warfare, indeed all warfare between close-order infantry with hand-held weapons:

The live sounds were more animal-like than human: the concerted groans of men exerting themselves, pushing forward in group effort with their bodies and shields against the immovable armour of the enemy – grunts such as one hears around men sweating at work in field or shop, for battle, after all, as Homeric man knew, was 'work' of the worst kind. Finally, whatever Tyrtaios advised about the hoplite 'biting his lip', there were all too often the noises of human misery. Here arose a tortured symphony of shrieks as a man went down with a wound to the groin, the steady sobbing of a soldier *in extremis*, a final gasp of fright as the spear thrust found its way home.[5]

Cinema portrays, in a way no other media can match, the sounds of battle. The scrape and clang of metal weapons against shields, the grunts of the attacker and the screams of the wounded defender. In many cases the authenticity of the sounds is hampered by background music though the level of drama is increased. Occasionally, as in *Rome*, the battle is unaccompanied by a soundtrack the better to appreciate the brutal noises of combat. Music aside these are the sights and sounds of ancient battle, a noisy place indeed.

Through these horrific sights and sounds, the films invite viewers to face that most important factor in the face of battle: morale. Some of the films make efforts to illustrate the stress of battle. *300* and *The Eagle* both capture shots of younger soldiers with fear and uncertainty on their face in response to an upcoming battle. Almost all the films, even when they do not focus on the fears of a few soldiers, present ancient battle, rightly, as a chaotic frightening affair. What made these warriors able to endure the horrors of battle is a question that often engages modern students of ancient military history. Keegan put nicely the importance of psychology for understanding battle:

What battles have in common is human: the behaviour of men struggling to reconcile their instinct for self-preservation, their sense of honour and the achievement of some aim over which other men are ready to kill them. The study of battle is therefore always a study of fear and usually of courage; always of leadership and usually of obedience. Above all it is always a study of solidarity and usually also of disintegration – for it is towards the disintegration of human groups that battle is directed.[6]

For those hoping to come to some understanding of ancient battle, morale, in this sense the will to fight, is of paramount importance. What could and did motivate the soldiers of the ancient world to stand firm in the face of death or horrific injury?

The films offer some solutions. Most involve the charisma of a leader who inspires his men with talk of victory and glory. Achilles encourages his Myrmidons as they are about to hit the shores of Troy: 'You know what is there, waiting, beyond that beach. Immortality! Take it! It's yours.' Leonidas too issues a call for glory, 'This is where we hold them! This is where we fight! This is where they die! Remember this day boys, for it will be yours forever!' Alexander, and Maximus too, make their speeches.

Many of the films also illustrate, however, that there is more to an effective commander than a stirring speech. An important element in leadership, especially the kind of leadership that kept morale high is the sharing of risks with one's soldiers. Aquila leads his squad into battle personally: he does not command from behind. Leonidas and his captain are in the first rank of the phalanx. Alexander, of course, leads his charging cavalry as does Maximus in *Gladiator*. Junior officers in *Centurion* are shown doing their part when the legion is ambushed by the Picts. They issue words of calm reassurance to the soldiers and stay beside them as the danger unfolds. Hector is at the forefront of the battle as are the heroic leaders of the Greeks; they take even greater risks than they demand of their soldiers.

Generals who take efforts to bond with their men are also highlighted in the films. And so Alexander spends the evening before Gaugamela walking round the campfires and talking to his soldiers as individuals. On the day of the battle, he is able to call his infantrymen by name and praise their records. *Gladiator* too shows Maximus surveying the troops and speaking kindly to his soldiers. Flavius Silva in Masada openly commiserates with his soldiers about their exhaustion with Judaea and their homesickness.

Many of the films go a step further. In addition to their speeches and their empathy, a number of commanders engage in spectacular displays of skill, personally throwing themselves into battle. *Troy*, *300*, *Alexander*, and *Gladiator* all display their heroes taking part in grand individual exploits. In some cases this is consistent with what is known about ancient battle. Homeric heroes seem to have displayed their courage and inspired others to follow by seeking out dangerous opponents. Alexander was notable for leading his Companion Cavalry personally in the major battles against the Persians. At times, however, the *aristeia* appears to be chosen more for its appeal to audiences than any accurate representation. Generals in Roman armies did not often lead their cavalry on charges as *Gladiator's* Maximus does. To do so would be to sacrifice any hope of making further tactical decisions in the battle. In *300* the *aristeias* that add to the coolness factor of the film, as noted, also make a mockery of the solidarity of the phalanx that the movie itself promotes.

Nor is this the only way to misrepresent a commander, however. *Masada* makes General Flavius softer, smoother edged. Early in the film a disgruntled homesick soldier stabs Flavius in an effort to assassinate him. Flavius summons the army and calls the would-be-assassin's best friend forth to execute the criminal. Before the execution takes place, though, Flavius substitutes a slap on the head in place of a sword stroke. He then gives a stirringly sympathetic speech to his legionaries including the plea: 'If I can't bring you home, who can?' Less artificially, Oliver Stone constructs a scene after the battle of Gaugamela where Alexander walks among the wounded Macedonians in a field hospital, nearly overwhelmed by the aftermath of the slaughter. He finishes the scene sitting in the battlefield crying, a scene tailor-made to humanize Alexander according to modern standards.

Though the emphasis on exceptional leaders can lead to hyperbole, these films do make an important point. One of the principles of excellent leadership is to lead from the front. The duelling commanders certainly show this but other films show the importance of the junior officers. *Centurion* and *Rome* are the most notable in this aspect. *Rome's* battle of Alesia scene in reality is a scene about the century in action and the film makes an effort to show the importance of order and the role of the centurion in keeping the formation operating smoothly. *Centurion* shows a different scenario, the army subject to an ambush. Before the trap is sprung, however, we see the junior officers, tribunes or centurions, keeping the soldiers calm and ready.

Ancient history, even more than history of other periods, cannot be reduced to simple categories of right or wrong, accurate or inaccurate. The evidence is often too patchy for such summary judgments. This is even more the case with films about ancient battle. Representing in sound and moving image something as complicated as an ancient battle is bound to result in a combination of more and less plausible features even when made with an attention to historical detail. Overall there are moments of genius in many of the films; soldiers are emphasized and a face of battle is sketched. In this sense, perhaps these films and this book can help broaden our appreciation of the mechanics of ancient battle.

Online Texts of Ancient Sources

It is increasingly the case that translations of the most commonly read Greek and Roman authors can be found online, often typed from scholarly translations such as the Loeb series. Most of the texts from Greco-Roman writers come from four sites. Bill Thayer's Lacus Curtius site presents a number of high quality public domain copies of ancient authors' works in the Loeb classical library series. Jona Lendering's Livius.org also houses a number of translations. The Internet Classics archive contains texts from a few of the ancient sources used in this book. Finally, the Greek and Roman section of the Perseus Project at Tufts University also provides a number of sources in translation accompanied by a full set of scholarly tools for reading the originals. The following list provides links to translations of the authors cited and quoted in this work.

Arrian, *The Anabasis*
Cornell University Internet Archive: http://archive.org/details/cu31924026460752

Appian, all books
http://www.livius.org/ap-ark/appian/appian.html

Caesar, *Gallic War*
http://classics.mit.edu/Caesar/gallic.html (Edwards trans.)

Cassius Dio
http://penelope.uchicago.edu/Thayer/E/Roman/Texts/Cassius_Dio/home.html (Cary trans).

Diodorus Siculus
http://penelope.uchicago.edu/Thayer/e/roman/texts/diodorus_
siculus/home.html (Oldfather trans)

Dionysius of Halicarnassus, *Roman Antiquities*
http://penelope.uchicago.edu/Thayer/E/Roman/Texts/dionysius_of_
halicarnassus/home.html (Cary trans.)

Homer, *The Iliad*
http://classics.mit.edu/Homer/iliad.html (Butler trans).

Herodotus, *History*
http://classics.mit.edu/Herodotus/history.html (Rawlinson trans).
http://www.perseus.tufts.edu/hopper/text?doc=Perseus%3Atext
%3A1999.01.0126%3Abook%3D1%3Achapter%3D1%3Asection%
3D0(Godley trans)

Josephus, *The Jewish War*
http://www.gutenberg.org/files/2850/2850-h/2850-h.htm#link62
H_4_0001 (Whiston trans)

Livy, *Ab Urbe Condita*
http://www.perseus.tufts.edu/hopper/text?doc=Perseus:text:
1999.02.0026 (Roberts trans, books 1–9)
http://www.perseus.tufts.edu/hopper/text?doc=Perseus%3Atext%
3A1999.02.0144%3Abook%3D21 (Roberts trans, books 21–45)

Plutarch's *Lives of Greeks and Romans*
http://penelope.uchicago.edu/Thayer/E/Roman/Texts/Plutarch/
Lives/home.html (Perrin trans).

Plutarch's *Sayings of Spartan Women*
http://penelope.uchicago.edu/Thayer/E/Roman/Texts/Plutarch/
Moralia/Sayings_of_Spartan_Women*.html (Babbit trans).

Polybius, *Histories*
http://penelope.uchicago.edu/Thayer/E/Roman/Texts/Polybius/home.html (Paton trans.)

Suetonius
http://penelope.uchicago.edu/Thayer/E/Roman/Texts/Suetonius/home.html (Rolfe trans.)

Tyrtaios
http://www.perseus.tufts.edu/hopper/text?doc=Perseus%3Atext%3A2008.01.0479%3Avolume%3D1%3Atext%3D2%3Asection%3D2 (Edmonds trans.)

Velleius Paterculus
http://penelope.uchicago.edu/Thayer/e/roman/texts/velleius_paterculus/home.html (Shipley trans.)

Xenophon, *Constitution of the Lacedaemonians*
http://www.perseus.tufts.edu/hopper/text?doc=Xen.+Const.+Lac.+1&fromdoc=Perseus%3Atext%3A1999.01.0210 (Bowersock trans.)

Notes and References

Introduction

1. John Keegan, *The Face of Battle: A Study of Agincourt, Waterloo, and the Somme* (New York, 1976) pp. 76–77.
2. See for example, Victor Hanson, *The Western Way of War: Infantry Battle in Classical Greece* (New York, 1989); Adrian Goldsworthy, *The Roman Army at War 100 BC–AD 200* (Oxford, 1996); Philip Sabin, 'The Face of Roman Battle', *Journal of Roman Studies* 90 (2000) pp. 1–17; and my own work, *The Cavalry of the Roman Republic: Cavalry Combat and Elite Reputations in the Middle and Late Republic* (London, 2002).
3. Jeremiah McCall, *The Sword of Rome: A Biography of Marcus Claudius Marcellus* (Barnsley, 2012) p. 110.
4. Robin Lane Fox, *The Making of Alexander* (Oxford, 2004) p. 31.

Chapter 1

1. Barry Strauss, *The Trojan War* (New York, 2006) xvii-xix, pp. 186–7.
2. For a recent reappraisal of Homer's relation to his subject, see Strauss, *The Trojan War*, esp. pp. 5–11. See also Hans van Wees, *Greek Warfare: Myths and Realities* (London, 2004) pp. 249–52.
3. Van Wees, *Greek Warfare* pp. 249–50. This argument was set out in detail decades ago by Moses Finley, *The World of Odysseus* (London, 1954). Finley, however, dated Homer to the tenth century. Succeeding scholarship has tended to move that date forward, as does van Wees.
4. Wolfgang Petersen, 'From Ruins to Reality', on *Troy*, Warner Brothers, 2004.
5. Peter Green, 'Heroic Hype, New Style: Hollywood Pitted against Homer', *Arion* 12 (2004) p. 177.
6. See Robin Archer, 'Chariotry to Cavalry: Developments in the Early First Millennium', in Garret G. Freeman and Matthew Trundle, eds. *New Perspectives on Ancient Warfare* (Leiden, 2010) pp. 57–80.

Archer summarizes the debate well and makes a compelling case for the importance of composite bows used in conjunction with chariots. See also Robert Drews, *The End of the Bronze Age: Changes in Warfare and the Catastrophe ca. 1200 BC* (Princeton, 1993) pp. 174–7; van Wees, *Greek Warfare* pp. 158–60.

7. Drews, *The End of the Bronze Age* pp. 174–7.
8. The Warrior Krater is housed at the National Archaeological Museum in Athens. The easiest way to get a look is to use a search engine on the Internet, but one could also see Drews, *The End of the Bronze Age* pp. 161–3 for a photo and discussion.
9. Van Wees, *Greek Warfare* pp. 154–65.
10. Karl G. Heider, *Grand Valley Dani: Peaceful Warriors* (New York, 1979) pp. 94–6 and Robert Gardner and Karl G. Heider, *Gardens of War: Life and Death in the New Guinea Stone Age* (London, 1968) pp. 139, 141. Cited by Hans van Wees, 'The Homeric Way of War: The Iliad and the Hoplite Phalanx (I)', *Greece and Rome* 41 (1994) p. 8. See also the photos of Dani Warfare in van Wees, *Greek Warfare* plates XIV – XVII.
11. Van Wees, 'The Homeric Way of War (I)' p. 8.
12. Homer, *Iliad* 2.363–8 (Fagles trans).
13. Kurt Raaflaub, 'Homeric Warriors and Battles: Trying to Resolve Old Problems', *The Classical World* 4 (2008) pp. 476–81; Anthony Snodgrass, 'The 'Hoplite Reform Revisited', *Dialogues D'histoire ancienne* 19 (1993) p. 48.
14. Homer, *Iliad* 2.427–32 (Fagles trans). Noted by Kurt Raaflaub 'Homeric Warriors and Battles' p. 480.
15. See van Wees, *Greek Warfare* pp. 166–174; Raaflaub, 'Homeric Warriors and Battles' pp. 478–9.
16. Homer *Iliad* 4. 422–429, 446–4564 (Fagles trans). Cited by Martin Winkler, 'Leaves of Homeric Storytelling: Wolfgang Petersen's Troy and Franco Rossi's Odissea', in E. Cavallini ed., *Omero Mediatico. Aspetti della ricezione omeric nella civilta contemporanea* (Bologna, 2007) (web: http://www.mythimedia.org/doc/Leaves%20of%20Homeric%20Storytelling.pdf)
17. VD Hanson, *The Western Way of War* pp. 171–84.
18. 1 Samuel 17.8–11.

19. Stephen P. Oakley, 'Single Combat in the Roman Republic,' *Classical Quarterly* 35 (1985) p. 393.
20. Jon E. Lendon, *Soldiers and Ghosts: A History of Battle in Classical Antiquity* (New Haven, 2006) pp. 22–3.

Chapter 2

1. Murray, Rebecca, 'Writer-Director Zack Snyder Discusses '300',' *About.com Hollywood Movies*, Web. 01 Sept. 2013 <http://movies.about.com/od/300/a/300zs022707.htm>
2. Hanson, *The Western Way of War* especially pp. 55–88.
3. Hanson, *The Western Way of War* pp. 76–83.
4. Anthony Snodgrass, *Early Greek Armour and Weapons: from the End of the Bronze Age to 600 BC* (Edinburgh 1964) pp. 20–31.
5. On the mechanics of Greek hoplite combat see Hanson, *Western Way of War* especially pp. 135–85; van Wees, *Greek Warfare* pp. 172– 195 (though he differentiates the mentality and fighting style of the hoplite in the Archaic period and up through the Persian Wars from the classical Hoplite. Lendon, *Soldiers and Ghosts* pp. 41–57.
6. Plutarch, *Moralia*, 241.16.
7. Lendon, *Soldiers and Ghosts* pp. 139–57.
8. Tyrtaios in M.L. Wes, trans. *Greek Lyric Poetry: The Poems and Fragments of the Greek Iambic, Elegiac, and Melic Poets (Excluding Pindar and Bacchylides) down to 450 BC* (Oxford 1993) p. 24.
9. Paul Cartledge, *The Spartans: The World of the Warrior Heroes of Ancient Greece* (New York, 2004) pp. 82–3.
10. Paul Cartledge, *The Spartans* p. 72.
11. John Marincola, *Greek Historians* (Cambridge, 2001) pp. 19–21, 24.
12. P.J. Stylianou 'Ephorus' in Nigel Wilson ed. *Encyclopedia of Ancient Greece* (New York) pp. 262–3.
13. Michael Lipka, *Xenophon's Spartan Constitution: Introduction, Text, Commentary* (Berlin, 2002) pp. 3–4.
14. Noted scholar of Greek history N.G.L. Hammond worked through the sources and used his own extensive knowledge of Greek topography to provide the account paraphrased here. See Hammond, 'Sparta at Thermopylae', *Historia: Zeitschraft für Alte Geschachte* 45 (1996) pp. 14–20. (JStor URL http://www.jstor.org/stable/4436404).

Hammond in turn is based on the accounts of Herodotus and Diodorus Siculus.

15. Herodotus 7.176 (Macaulay trans).
16. Xenophon, *Constitution of the Spartans* 8 (Dakyns trans).
17. Xenophon, *Constitution of the Spartans* 15 (Dakyns trans).
18. Paul Cartledge *Thermopylae: The Battle that Changed the World* (New York, 2006) pp. 78–9.
19. Xenophon *Constitution of the Spartans* 13.2–4 (Bowersock trans).
20. Cartledge, *The Spartans* pp. 72–3.
21. Plutarch *Moralia* 241D (Babbit trans).
22. Cartledge, *The Spartans* p. 93.
23. Cartledge, *The Spartans* pp. 70, 73.
24. Francois Ollier, *Le mirage spartiate: étude sur l'idéalisation de Sparte dans l'antiquité grecque de l'origine jusqu'aux cyniques* (Paris, 1933).
25. Xenophon *Constitution of the Spartans* 2.1–5 (Bowersock trans).
26. Xenophon *Constitution of the Spartans* 2.1–11 (Bowersock trans).
27. Xenophon *Constitution of the Spartans* 3.1–5 (Bowersock trans).
28. See Cartledge, *The Spartans* pp. 69–70 for a summary.
29. Plutarch, *Life of Lycurgus* 6 (Perrin trans).
30. Xenophon, *Constitution of the Spartans* 3.
31. Cartledge, *Thermopylae* pp. 81–3.
32. Herodotus 7.213 (Rawlinson trans).
33. Plutarch, *Life of Lycurgus* 15.
34. Tyrtaios (Edmonds trans).
35. Herodotus 7.61–88.
36. Herodotus 7.61 (Macaulay trans.).
37. Philip de Souza, *The Greek and Persian Wars 499–386 BC* (New York, 2003) p. 35.
38. Plutarch, *Moralia* 225D.
39. Diodorus Siculus 11.7 (Oldfather trans).
40. Homer *Iliad* 5.158–85 (Fagles trans).
41. Herodotus 7.211–12.
42. John Keegan, *The Face of Battle* 146–153; McCall, *Cavalry of the Roman Republic* pp. 66–7.
43. Herodotus 7.84.
44. Herodotus 7. 209–12; Diodorus Siculus 9.7–8.

45. Diodorus Siculus 9.7.4 (Oldfather trans).
46. Herodotus 7.83.1–3 (Godley trans).
47. Herodotus 7.211.1–3 (Godley trans).
48. Diodorus Siculus 11.8.1–3 (Oldfather trans).
49. Herodotus 7.218–21.
50. Herodotus 7.228.2.

Chapter 3
 1. Robin Lane Fox, *Alexander the Great* (London, 1973).
 2. Oliver Stone and Robin Lane Fox, *Alexander* (DVD Commentary) 2005, Warner Brothers.
 3. Rob S. Rice, Simon Anglim, Phyllis Jestice, Scott Rusch, and John Serrati, *Fighting Techniques of Ancient World* (New York, 2003) p. 31.
 4. Fox, *Alexander the Great* p. 72. See also Paul Cartledge, *Alexander the Great* (Oxford 2004) pp. 164–6, and Philip Freeman, *Alexander the Great* (New York 2011) pp. 10–14.
 5. Fox, *Alexander the Great* pp. 76–7.
 6. Rice et al., *Fighting techniques of the Ancient World* p. 33.
 7. Fox, *Alexander the Great* p. 76.
 8. Fox, *Alexander the Great* p. 76.
 9. Rice et al., *Fighting techniques of the Ancient World* p. 36.
10. Rice et al., *Fighting techniques of the Ancient World* p. 36; Cartledge, *Alexander the Great* pp. 163–4; Freemen, *Alexander the Great* pp. 12–13.
11. Fox, *Alexander the Great* pp. 76–8.
12. Fox, *Alexander the Great* p. 78.
13. Freeman, *Alexander the Great* p. 13.
14. Fox, *Alexander the Great* pp. 73–4.
15. Fox, *Alexander the Great* pp. 74–5.
16. Fox, *Alexander the Great* pp. 75–78.
17. Fox, *Alexander the Great* p. 79.
18. Cartledge, *Alexander the Great* pp. 47, 87, 88.
19. Cartledge, *Alexander the Great* p. 89; Freeman, *Alexander the Great* p. 72.
20. J.R. Hamilton, 'Introduction' in Aubrey De Selincourt, *Arrian: The Campaigns of Alexander* (London 1971) pp. 19–21.
21. Fox, *Alexander the Great* p. 50.

22. Modern accounts of Issus: Fox, *Alexander the Great* pp. 164–74; Cartledge, *Alexander the Great* pp. 144–46; Freeman, *Alexander the Great* pp. 107–42.
23. For these details, see the timeline in Cartledge, *Alexander the Great* pp. 15–18.
24. Modern accounts of Alexander's strategy at Gaugamela: Fox, *Alexander the Great* pp. 230–41; Cartledge, *Alexander the Great* pp. 151–52, 179–82; Freeman, *Alexander the Great* pp. 176–80.
25. Diodorus Siculus 17.57.1–4 ; Arrian, *Anabasis* 3.11.
26. Oliver Stone and Robin Lane Fox, *Alexander* (DVD Commentary).
27. Fox, *Alexander the Great* pp. 229–36.
28. Arrian, *Anabasis* 3.8–9.
29. Arrian, *Anabasis* 3.12. For modern accounts of the battle plan: Fox, *Alexander the Great* pp. 233–5; Cartledge, *Alexander* pp. 178–82; Freemen, *Alexander the Great* pp. 176–8.
30. Oliver Stone and Robin Lane Fox, *Alexander* (DVD Audio Commentary).
31. See for example, the plate in Nicholas V. Sekunda, 'The Persians' in John Hackett ed., *Warfare in the Ancient World* (New York 1989) pp. 83, 87.
32. Oliver Stone and Robin Lane Fox, *Alexander* (DVD Audio Commentary).
33. On the numbers, see Paul Cartledge, *After Thermopylae: The Oath of Plataea and the End of the Graeco-Persian Wars* (Oxford, 2013) pp. 91–3.
34. Arrian, *Anabasis* 3.9–10.
35. Cartledge, *Alexander the Great* p. 185.
36. Arrian 6.26 (De Selincourt trans).
37. Points noted by Stone and Fox in Oliver Stone and Robin Lane Fox, *Alexander* (DVD Audio Commentary).
38. Polybius 18.30.
39. Diodorus 17.58.2–5 (Oldfather trans).
40. Waldemar Heckel, Carol Willekes, Graham Wrightson, 'Scythed Chariots at Gaugamela: A Case Study', in Elizabeth Carney and Daniel Ogden, eds. *Philip II and Alexander the Great: Father and Son, Lives and Afterlives* (Oxford, 2010) pp. 103–112.

41. Polybius 18.30.9–11.
42. Polybius makes this point 18.30.
43. Fox, *Alexander the Great* pp. 240–2.

Chapter 4

1. Goldsworthy, *Roman Army at War* p. 209; M.C. Bishop and J.C.N. Coulston, *Roman Military Equipment from the Punic Wars to the Fall of Rome* 2nd Edition (Oxford, 2006) p. 91.
2. Polybius 6.23.
3. Goldsworthy, *Roman Army at War* pp. 209–212.
4. Bishop and Coulston, *Roman Military Equipment* p. 92.
5. Polybius 6.23.13.
6. Polybius 6.23.14.
7. Bishop and Coulston, *Roman Military Equipment* pp. 50–2.
8. Bishop and Coulston, *Roman Military Equipment* p. 78.
9. Graham Webster, *The Roman Imperial Army*, Third Edition (Totowa, NJ, 1985) pp. 128–129; Bishop and Coulston, *Roman Military Equipment* pp. 54–6.
10. Livy 8.8 (Roberts trans).
11. See Philip Sabin, 'The Roman Face of Battle', *Journal of Roman Studies* 90 (2000) p. 7.
12. Jon Solomon, 'In the Wake of 'Cleopatra': The Ancient World in the Cinema since 1963,' *The Classical Journal* 91 (1996) p. 113.
13. Solomon, *The Ancient World in the Cinema, Revised and Expanded Edition* (New Haven, 2001) p. 49.
14. Polybius 6.19.2.
15. Lawrence Keppie, *The Making of the Roman Army from Republic to Empire* (Norman OK, 1984) pp. 32,33 51–5.
16. Keppie, *The Making of the Roman Army* pp. 33–4, 51–55, 61–7.
17. Keppie, *The Making of the Roman Army* pp. 61–7.
18. M.J.V. Bell, 'Tactical Reform in the Roman Republican Army', *Historia: Zeitschrift für Alte Geschichte* 14 (1965) pp. 404–22; Webster, *The Roman Imperial Army* pp. 15–24, Keppie, *The Making of the Roman Army* pp. 61–7.
19. McCall, *The Cavalry of the Roman Republic* esp. pp. 100–37.

20. For readers interested in delving into the historical sources for the Spartacus Revolt, see Brent Shaw, *Spartacus and the Slave Wars: A Brief History with Documents* (Boston, 2001).

21. Duncan L. Cooper, 'Who Killed Spartacus? Production, Censorship, and Reconstruction of Stanley Kubrick's Epic Film', in Martin M. Winkler, ed., *Spartacus: Film and History* (Oxford, 2007) esp. pp. 26–34.

22. Caption to figure 9 in Winkler ed., *Spartacus: Film and History*.

23. Cooper, 'Who Killed Spartacus?' p. 28.

24. Sabin, 'The Roman Face of Battle' p. 7.

25. Goldsworthy, *Roman Army at War* pp. 137–9.

26. 'Training + Tactics = Roman Battle Success', from the Spartacus souvenir program, reproduced in Winkler ed., *Spartacus: Film and History* pp. 124–7.

27. Bishop and Coulston, *Roman Military Equipment* p. 91.

28. Bishop and Coulston, *Roman Military Equipment* pp. 101–102. Wikimedia commons has an excellent photograph of an Imperial Gallic helmet: http://en.wikipedia.org/wiki/File:Helmet_typ_Weissenau _01.jpg.

29. Allen M. Ward, 'Spartacus: History and Histrionics', in Winkler ed. *Spartacus: Film and History* p. 95.

30. Appian, *Civil Wars* 1.120. Plutarch, *Life of Crassus* 11.

31. Appian, *Civil Wars* 1.116–117.

32. Plutarch, *Life of Crassus* 11.6–7.

33. Vegetius *De Re Militari* 1.12.

34. Keppie, *The Making of the Roman Army* pp. 181–4.

35. Caesar , *Gallic Wars* 5.44. (Edwards trans, slightly modernized by the author.)

36. Bishop and Coulston, *Roman Military Equipment* p. 91.

37. Caesar, *Gallic Wars* 1.24–5, 52.

38. Goldsworthy, *The Roman Army at War* pp. 197–201.

39. Caesar, *Gallic Wars* 1.28.

40. Caesar, *Gallic Wars* 1.52, 6.8, 7.52; Caesar, *Civil Wars* 3.46, 3.92.

41. Caesar, *Gallic Wars* 1.52.

42. Peter Connolly, 'The Roman Army in the Age of Polybius', in Hackett, *Ancient Warfare* pp. 162–3; JFC Fuller, *Julius Caesar: Man, Soldier, and Tyrant* (New Brunswick NJ, 1965) pp. 90–1.

43. Goldsworthy, *The Roman Army at War* p. 208.
44. According to Plutarch, *Life of Caesar* 66.
45. Plutarch, *Life of Antonius* 22.2; Suetonius, *Life of Augustus* 91.1. Appian, *Civil Wars* 4.108.1. Velleius Paterculus 2.70.1 argues Octavian soldiered on and commanded despite his illness.
46. Velleius Paterculus 2.70; Plutarch, *Life of Antonius* 22; Suetonius, *Life of Augustus* 91. Appian, *Civil Wars* 4.105–131. See also Lawrence Keppie 'The Roman Army of the Later Republic', pp. 188–90.
47. See above, note 33.

Chapter 5
1. Bishop and Coulston, *Roman Military Equipment* p. 95; Chris Thomas, 'Claudius and the Roman Army Reforms', *Historia: Zeitschrift für Alte Geschichte* 53 (2004) pp. 424–452, esp. 443ff.
2. Bishop and Coulston, *Roman Military Equipment* p. 95; Webster, *The Roman Imperial Army* p. 122.
3. Webster, *The Roman Imperial Army* pp. 122–5.
4. Bishop and Coulston, *Roman Military Equipment* pp. 110–11.
5. Bishop and Coulston, *Roman Military Equipment* pp. 111, 113.
6. Webster, *The Roman Imperial Army* pp. 125–6; Yann le Bohec, *The Imperial Roman Army* (Raphael Bate, trans.) (London, 1994) pp. 122; Bishop and Coulston, *Roman Military Equipment* pp. 100–104.
7. Goldsworthy, *Roman Army at War* pp. 13–16.
8. Goldsworthy, *Roman Army at War* pp. 18–20.
9. Goldsworthy, *Roman Army at War* pp. 137, 197–8.
10. Goldsworthy, *Roman Army at War* pp. 137, 28.
11. Allen Ward, 'Gladiator in Historical Perspective', in Martin Winkler ed., *Gladiator: Film and History* (Malden MA, 2004) especially pp. 30–32.
12. Goldsworthy, *Roman Army at War* pp. 44–5.
13. Tacitus, *Germania* p. 6.
14. Goldsworthy, *Roman Army at War* pp. 46–8.
15. Ward, 'Gladiator in Historical Perspective', p. 32.
16. Goldsworthy, *The Roman Army at War* pp. 147–48 talks about the air of camaraderie that could exist between general and soldiers.
17. Tacitus *Histories* 3.23.

18. Keppie, 'The Roman Army of the Later Republic', in Hackett ed., *Ancient Warfare* p. 179.
19. Goldsworthy, *Roman Army at War* pp. 176–8.
20. Goldsworthy, *Roman Army at War* pp. 177–80.
21. McCall, *The Cavalry of the Roman Republic* pp. 20–23, 55–61; I.G. Spence, *The Cavalry of Classical Greece* pp. 108.
22. Goldsworthy, *Roman Army at War* pp. 182, 205.
23. Bishop and Coulston, *Roman Military Equipment* pp. 51–2; Goldsworthy, *The Roman Army at War* pp. 198–9
24. Bishop and Coulston, *Roman Military Equipment* p. 52; Goldsworthy, *The Roman Army at War* p. 198.
25. For references, see Goldsworthy, *The Roman Army at War* pp. 202–4.
26. Vegetius 1.12: Not to Cut, but to Thrust with the Sword (Clarke Trans.)
27. Goldsworthy, *Roman Army at War* pp. 192–218.
28. Goldsworthy, *Roman Army at War* pp. 208, 22.
29. Goldsworthy, *Roman Army at War* p. 197.
30. See page 111.
31. On soldiers as an important source of Mithras worshippers, see Manfred Clauss, *Mithras: The Roman God and His Mysteries* Richard Gordon, trans. (London, 2001) pp. 33–36.
32. See above, Chapter 4, note 33.
33. Dio Cassius 49.29.2–4 (Cary trans); Cited by Charles Knapp, 'Testudo', *The Classical Weekly* 22 (1928) p. 57.
34. Dio Cassius 49.30.1–4 (Cary trans); Cited by Knapp, 'Testudo' p. 57.
35. Liv 31.39.13–14; 34.39.2–6 are cited by Alexander Zhmodikov, 'Roman Republican Heavy Infantrymen in Battle', *Historia: Zeitschrift für Alte Geschichte* 49 (2000) pp. 67–78; Goldsworthy, *Roman Army at War* p. 234 provides Plutarch, *Life of Antonius* p. 45.
36. See above, Chapter 4, note 33.
37. Miles Russell, 'The Roman Ninth Legion's mysterious loss', *BBC News Magazine* http://www.bbc.co.uk/news/magazine-12752497 (accessed November 30, 2013).
38. Livy 23.24.6–13 (Roberts trans).
39. Velleius Paterculus 2.119.

Chapter 6

1. Steve Mason, *Life of Josephus: Translation and Commentary* (Leiden, 2001) p. x.
2. Noted by Lendon, *Soldiers and Ghosts* pp. 242–6.
3. Lendon, *Soldiers and Ghosts* p. 242.
4. Lendon, *Soldiers and Ghosts* pp. 243 -252.
5. Josephus, *Jewish War* 3.7.9; Paul B. Kern, Ancient Siege Warfare (Bloomington IN, 1999) pp. 310–11.
6. Josephus, *Jewish War* 3.7.19–8–24.
7. Josephus, *Jewish War* books 5 and 6 provide a highly detailed account of the siege; see also Kern, *Ancient Siege Warfare* pp. 314–22.
8. Josephus, *Jewish War* 6.4.5–6.
9. Kern, *Ancient Siege Warfare* pp. 313–321.
10. Josephus, *Jewish War* 4.7.2 (Whiston trans).
11. Josephus, *Jewish War* 7.8.1.
12. Josephus *Jewish War* 7.8.
13. Josephus *Jewish War* 7.8.5–6 (Whiston trans).
14. The easiest way to look at large segments of the column is to visit http://cheiron.mcmaster.ca/~trajan/index.html. The site contains a great number of photographs and diagrams that reconstruct the whole of the column for those interested.
15. Noted by Josephus, *Jewish War* 7.8.5.
16. Kenneth Atkinson, 'Noble Deaths' in Zuleika Rodgers ed., *Making History: Josephus and Historical Method* (Leiden, 2007) pp. 351–3.
17. Atkinson, 'Noble Deaths', pp. 353–4.
18. Atkinson 'Noble Deaths', p. 355.
19. Josephus, *Jewish War* 3.19 (Whiston trans).
20. Josephus, *Jewish War* 7.8.5–6 (Whiston trans).
21. Josephus, *Jewish War* 7.9.1–2, 10.1 (Whiston trans).
22. Josephus, *Jewish War* 3.7.31 (Whiston trans).
23. Josephus, *Jewish War* 3.7.34 (Whiston trans).
24. Josephus, *Jewish War* 3.9.2–3 (Whiston trans).
25. Josephus, *Jewish War* 3.10.5 (Whiston trans).
26. Josephus, *Jewish War* 6.9.1–2.
27. Kern, *Ancient Siege Warfare* pp. 323–6.

Conclusion

1. Ardant du Picq, *Battle Studies: Ancient and Modern Battle*, Chapter 5: Morale in Ancient Battle. Web: http://www.gutenberg.org/files/7294/7294-h/7294-h.htm.
2. From the Elegiac Poems of Tyrtaios 1.2.1 in *Elegy and Iambus*, Volume I J. M. Edmonds, Ed. Perseus Digital Library. Web: http://www.perseus.tufts.edu/hopper/text?doc=Perseus%3Atext%3A2008.01.0479%3Avolume%3D1%3Atext%3D2%3Asection%3D2. Word choices slightly modernized by the author.
3. Homer, *Iliad* 5.64–88 (Fagles trans).
4. See Christine F Salazar, *The Treatment of War Wounds in Graeco Roman Antiquity* (Leiden, 1999).
5. Hanson, *Western Way of War* p. 154.
6. Keegan, *Face of Battle* pp. 297–298.

Bibliography

Anglim, Simon and Phyllis G, Jestice, Rob S. Rice, Scott M. Rusch, and John Serrati, *Fighting Techniques of the Ancient World 3000 BC–AD 500: Equipment, Combat Skills, and Tactics* (New York, 2002).

Archer, Robin, 'Chariotry to Cavalry: Developments in the First Millennium', in Fagan, Garrrett G. and Matthew Trundle, eds., *New Perspectives on Ancient Warfare* (Leiden, 2010).

Atkinson, Kenneth, 'Noble Deaths at Gamla and Masada? A Critical Assessment of Josephus' Accounts of Jewish Resistance in Light of Archaeological Studies', in Xuleika Rodgers, ed., *Making History: Josephus And Historical Method* (Leiden, 2007) pp. 349–72.

Bishop, M.C. and J.C.N. Coulston, *Roman Military Equipment: From the Punic Wars to the Fall of Rome* Second Edition (Oxford, 2006).

Le Bohec, Yann, *The Imperial Roman Army* (Raphael Bate, trans.) (London, 1994).

Cartledge, Paul, *Alexander the Great* (Woodstock, NY 2004).

Cartledge, Paul, *The Spartans: The World of the Warrior Heroes of Ancient Greece* (New York, 2004).

Cartledge, Paul, *Thermopylae: The Battle that Changed the World* (New York, 2007).

Cartledge, Paul, *After Thermopylae: The Oath of Plataea and the End of the Graeco-Persian Wars* (Oxford, 2013).

Cartledge, Paul and Fiona Rose Greenland, eds., *Responses to Oliver Stone's Alexander: Film, History, and Cultural Studies* (Madison, WI, 2010).

Chrissanthos, Stefan G, *Warfare in the Ancient World: From the Bronze Age to the Fall of Rome* (Westport, CT, 2008).

Clauss, Manfred, *Mithras: The Roman God and His Mysteries* (Richard Gordon, trans.) (London, 2001).

Cooper, Duncan L, 'Who Killed Spartacus? Production, Censorship, and Reconstruction of Stanley Kubrick's Epic Film', in Martin M. Winkler, ed., *Spartacus: Film and History* (Malden MA, 2007) pp. 14–55.

Cowan, Ross, *Roman Battle Tactics 109 BC to AD 313* (Oxford, 2007).

Devine, A.M, 'Grand Tactics at Gaugamela', *Phoenix* 29 (1975) pp. 374–85.

Drews, Robert, *The End of the Bronze Age: Changes in Warfare and the Catastrophe ca, 1200 B.C.* (Princeton, 1993).

Flower, Mark A, 'Simonides, Ephorus, and Herodotus on the Battle of Thermopylae', *Classical Quarterly* 48 (1998) pp. 365–79.

Fox, Robin L, *Alexander the Great* (London, 1973).

Fox, Robin L, *The Making of Alexander* (Oxford, 2004).

Freeman, Philip, *Alexander the Great* (New York, 2011).

Goldsworthy, Adrian K, *The Roman Army at War, 100 BC–AD 200* (Oxford, 1996).

Green, Peter, 'Heroic Hype, New Style: Hollywood Pitted Against Homer', *Arion* 1 (2004) pp. 171–87.

Griffith, G.T, 'Alexander's Generalship at Gaugamela', *The Journal of Hellenic Studies* 67 (1947) pp. 77–89.

Hamilton, J.R, 'Introduction' in Aubrey De Selincourt, trans. *Arrian: The Campaigns of Alexander* (London, 1971) pp. 13–40.

Hammond, N.G.L, 'Sparta at Thermopylae', *Historia: Zeitschraft für Alte Geschachte* 45 (1996) pp. 1–20.

Hanson, Victor D, *The Western Way of War: Infantry Battle in Classical Greece* (New York, 1989).

Heckel, Waldemar, Carol Willekes, and Graham Wrightson, 'Scythed Chariots at Gaugamela: A Case Study', in Elizabeth Carney and Daniel Ogden, eds., *Philip II and Alexander the Great: Father and Son, Lives and Afterlives* (Oxford, 2010) pp. 103–112.

Keppie, Lawrence, *The Making of the Roman Army: From Republic to Empire* (Norman OK, 1984).

Keppie, Lawrence, 'The Roman Army of the Later Republic', in John Hackett, ed., *Warfare in the Ancient World* (New York, 1989) pp. 169–91.

Kern, Paul B, *Ancient Siege Warfare* (Bloomington IN, 1999).

Knapp, Charles, 'Testudo', *The Classical Weekly* 22 (1928) pp. 57–8. Stable URL: http://www.jstor.org/stable/4389222.

Lendon, J.E, *Soldiers and Ghosts: A History of Battle in Classical Antiquity* (New Haven, 2005).

Lipka, Michael, *Xenophon's Spartan Constitution: Introduction. Text. Commentary* (Berlin, 2002).

Marincola, John, *Greek Historians* (Cambridge, MA, 2001).

Macaulay, G. C, trans. *The History Of Herodotus, by Herodotus* Vol. 1. (ebook) Project Gutenberg, 1 Dec. 2008. Web. 1 Sept. 2013. <http://www.gutenberg.org/files/2707/2707-h/2707-h.htm>.

Macaulay, G. C, trans. *The History of Herodotus* Vol. 2. (ebook) Project Gutenberg, 1 Dec. 2008. Web. 1 Sept. 2013. <http://www.gutenberg.org/files/2456/2456-h/2456-h.htm>.

Mason, Steve, *Life of Josephus: Translation and Commentary* (Leiden, 2001).

Mogens, Herman Hansen, 'The Battle Exhortation in Ancient Historiography. Fact or Fiction?' *Historia* 42 (1993) pp. 161–80.

Murray, Rebecca, 'Writer-Director Zack Snyder Discusses "300"' *About. com Hollywood Movies* N.p., n.d. Web. 01 Sept. 2013. <http://movies.about.com/od/300/a/300zs022707.htm>.

Petersen, Wolfgang, 'From Ruins to Reality' on *Troy* (Warner Brothers, 2004).

Raaflaub, Kurt, 'Homeric Warriors and Battles: Trying to Resolve Old Problems', *The Classical World* 101 (2008) pp. 469–83.

Richmond, I.A, 'The Roman Siege-works of Masada, Israel', *The Journal of Roman Studies* 52 (1962) pp. 142–55.

Russell, Miles, 'The Roman Ninth Legion's mysterious loss', *BBC News Magazine* http://www.bbc.co.uk/news/magazine-12752497 (accessed November 30, 2013).

Sabin, Philip, 'The Face of Roman Battle', *The Journal of Roman Studies* 90 (2000) pp. 1–17.

Shaw, Brent D, *Spartacus and the Slave Wars: A Brief History with Documents* (Boston 2001).

Snodgrass, Anthony, *Early Greek Armour and Weapons: From the End of the Bronze Age to 600 B.C.* (Edinburgh, 1964).

Snodgrass, Anthony, 'The "Hoplite Reform" Revisited', *Dialogues D'Histoire Ancienne* 19 (1993) pp. 47–61.

Solomon, Jon, 'In the Wake of *Cleopatra*: The Ancient World in the Cinema Since 1963', *The Classical Journal* 91 (1995) pp. 113–40.

Solomon, Jon, *The Ancient World in the Cinema, Revised and Expanded Edition* (New Haven, 2001).

de Souza, Philip, *The Greek and Persian Wars 499–386 BC* (New York, 2003).

Spence, I.G, *The Cavalry of Classical Greece* (Oxford, 1993).

Stone, Oliver and Robin Lane Fox, *Alexander* (DVD Audio Commentary) (Warner Brothers, 2005).

Strauss, Barry, *The Trojan War: A New History* (New York, 2006).

Stylianou, P.J, 'Ephorus' in Nigel Wilson ed., *Encyclopedia of Ancient Greece* (New York, 2006) pp. 262–3.

Thomas, Chris, 'Claudius and the Roman Army Reforms', *Historia: Zeitschrift für Alte Geschichte* 53 (2004) pp. 424–52.

Sekunda, Nicholas V, Simon Northwood, and Michael Simkins, *Caesar's Legions: The Roman Soldier 753 BC to AD 117* (Botley UK, 2000).

Sekunda, Nicholas V, 'The Persians' in John Hackett ed., *Warfare in the Ancient World* (New York 1989) pp. 82–103.

van Wees, Hans, 'The Homeric Way of War: The *Iliad* and the Hoplite Phalanx' (I), *Greece & Rome* 41 (1994) pp. 1–18.

van Wees, Hans, 'The Homeric Way of War: The *Iliad* and the Hoplite Phalanx' (II), *Greece & Rome* 41 (1994) pp. 131–55.

van Wees, Hans, *Greek Warfare: Myths and Realities* (London, 2004).

Ward, Allen M, 'Spartacus: History and Histrionics', in Martin Winkler ed., *Spartacus: Film and History* (Maldon, MA, 2004) pp. 87–111.

Webster, Graham, *The Roman Imperial Army* Third Edition (Totowa, NJ, 1985).

Wes, ML trans. *Greek Lyric Poetry: The Poems and Fragments of the Greek Iambic, Elegiac, and Melic Poets (Excluding Pindar and Bacchylides) down to 450 BC* (Oxford 1993).

Winkler, Martin, 'Leaves of Homeric Storytelling: Wolfgang Petersen's Troy and Franco Rossi's Odissea' in E. Cavallini ed., *Omero Mediatieo. Aspetti della ricezionc omerica nella civilta* (Bologna, 2007).

Winkler, Martin, ed., *Gladiator: Film and History* (Maldon, MA, 2004).

Winkler, Martin, ed., *Spartacus: Film and History* (Maldon, MA, 2007).

Wyke, Maria, *Projecting the Past: Ancient Rome, Cinema, and History* (New York, 1997).

Wyke, Maria, 'Are You Not Entertained?: Classicists and Cinema', *International Journal of the Classical Tradition* 9 (2003) pp. 430–45.

Zhmodikov, Alexander, 'Roman Republican Heavy Infantrymen in Battle', *Historia: Zeitschrift für Alte Geschichte* 49 (2000) pp. 67–78. Stable URL: www.jstor.org/stable/4436566.

Index

Achilles, 1, 15, 17, 20–1
Agamemnon, 3, 10, 14–15, 19–20
Agoge, 36, 40–4
Alesia, siege of, 98, 106, 108–9
Alexander the Great:
    invasion of Persian Empire, 69–70
    leadership, 78–9
    strategy at Gaugamela, 72
Archaic period of Greece, 2, 5
Armor:
    Archaic Greek, 7
    Homeric, 4
    hoplite *see* Hoplite, armor
    in *Alexander*, 74, 77
    in *Centurion*, 146
    in *Gladiator*, 121–2, 126, 128
    in *Spartacus*, 99
    in *The Eagle*, 138
    in *Troy*, 12–14
    Macedonian, 66
    Mycenaean, 7
    Persian, 48, 50, 51–2, 75
    Roman:
        hastati and principes, 91
        leather inaccurately depicted,
          93, 104
        legionaries, 97, 101–2, 104,
          123–4, 156, 165
        worn during sieges, 165
Arrian, 68–9, 71, 78–9
Artillery, 130–1
Auxilia, Roman, 105, 139, 151,
    155–6, 168

    at Masada, 154
    cavalry, 125
    superseded legionaries in combat,
      155–6

Battering ram, 157–8, 164, 170
Battle speeches, 183–4
    Alexander's, 77–80
    Maximus's (in *Gladiator*), 128–9
Brutus, Marcus Iunius, 106, 114–15,
    117–18

Cabiria, 93–4, 123, 189
Caliga, 124
Capite censi, 96
Cataphracti, 75
Cavalry:
    Archaic Greek, 55
    Persian, 55–6
    Roman 103, 119
    see also Companion Cavalry
Changes in Greek Battle, 87–8
Charge:
    cavalry, 55, 133–4
    infantry, 16–18, 49, 136, 143
Chariots:
    Eastern Mediterranean, 6, 189–90
    in *Alexander*, 81–3
    in *The Eagle*, 144
    Mycenaean, 3, 6
    Persian, 72, 82–3
Cohort, Roman, 112, 125
    deployment in *Spartacus*, 99–100

depth of a, 132–3
  size of an imperial, 124
  transition from maniple to, 97–8
Comitatus, 127–8
Companion Cavalry:
  commanded by Philotas at
    Gaugamela, 71
  equipment of, 67
  in Alexander, 75, 85
  part of Philip's army, 65
  used as a shock force, 66–7
  wedge formation of, 67–8

Dani Warriors of New Guinea, 8–9,
    190
Darius:
  Alexander's opponent, 70, 72–3,
    77, 80, 84–6
  invader of Greece, 31
Dark Age of Greece, 2
Diodorus Siculus:
  account of Gaugamela, 71, 82
  describes Philip of Macedon, 65
  describes Thermopylae, 52, 55–7,
    59
  source for Alexander's campaigns,
    68–9
  source for the Persian Wars, 30
Diomedes,
  aristeia in the Iliad, 53–4
Domitius Ahenobarbus, altar of, 102
Duels:
  between Achilles and Boagrius,
    20–1
  between Hector and Ajax, 18–19
  between Hector and Patroclus, 21
  between Paris and Menelaus,
    14–15
  in Archaic Greece, 9–12
  in the Iliad, 21–2
Earth and water, Persian terms of
  surrender, 34–5

Eleazar, 161–3, 165–7, 171, 173–5
Ephialtes, 23, 44–7, 60
Ephors, 35–9, 44
Ephorus, 30, 65

Face of Battle, vi–vii
Film, compared to textual history,
    vi–ix
Flaming objects, 102, 147
Flavius Silva, Roman commander at
    Masada, 161–2, 164, 176
Foot Companions, Macedonian,
    65–7
Formation, 11–12
  battle standards for, 14, 17, 135,
    146
  disordered, 16, 19, 135, 144
  maintaining order of:
    advantage of, 135, 179–80
    difficulty of, 14–16, 74–5, 137
  open, 8–9, 19, 24
  wedge, 55, 67–8
  width and depth of Roman, 131–3
Fort, Roman, 139

Gaugamela, Battle of:
  Alexander's strategy at, 71–3
  size of armies at, 72
Gauls, 106–7, 111
Germanic Peoples, 127–8
Gladius, 92, 97, 101, 132
Gorgo, queen of Sparta, 40, 51
Granicus, Battle of, 69, 85

Hastati see Maniple, Roman
Hammer and anvil tactics, 67
Hand–to–hand combat, 11, 18, 84,
    102, 178
  see also Melee
Hector, 14–15, 18–19, 21
Hellenic League, 32, 34
Helots, 29, 32, 34, 39, 41

Herodotus:
  describes Ephialtes, 44–5
  describes Persians, 48, 57
  describes Spartans, 37
  describes Thermopylae, 33, 55–6,
    60
  source for Persian Wars, 23, 29
Homer, 7–10, 15
  composed *Iliad* and *Odyssey*, 1–2
  describes battle wounds, 17–18,
    181
  describes Diomedes' *aristeia*, 53–4
  relation to Mycenaeans, 3–5
  simile of Trojans as a wave, 16–17
  see *also Iliad*
Homeric Warfare, 11–12
Hoplite:
  armor, 4, 24–5
  competition between, 27–8
  effectiveness of, 51
  ethos of, 27–8, 45–6, 53
  weaponry, 26
Hypaspist, 67, 71, 81

Iliad, 1, 3, 14–15
  army in formations as described
    by, 9–10
  combat described in, 5, 6–12, 17,
    21–2, 53–4, 181
  historical period described by, 1,
    3–4
Immortals, 57–9
Imperial Gallic helmet, 102, 124,
  126, 146
Ionian Revolt, 31

Jerusalem, siege of, 153, 155, 157–9
Josephus, 167, 173, 175–6
  as a source, 154–5
  commander at Jotapata, 157, 170,
    175

describes Sicarii negatively,
  159–60, 162
describes siege of Jerusalem, 159,
  168, 176
describes siege of Masada, 163–4,
  170–1, 173
Jotapata, siege of, 155–7, 163, 170,
  175
Julius Caesar, 113–14
Jupiter's Darling, 94

Krypteia, 41

Legionaries:
  as combat engineers, 155–6
  equipment, *see* armor, *pilum*,
    shield, sword
  organization, 124–5
Leonidas:
  at Thermopylae, 34, 52, 59–60
  commanded forces of Hellenic
    League, 32–3
  in *300*, 23, 34–5, 36–8, 40, 45–6,
    48–9, 53–5, 56, 60, 183
  sayings of, 51
Lorica segmentata, 121, 123–4, 126,
  146, 150
  anachronistically depicted, 95,
    104, 123, 138
  in leather 140
Lycurgus, 30, 41, 43

Macedonia, 64
Maniple, Roman 84, 90–3, 97
Marius, 96–7
Masada:
  defenders' counter-wall, 170–2
  described by Josephus, 159–60
  Roman siege and siegeworks at,
    163–6, 167–9

Melee, 132, 136, 155, 178–9
    see also hand–to–hand combat
Morale, 56, 76, 132, 179
    commander's efforts to manage,
        182–5
Mycenaean Greeks, 1–7

New Guinea, Dani Warriors *see*
    Dani Warriors of New Guinea
Ninth Legion, 123, 137–8, 145

Octavian, 90, 106, 114–18
Officer, Roman, 124, 135, 137,
    146–7, 185

Parmenio, 68, 70–1, 85
Persian Army, size of:
    at Gaugamela, 72
    in Persian Wars, 48
Persian infantry, 47–9
Phalanx:
    against Roman maniples, 83–4
    Archaic Greek, 11–12, 24–8
    depicted in *300*, 46–9, 53, 59–60
    gave advantage at Thermopylae,
        51–2, 61
    Macedonian, 65–7, 74, 81–4, 88
    othismos, 19
    Roman, 90
Postumius, Lucius:
    led army into Gallic ambush,
        148–9
Philip II, 62–3
    invasion of Persia, 68
    military reforms of, 64–5, 67
Philippi, Battle of, 113–19
Phocians:
    at Thermopylae, 33
Pilum:
    carried by *hastati* and *principes*, 92
    carried by legionaries of late
        Republic, 97

construction, 127
    designed to pierce shields and
        armor, 92
    effective range of, 92, 135
    in *Rome*, 106, 115
    volley, 111–12, 118, 125, 135–6
Plutarch, 30, 40, 45, 51, 69, 105
Polis, 2, 28–9
Principes see Maniple, Roman
Promachoi, 11, 19, 22, 53
Property requirements for Roman
    infantry, 96
Ptolemy, 62–3, 69, 71
Pullio, Titus, 109–10

Rome, history 89–90

Sacking cities:
    Roman practices, 175–6
Sarissa, 66, 71, 74, 81, 83–4
Scipio L'Africano, 94, 123
Shield:
    Homeric, 4, 7, 17
    Hoplite, 11–12, 25–7, 49–50,
        52
    Importance at Thermopylae of
        52
    in *Troy*, 12–14, 16, 18
    Macedonian, 65–7, 73–4, 80–3
    Mycenaean, 7
    Persian, 36, 48, 55, 58, 75
    Roman, 91, 101, 107, 110, 122,
        127, 131
Sicarii, 159–60, 162, 170, 172
Sieges, Roman, 155–8
    see also Sacking cities, Roman
        practices
Slaves:
    in Greek society 38–9
Snyder, Zach, 23–4, 191
Sounds of battle, 180–2
Spartacus, 98–106, 177

Spartans:
  education, *see agoge*
  lack of sources for, 30
  mirage, 41
  religious scruples, 37–8
  virtue of obedience, 43–4
Spear:
  in *Troy*, 13–14
  of Companion cavalry, 67
  of Dani warrior, 8–9
  of hoplite, 26, 90
  of Immortals, 58
Stone, Oliver, 63–4, 73–4
Sword, 67, 84, 106–107, 111, 120,
    125, 128
  of hoplites, 26, 47, 53
  see also Gladius
Syntagma, 73

Testudo, 116, 141–3
Teutones and Cimbri, 96–7
Thermopylae:
  geography of, 32–3, 35, 45
  Greek forces at, 23–4, 33, 56
The 300 Spartans, 39
Titus, Roman emperor, 146, 155,
    157–9, 163, 176

Trajan's column, 137, 155, 165
Triarii see Maniple, Roman
Triclinia, 168
Triplex acies, 100, 118, 125
Tyrtaios:
  elegies of, 27–8, 30, 46, 180

Varenus, Lucius, 109–10
Varus:
  led army into German ambush,
    149–50
Vegetius, 107, 136–7
Vercingetorix, 109, 111
Vespasian, emperor, 155–8, 160–1,
    163, 166

Warfare, Homeric *see* Homeric
    Warfare
Warrior Krater, 7, 13–14, 190
Weapons *see pilum, sarissa*, sword,
    spear
Wedge *see* Formation, wedge

Xenophon, 30, 35–6, 38, 43–4
Xerxes, 31, 34, 36, 38, 57–8